# Business Decisions and the Federal Taxing System

# Business Decisions and the Federal Taxing System

## A SIMPLIFIED GUIDE FOR MANAGERS

John L. Kramer

Sandra S. Kramer

A RONALD PRESS PUBLICATION
**JOHN WILEY & SONS**
New York · Chichester · Brisbane · Toronto · Singapore

*Library of Congress Cataloging in Publication Data:*

Kramer, John L.
   Business decisions and the federal taxing system.

   "A Ronald Press publication."
   Includes index.
   1. Business enterprises—Taxation—United States.
2. Tax planning—United States.  3. Corporate planning—
United States.  I. Kramer, Sandra S.  II. Title.

KF6450.K73  1985    658.1′5    84-25641
ISBN 0-471-89594-6

# PREFACE

As the title *Business Decisions and the Federal Taxing System: A Simplified Guide for Managers* suggests, this book attempts to integrate the federal taxing system with the various types of business decisions that a manager or owner of a business will face. This book is not complicated and requires no prior background in accounting and taxation. However, it does attempt to keep the taxing authorities from sharing to an even greater extent (than they presently do) in business profits by making the owner and manager aware of the implications that the tax laws have on selected business decisions.

All types of business entities are examined—proprietorships, partnerships, regular corporations, and S corporations. In addition, we examine extensively the tax implications of various kinds of business decisions for each of these entities. Decision areas reviewed include the formation of a business entity; acquisition and use of business assets; disposition of business and investment assets; employee compensation; nonliquidating distributions; and liquidating distributions.

Although we are concerned primarily with business taxation, we have included coverage of items that may be of particular interest to managers or owners in their personal tax planning. For example, we devote a separate chapter to tax shelters. In addition, coverage is provided for the office-in-home rules, the hobby loss rules, and the tax planning for the sale of stocks and securities.

This book is not intended to provide all the answers regarding complicated tax matters. We can only make the reader aware of the tax consequences for selected types of business decisions and hope that competent tax advice from a CPA or an attorney is obtained when needed.

The reader needs to remember that the tax laws are dynamic and constantly changing. The tax law that is included in the book is current through the revisions made in late summer in the Tax Reform Act of 1984. Many of these changes are effective for 1984 while others are not effective until 1985. Where differences in the tax treatment exist between 1984 and 1985 law, we have tried to reference both sets of laws. Other tax law changes may take place after this book is published. The reader needs to make sure that the tax law has not changed and that the law being used is current.

We express our thanks to the many individuals who have assisted in the preparation of this book. We have thoroughly enjoyed preparing it and believe the reader will find it useful in saving tax dollars.

JOHN L. KRAMER
SANDRA S. KRAMER

*Gainesville, Florida*
*March 1985*

# CONTENTS

# 1

# INTRODUCTION TO THE U.S. INCOME TAX SYSTEM

*Over and over again courts have said that there is nothing sinister in so arranging one's affairs as to keep taxes as low as possible. Everybody does so, rich and poor; and all do right, for nobody owes any public duty to pay more than the law demands: taxes' are enforced exactions, not voluntary contributions. To demand more in the name of morals is mere cant.*

JUDGE LEARNED HAND
COMMISSIONER V. NEWMAN[1]

In a few terse sentences Judge Learned Hand's comments from a 1947 case sum up what this book is about—paying no more tax than the law demands. The tax laws offer many opportunities for an individual to legally reduce his or her tax liability through tax avoidance. Tax avoidance, the legal reduction of one's tax liability, should not be confused with tax evasion. Tax avoidance is the proper use of tax laws to avoid paying too much of your income to the federal government. Tax evasion, on the other hand, is an illegal action using means outside the tax laws to reduce your tax liability.

An illustration of how tax avoidance can reduce a taxpayer's tax liability is found in a recent campaign statement filed by one gubernatorial candidate. The candidate, a member of a family that owns a chain of drug stores, has a personal net worth of about 25 million dollars. According to his campaign statement, the individual had income (net of business deductions) totaling $920,651. This income came from a salary of $76,626, dividends of $672,006, interest income of $71,626, and capital gains of $236,358. If a taxpayer had this amount of income but the minimum itemized deductions and only two personal exemptions (one for the taxpayer and one for his wife), his tax bill for the year in question would have been $609,779. This bill represents more than 66 cents out of each dollar earned. However, this political candidate claimed enough personal deductions and tax credits to legally reduce his tax liability to $121,706. Through tax avoidance a taxpayer who could have paid an average of 66 cents out of each dollar of income to the government was able to reduce his tax liability so that he only paid an average of 13 cents out of each dollar. The authors cannot guarantee you the same kind of success. However, we do hope to make each reader more aware of the consequences that the tax laws have upon many common business decisions.

This book is divided into five sections. The first section (Chapters 1 through 6) provides a framework for the federal income tax system including a discussion of the basic income and deduction concepts employed to arrive at one's tax liability, the basics of tax planning, and separate chapters covering the taxation of individuals, regular corporations, S corporations and partnerships. The second section (Chapter 7) examines the formation of a business including the tax consequences of creating a corporation or a partnership and the tax ramifications of alternative capital structures for the business. The third section (Chapters 8 through 11) explores the tax implications of a number of basic day-to-day operating decisions including the acquisition, use, and disposition of business and investment assets, the selection of an employee compensation package, and the making of nonliquidating distributions. The fourth section (Chapter 12) covers the tax impact of liquidating a corporation or a partnership. The final section (Chapter 13) looks at a specialized tax concept—tax shelters. The chapter on tax shelters uses the concepts developed earlier in the book to examine selected forms of tax shelters.

A functional approach is taken in investigating the impact of taxation on business decisions. Each chapter in the second, third, and fourth sections of the book examines a specific type of business decision that is faced by middle management of large firms or by individuals operating small to medium-sized business enterprises. As such, the book is written for a businessperson and not a tax practitioner. An accounting or tax background is not required in order to successfully use this book.

## TYPES OF TAX ENTITIES

Five different forms of business entities can be found discussed within the federal taxing system. Some pay federal income taxes, others are only conduits and all of their income, expenses, losses, and credits are passed through to their owners. Each of the five basic forms of tax entities are examined below.

### Individuals

Individuals are the most common taxpayer. During 1981, over 95 million individual tax returns were filed resulting in the collection of 284 billion dollars of tax receipts.[2] Some of these returns were simple with little income being reported. Other returns were more complex and contained more than 100 million dollars of income. The most complex of these individual returns generally contained not only an individual's salary and investment income, but also income derived from the individual's conduct of a trade or business.

An individual who operates a proprietorship does not file a separate tax return reporting his trade or business activities. The proprietorship's activities are an extension of the individual taxpayer and are reported on a special schedule that is a part of the individual taxpayer's federal income tax return. The proprietorship does not pay any income taxes. The proprietorship's income is combined with the individual's other income such as salaries, dividends, and interest and the total income is taxed at the individual tax rates. The proprietorship income is not taxed again when it is withdrawn.

### Partnerships

A partnership is a conduit whose income, expenses, losses and credits are passed through to its owners. A partner may be an individual, a corporation, a second partnership, a trust, or an estate. Unlike the proprietorship, a partnership must file a separate federal income tax return. The income, deductions, and losses reported on this return are not taxed to the partnership. Instead, they are allocated to the various partners who report the income, deduction, or loss on their own tax returns whether or not they have received any distributions from the business. The income or loss reported on the partners' individual tax returns is taxed according to the rules that apply to that partner. Partnership income is not taxed again when it is withdrawn.

### Corporations

Corporations are the most common form of business entity. During 1981 over 2.7 million corporate tax returns were filed resulting in the collection of 61 billion dollars of tax receipts.[3] Some of these corporations represent one-man operations where the owner incorporates the business primarily for nontax reasons. Other small corporations represent professional activities where the owner incorporates the business primarily because of tax savings motives. At the other extreme are the large multinational corporations such as General Motors and Exxon whose employees number into the thousands and whose revenues are in the billions.

Two different sets of tax rules can apply to the corporation and its owners. The first set applies to corporations that are taxpaying entities, or *regular corporations*. A regular corporation (also known as a C corporation) files an income tax return that includes its income, deductions, and losses. These amounts form the basis for determining the corporation's income tax liability. Distributions of the corporation's after-tax profit as a dividend result in the earnings being taxed a second time at the shareholder level. The second set of rules applies to corporations that elect to be taxed like a partnership, or *S corporations*. The S corporation files a federal income tax return. The income, deductions, and losses reported on this return are not taxed except in unusual circumstances. Instead, these amounts are allocated to the shareholders who report the income, deductions, or loss on their own tax return whether or not it has been distributed. The income or loss reported on the shareholder's tax return is taxed according to the rules that apply to that shareholder. The S corporation income is not taxed again when it is withdrawn.

### Trusts

A trust is a legal entity that is created by a grantor subject to the terms of a trust agreement. The trust is funded with property that is transferred by the grantor to a trustee. The title to this property is held by the trustee in the name of the trust. The income from the property, and perhaps the property itself, is distributed to the trust beneficiary(ies) according to the terms of the trust agreement. A beneficiary may be an individual, corporation, partnership, another trust, or an estate. Most often it is an individual. Trusts fall into one or two categories. An *inter vivos trust* is created by a living grantor usually as the result of a gift. A *testamentary trust* is created by a grantor under the terms of his will.

Because the trust is a separate legal entity, its income ordinarily is reported separate from the income that is reported by its grantor or by its beneficiary. The trust reports its income, deductions, and losses on a fiduciary income tax return. The trust can claim a deduction for income amounts that are distributed to its beneficiary(ies). Income which is distributed is included in the beneficiary's tax return and taxed according to the rules that apply to that beneficiary. Any income that is not distributed is taxed to the trust. These undistributed amounts may be taxed again when distributed to a beneficiary.

### Estates

Even death is no escape from taxes. At death, an individual ceases to be a taxpaying entity but his estate becomes a taxpayer. An estate is a separate legal entity that comes into existence when the individual dies and includes all of the property that the decedent owned at his death. The estate is a separate taxpaying entity for federal income tax purposes and reports all of the decedent's postdeath income, deductions, and losses. Don't get confused. The estate is subject to two very different taxes. First, it must pay income taxes on all income earned on property held in the estate (for example, rental income, dividends, interest, and royalties). In addition, there is a one-time tax—the estate tax—which is based on the fair market value of all the property included in the estate. At this point we are only discussing the income tax paid by the estate. The estate remains in existence until the final distribution of estate properties to the beneficiary(ies) occurs. Ordinarily the beneficiary of an estate will be an individual or a trust.

The estate reports its income, deductions, and losses on a fiduciary income tax return. The estate can claim a deduction for income amounts that are distributed to its beneficiary(ies). These amounts are included in the beneficiary's tax return and taxed according to the rules that apply to the beneficiary. Any undistributed income amounts are taxed to the estate and are not taxed again when distributed to a beneficiary.

## COMPUTATION OF THE INCOME TAX LIABILITY

Each profession has its own technical terminology or jargon and taxation is no exception. Many of the technical tax terms have developed because of the need to compute a taxpayer's income tax liability. While the tax computation varies slightly from one tax entity to another, the same basic terminology applies to each of the forms. Familiarity with some of the basic terms makes the remaining discussions easier to understand. (Besides, you can always use buzz

**FIGURE 1-1**   Basic income tax framework.

| | |
|---|---|
| | Income from whatever source derived |
| Less: | Exclusions |
| Equals: | Gross income |
| Less: | Business deductions |
| | Certain nonbusiness deductions (for individuals only) |
| | Special deductions |
| Equals: | Adjusted gross income (for individuals only) |
| Less: | Excess itemized deductions (for individuals only)[a] |
| | Personal and dependency exemptions |
| Equals: | Taxable income (or net operating loss) |
| Times: | Tax rate(s) |
| Equals: | Gross tax liability |
| Less: | Tax credits |
| | Prepayments |
| Equals: | Net tax liability (or net refund due) |

| | |
|---|---|
| | [a] Itemized deductions |
| Less: | Zero bracket amount |
| Equals: | Excess itemized deductions |

words to *sound* impressive.) Accordingly, the terminology is presented below in conjunction with the basic income tax framework found in Figure 1-1.

### Income

Income has been defined by one court as the return in money from one's business, labor, or capital invested; gains, profits, or private revenue.[4] Income does not include gains that simply accrue to capital or a growth in the value of an investment until the gain or income is separated from the capital in a sale or an exchange transaction. Some differences do exist between the time when income is recognized for financial accounting purposes and when it is recognized for tax purposes. For example, some prepaid income items may be recognized for tax purposes when collected. This recognition point will be earlier than when the monies are earned and recognized for financial accounting purposes. Other income items may be realized and included in financial accounting income before they are taxed. One example of such a tax deferral is the recognition of income on a long-term construction contract as it is earned for financial accounting purposes by using the percentage of completion accounting method, and reporting it for tax purposes at the time the contract is completed by using the completed contract accounting method.

### Exclusions

The Sixteenth Amendment to the Constitution, which enacted the modern-day income tax in 1913, granted Congress the "power to lay and collect taxes on incomes, from whatever source derived . . ." As such, all income earned by a taxpayer is subject to tax unless some authority can be found within the tax laws to exempt, or exclude, it from taxation. Most items of income that are excluded from taxation do not have to be reported on the taxpayer's income tax return. The $100 or $200 dividend exclusion available to an individual taxpayer is an exception to this rule. It is reported on the tax return but is excluded from gross income.

### Gross Income

Gross income equals the total of the taxpayer's income (from whatever source derived) minus all excluded income. The U.S. income tax is based upon a "net" concept which permits the taxpayer to further reduce his gross income by the amount of all deductions he can claim before he applies his tax rate(s) to the residual amount.

### Deductions

Deductions and exclusions both work in the same way to reduce taxable income. A deduction ordinarily is an outlay made, or loss incurred, by a taxpayer that reduces taxable income. There are a few "special deductions" that do not require an economic outlay.

There are different rules for reporting the deductions of a corporate taxpayer and a noncorporate taxpayer. All of a corporation's business deductions are considered incurred in connection with the conduct of a trade or business and are deductible from gross income. Individual taxpayers, on the other hand, must divide their deductions up into two categories—items which are deductible for determining adjusted gross income and items which are deductible from adjusted gross income.

The items deductible for determining adjusted gross income (FOR A.G.I. deductions) include the individual taxpayer's business deductions, such as the expenses of a sole proprietorship, certain employee expenses, such as moving expenses and business travel expenses, and certain nonbusiness expenses, such as alimony and expenses associated with rental property. The deductions from adjusted gross income (FROM A.G.I. deductions) are (1) any itemized deductions that exceed a zero bracket amount and (2) personal and dependency exemption amounts.

Congress, at least in theory, tries to match a taxpayer's tax bill with his ability to pay that bill. Accordingly Congress recognizes that some personal expenditures such as large medical bills, other taxes, interest expenses, and casualty losses may significantly alter a taxpayer's ability to pay. Within the categories approved by Congress, a taxpayer can deduct his personal expenses and losses. In order to minimize the need for small taxpayers to keep records and to simplify the administration of the tax system, Congress has established levels of itemized deductions which virtually *every* taxpayer is presumed to have. This established level is called the zero bracket amount and is built into the tax tables and schedules. (See Appendix A.) Therefore this zero bracket amount of deductions does not have to be subtracted to arrive at taxable income. If a taxpayer totals his itemized deductions and they exceed the applicable zero bracket amount, he only needs to deduct the excess amount. (Remember, the tables and schedules in effect deduct the zero bracket amount for you.) Logically, these excess amounts are called excess itemized deductions. Notice that itemized deductions benefit a taxpayer by reducing taxable income *only* if the total itemized deductions exceed the zero bracket amount.

All individual taxpayers, whether or not they have excess itemized deductions, can claim both personal and dependency exemptions. If the taxpayer has no excess itemized deductions he reduces the A.G.I. by $1,000 ($1,041 for 1985) times the number of his personal and dependency exemptions. An election to itemize deductions permits the A.G.I. to be reduced by the sum of the excess itemized deductions plus $1,000 ($1,041 for 1985) times the number of personal and dependency exemptions claimed ($1,041 equals the $1,000 basic exemption amount plus an inflation adjustment).

Individual and corporate taxpayers both can claim "special deductions." Two-wage-earner couples are eligible for a special two-wage-earner deduction of up to $3,000. Corporations can claim a special deduction equal to 85 or 100% of certain dividend income amounts. This deduction reduces the amount of the distribution that is taxed in order to mitigate the double taxation that occurs when the profits are taxed to the distributing corporation at the time they are earned and again taxed to the shareholder at the time they are received as a dividend. No economic outlay is required of the individual taxpayer or the shareholder corporation to obtain these deductions.

### Adjusted Gross Income (A.G.I.)

The adjusted gross income concept is found only in the individual tax computation. This amount serves as a base for determining the maximum amount of deductible charitable contributions, and the nondeductible portions of the medical expenses and casualty losses.

### Taxable Income

Taxable income is the tax base used when applying the individual, corporate, or trust and estate income tax rates.

### Tax Rates

The various taxpaying entities have different tax rate schedules. Appendix A contains the rate schedules for individuals, trusts, and estates. Individuals have four rate schedules. (See Chapter 3.) Trusts and estates use special tax rate schedule that looks much like the individual rate schedules.

Each rate schedule is composed of a series of rates that range from 0 to 50%. Each of these tax rates represents a separate tax bracket. Taxpayers always start in the first tax bracket (for individuals the zero bracket where no tax is owed) and work their way down the schedule to succeeding tax brackets where higher tax rates apply. The tax rate that is applied to the last dollar of income is known as the marginal tax rate. Because the tax schedules are structured as they are, an individual taxpayer can never pay more than 50 cents of his last dollar of income earned in a year as federal income taxes.

### Gross Tax Liability

The product of the tax base (taxable income) and the marginal tax rate is the taxpayer's gross tax liability. A taxpayer can reduce his gross tax liability by tax credits and prepayments in determining the final tax due (or net refund available) that is shown on the income tax return.

### Tax Credits

A tax credit is a dollar-for-dollar reduction in the amount of the gross tax liability. A tax credit is more valuable than a deduction of the same dollar amount. The value of a deduction is the tax savings that results from including the deduction in the taxable income computation. As such, its value equals the amount of the deduction times the taxpayer's marginal tax rate (s) and has a maximum value equal to one-half of its dollar amount. A tax credit, on the other hand, is more valuable because it provides a dollar-for-dollar reduction in the tax liability. One common tax credit is the investment tax credit, which permits a reduction in the gross tax liability equal to 10% of the cost of selected asset purchases. (See Chapter 8 for more details.)

### Prepayments

The federal income tax is a pay-as-you-go system whereby taxpayers make payments throughout the year, and then pay a final balance or get a refund at the time they file their income tax return. Wage earners pay their income taxes through the withholding system where employers withhold income taxes from the salary payments made to the taxpayer.

Taxpayers who have income from sources that are not subject to withholding (e.g., investment income or partnership or proprietorship income) may have to make estimated tax payments. These estimated taxes are paid four times a year and usually equal the difference between the taxpayer's estimate of the amount to be withheld from any salary income and the total amount to be owed to the government.

### Net Tax Liability (or Net Refund Due)

A taxpayer's net tax liability is the balance of the income tax liability for the year. This amount must be paid with the income tax return. For some taxpayers, the total tax credits and prepayments will exceed the gross tax liability and result in a refund.

**EXAMPLE 1-1.** Tax A. Voider is married and files a joint tax return with his wife for 1984. He reports income from all sources of $450,000, exclusions of $150,000, deductions FOR A.G.I. of $50,000, itemized deductions of $49,400, and four personal and dependency exemptions. Taxable income is determined as follows:

|          | Income                    |           | $450,000  |
|----------|---------------------------|-----------|-----------|
| Less:    | Exclusions                |           | (150,000) |
| Equals:  | Gross income              |           | $300,000  |
| Less:    | FOR A.G.I. deductions     |           | (50,000)  |
| Equals:  | A.G.I.                    |           | $250,000  |
| Less:    | Itemized deductions       | $49,400   |           |
|          | Less: Zero bracket amount | (3,400)   | (46,000)  |
| Less:    | Exemptions                |           | (4,000)   |
| Equals:  | Taxable income            |           | $200,000  |

Tax A. Voider's marginal tax rate is 50% (see Appendix A). This rate applies to taxable income in excess of $162,400 and results in a gross tax liability of $81,400 [$62,600 + 0.50 ($200,000 −

$162,400)]. Tax A. Voider's average tax rate is 40.7% ($81,400 ÷ $200,000). Because of the large amount of excluded income and tax deductions, the 40.7% average tax rate is substantially higher than Tax A. Voider's 18.1% effective tax rate ($81,400 ÷ $450,000).

Now that we have completed our overview of the tax calculation, we need to examine some of the concepts in greater detail.

## GROSS INCOME

To begin the calculation of tax due, a taxpayer must determine his *gross income.* This section presents the general statutory definition of gross income without examining the rules that have limited applicability to a particular class of taxpayers (e.g., the employee compensation rules presented in Chapter 10).

### Section 61: Gross Income Defined

The starting point for defining gross income must be the Internal Revenue Code itself. Section 61 of the Code defines gross income in *extremely* broad terms.

*General Definition.   Except as otherwise provided in this subtitle, gross income means all income from whatever source derived, including (but not limited to) the following items:*

(1)   *Compensation for services, including commissions, fringe benefits, and similar items;*
(2)   *Gross income derived from business;*
(3)   *Gains derived from dealings in property;*
(4)   *Interest;*
(5)   *Rents;*
(6)   *Royalties;*
(7)   *Dividends;*
(8)   *Alimony and separate maintenance payments;*
(9)   *Annuities;*
(10)   *Income from life insurance and endowment contracts;*

(11)  *Pensions;*
(12)  *Income from discharge of indebtedness;*
(13)  *Distributive share of partnership gross income;*
(14)  *Income in respect of a decedent; and*
(15)  *Income from an interest in an estate or trust.*

While this definition presents an extensive list of income items, it does provide that some items are excluded from gross income. A literal interpretation of the statute seems to imply that no income can be excluded unless it is so listed in the Code. This is not completely correct, and exclusions come from four sources—the Constitution, the Internal Revenue Code, the definition of income, and administrative rulings of the IRS.

The most common of the four types of exclusions is the statutory exclusion found in the Internal Revenue Code. For example, Section 103 specifically excludes interest income earned on certain state and local obligations. Such a statutory exclusion restricts the general rule found in Section 61 that makes all interest income taxable. A good general rule to follow is that if the Internal Revenue Code does not specifically state that an item is excluded from the definition of gross income, you should assume that it is part of gross income even if it is not on the list provided by Section 61.

Some income items are excluded from taxation because they do not fit within the definition of income. For example, only the *gain* derived from dealings in property is included in income under Section 61 since a return of the taxpayer's investment in property is generally tax-free. As a result, if Tax A. Voider purchases a share of stock for $40 and later sells that share for $60, his income from the sale includes only the $20 that he received in excess of his original capital investment. This return of capital doctrine has been used by the courts to exempt from taxation loan proceeds, some annuity payments, and payments for injury to one's reputation. Sometimes the distinction between capital and income is not so clear. For example, it took the Supreme Court in the *Eisner* v. *Macomber* case[5] to finally determine that stock dividends did not constitute income and thus could not be taxed. This exclusion is now part of the Internal Revenue Code, although the exemption has been restricted to include only certain types of stock dividends.

## Items Included in Gross Income

A list of items that are included in gross income for all categories of taxpayers is provided in Figure 1-2. Similarly, Figure 1-3 lists items that are excluded from gross income. Figure 1-3 represents a good

**FIGURE 1-2**    Items included in gross income.

Alimony

Annuities (income portion only)

Awards

Bad debt recoveries

Bargain purchase of property representing compensation or dividend

Barter income

Bonuses

Business profits

Commissions

Compensation for services

Damages for loss of business profits

Damages for patent infringement

Director's fees

Distributions from an estate or trust

Dividends

Employee awards

Estate or trust income (distributive share of undistributed income)

Executors' fees

Farming income

Gain from sale or exchange of property

Gambling winnings

Hobby income

Illegal transaction income

Income from the discharge of an indebtedness

Interest (including amortization of discount and imputed amounts)

Lease cancellation payments

Meals and lodging

Mileage allowance

Money expense reimbursement

Partnership income (distributive share of)

Pensions

Prepaid income items (e.g., rent and interest)

Prizes

Professional fees

Property received as compensation

Rents

Royalties

Salaries

Severance pay

Sick pay

Social Security benefits

Social Security taxes paid by employer

Stock options

Supplemental unemployment benefits

Tax refund (of taxes paid and deducted in prior year)

Tips

Unemployment compensation

Wages

**FIGURE 1-3**  Income items excluded from gross income.

Accident and health insurance premiums paid by employer

Accident and health benefits paid on policy purchased by the taxpayer

Annuities (recovery of investment in annuity)

Awards for recognition of certain kinds of achievements

Bad debt recovery which did not result in a tax benefit

Capital contributions

Child care provided by employer

Child support payments

Cost sharing payments paid by the federal government under certain Acts

Damages for personal injuries or sickness

Damages for slander or libel

Disability payments

Distributions from a partnership

Dividends (up to $100/$200 for individual)

Dividends paid on life insurance policies

Dividends reinvested under a public utility company reinvestment plan

Educational assistance program benefits provided by employer

Employee death benefits (up to $5,000)

Extraordinary dividends

Federal tax refunds

Fellowships

Foreign earned income (for extended periods of non-U.S. residence)

Gain on involuntary conversion (to extent reinvested)

Gain on like-kind exchange

Gain on sale of personal residence (to extent reinvested in new residence or up to $125,000 by taxpayer age 55 or older)

Gain on transfer of property incident to divorce

Gifts

Group term life insurance premiums (up to $50,000 death benefit amount)

Income from discharge of an indebtedness (for bankrupt or insolvent taxpayer, or for which special basis adjustment election is made)

Inheritances

Interest on:
    proceeds of life insurance policy reinvested (up to $1,000)
    state and local obligations

Lessee improvements acquired by lessor at end of lease term

Living expense reimbursement paid following damage to or destruction of personal residence

Meals and lodging furnished for the convenience of the employer

Medical reimbursements under employer-provided accident and health plan

Prepaid income items (e.g., prepayments for merchandise and services in certain cases)

Prizes for recognition of certain kinds of achievements

Scholarships

Social Security benefits (not in excess of income "ceiling")

State tax refunds (of taxes that did not provide a tax benefit in a prior year)

Stock dividends

Stock options (incentive stock options only)

Stock rights

Transportation provided by employer (van, etc.)

Unemployment compensation (not in excess of income "ceiling")

Veterans Administration benefits

Workmen's compensation

starting point for tax planning. Maximizing exclusions results in minimizing tax! Further discussion of the income and exclusions primarily applicable to individual taxpayers is presented in Chapter 3.

## DEDUCTIONS

After gross income is calculated, numerous deductions are allowed which reduce gross income to taxable income. Like most exclusions, deductions exist only if there is authorization for the reduction in the tax laws. Many deductions are available for all business entities while a few deductions are restricted to individual taxpayers only. In this section we will examine those deductions available to all business entities.

While the reporting requirements may differ, the deductions available to a business entity are largely the same regardless of the formal business structure used. As we shall see in Chapter 4, there are a few deductions available *only* for corporations. A corporation reports its deductions on its own tax return and pays the tax due. A partnership or S corporation files an information return delineating their deductions and each partner or shareholder reports his appropriate share of the deduction. A sole proprietorship's deductions are reported on a special schedule that is included as part of the proprietor's individual tax return. Nevertheless, the kinds of items that are deductible vary only slightly among business forms so the discussion that follows relates to all business entities unless otherwise noted.

### Ordinary and Necessary Business Expenses

A number of Code sections provide authority for business and individual deductions. The most important section for business entities is Section 162, which begins,

> There shall be allowed as a deduction all the ordinary and necessary expenses paid or incurred during the taxable year in carrying on any trade or business. . . .

Expenses are deductible under Section 162 only if incurred in the taxpayer's "trade or business." However, the Code does not define what a trade or business is. In general, an activity must be entered into in order to make a profit and the taxpayer's operation and management activities must be extensive enough to indicate that a trade or business is being carried on. For example, taxpayers who own a few stocks and bonds are not in the trade or business of investing but a securities broker clearly is. (Don't despair. Expenses for the passive investor are still deductible. They just are not deductible as trade or business expenses. We will see how the treatment differs shortly.)

As you might expect, the definitions of the words "ordinary and necessary" are also critical to the interpretation of the law. The courts have held that an expense is *necessary* if a prudent businessman would incur the expense and the expense is expected to be helpful in the taxpayer's business. For an expense to be *ordinary,* the courts have held that it first must *not* be a capital improvement and it must be usual or customary in the type of business conducted by the taxpayer. To be deductible the expense must be both ordinary and necessary. Most business expenses are deductible under this criteria. A few of the expenses that can be deducted under Section 162 are the cost of materials and supplies used in inventory production, rents for facilities or equipment, licenses and fees, professional fees (i.e. accounting expenses), utilities, maintenance expenses, and interest on borrowed funds.

Section 162 provides that an ordinary and necessary expense is deductible only if it is also reasonable in amount. Hundreds of court cases in this area testify to the difficulty of determining what constitutes a reasonable salary for an employee (especially for a shareholder-employee of a family owned corporation). This question must be carefully considered. If the IRS and the courts determine that a salary payment made to a shareholder-employee is not deductible by the corporation because it is unreasonable in amount, the payment is likely to be taxed as a dividend to the shareholder-employee.

Certain expenditures are not deductible as ordinary and necessary expenses because they are contrary to public policy. Fines and penalties are generally not deductible. For example, speeding fines paid by long-haul truck drivers may be argued to be ordinary and necessary in that business but they cannot be deducted. A deduction is also disallowed for any payment which is an illegal bribe or kickback, or any payment which is illegal under the Foreign Corrupt Practices Act of 1977. Notice, however, that the ordinary and necessary expenses of even an illegal business are deductible except for payments which represent fines, bribes, kickbacks and so on. For example, an illegal gambling house can claim deductions for utilities, rents, salaries, supplies and similar items but cannot claim a deduction for bribes paid to the local police nor for fines incurred when the house is raided. As a new exception to this rule, *no* deduction is allowed for expenditures made in connection with the illegal sale of drugs.

An outlay made in connection with a trade or business may meet the above criteria and still be nondeductible if it is a capital expenditure. The most common capital expenditure is for plant and equipment and other long-lived assets. The cost of these properties must be capitalized and recovered through depreciation and amortization. Depreciation and amortization represent deductible expenses, but because of their importance they will be separately covered in Chapter 8.

A summary listing of common deductible and nondeductible expenditures can be found in Figures 1-4 and 1-5. Some caution should be exercised about deducting an expense listed in Figure 1-4. Sometimes the expense is deductible only if related to the conduct of a trade or business or to a transaction entered into with a profit mo-

**FIGURE 1-4**   Common deductible expenditures.

| | |
|---|---|
| Accounting fees | Contribution to Individual Retirement Accounts (IRAs) |
| Advertising | Contribution to nonqualified pension plan |
| Alimony | |
| Attorneys fees | Contribution to qualified pension, profit sharing, stock bonus plan |
| Automobile operating expenses, related to business, medical, or charitable use | Contribution to self-employed pension (H.R. 10) plan |
| Bad debts | Depletion (percentage or cost) |
| Bond premium, amortization of | Depreciation: |
| Business expenses | income-producing properties |
| Business gifts | trade or business properties |
| Charitable contributions | Dues |
| Club dues | Educational expenses |
| Commissions | Employee expenses: |
| Compensation | automobile |
| | reimbursed expenses |

**FIGURE 1-4** *(Continued)*.

transportation
travel

Entertainment facilities

Entertainment of:
customers
employees

Finance charges

Gambling losses (but not in excess of winnings)

Insurance premiums

Intangible drilling costs

Interest

Investment expenses

Legal fees

Licenses

Liquidation expenses incurred by a corporation

Lobbying expenses

Losses:
abandonment
casualty
hedging transactons
net operating losses
sale of property
theft
worthless securities

Medical and dental expenses (individual only if greater than 5% of A.G.I.)

Mortgage prepayment penalty

Moving expenses

Nonbusiness bad debts (treated as short-term capital loss)

Office expenses

Organizational expenses, amortization of
corporation
partnership

Outside salesman expenses

Partnership guaranteed payments

Penalty on early withdrawal of investment income

Points on mortgage

Postage

Professional journals

Reimbursed expenses

Rentals

Repairs

Research and experimentation expenses

Royalties

Safe deposit box

Salaries

Start-up expenses, amortization of

Supplies

Tax return preparation fees

Taxes:
employment (employer only if trade or business or profit-making related)
franchise
income (state, local, and foreign)
personal property
real property
sales

Tools

Transportation

Travel

Two-wage-earner deduction

Uniforms

Union dues

Utilities

Workmen's compensation

Work shoes

**FIGURE 1-5** Nondeductible expenditures.

Appraisal fees, related to acquisition of property

Attorney fees:
obtaining a divorce
preparation of a will

Automobile operating expenses, related to personal use

Child care

Child support

Clothing, personal

Commission on a sale of property by a nondealer

Commuting costs

Depreciation, of personal asset

Dues for personal memberships

Educational expenses designed to prepare one for entry into a career or a new trade or business

Entertainment expenses incurred primarily for the benefit of the individual or that are improperly substantiated

"Excess" compensation paid on "golden parachute" contracts

Funeral expenses

Gifts, nonbusiness

Hobby losses

Illegal payments

Insurance:
life
personal assets

Interest and taxes during construction period

Interest related to earning tax-exempt income

Investigation of a new business

Land clearing expenses on farmland

License on personal auto

Lobbying expenses incurred to influence voters

Losses:
like-kind exchanges
related-party transactions
sale of personal assets

Medical and dental expenses (up to 5% of A.G.I. for individual)

Organizational expenditures:
corporation
partnership

Political contributions

Prepaid interest

Rental of personal assets

Safe deposit box rented to store personal assets

Soil and water conservation expenses for farmland

Taxes:
employment (employee portion)
estate
excise (on personal assets)
gift
income (federal)
inheritance
self-employment

Tax penalty payments

Trademark, acquisition of

Trade name, acquisition of

Travel expense incurred
primarily for the benefit of the individual or that are improperly substantiated

Unreasonable compensation and other expenditures

tive. If the expense is incurred for personal motives, it may be non-deductible.

## Nontrade or Business Expenses

Section 212 of the Internal Revenue Code permits a taxpayer to deduct some expenses incurred outside of a trade or business. For such an outlay to be deductible, it must be ordinary, necessary, reasonable in amount, and related to (a) the production or collection of income, (b) the management, conservation, or maintenance of property held for the production of income, or (c) the determination, collection, or refund of any tax. The first category of expenses can be related either to the production of current income or to income of an earlier or later taxable year; the income can be either ordinary income or capital gain. The second category of expenses can be related to property that is currently producing income or to property that is not currently producing income but is expected to produce income in a future period. Like the first category of expenses, the income that is expected to be realized can be either ordinary income or capital gain. The final category of expense permits a deduction to be claimed for the preparation of a tax return, the contesting of a tax liability, the collection of a tax refund, or the obtaining of tax advice. The tax to which the expense relates may be levied by federal, state, or local authorities and may be of an income, estate, gift, property, or excise tax nature.

## Losses

The tax laws permit a taxpayer to deduct any loss sustained during the taxable year that is not compensated for by insurance or other means. Some limitations are placed on the deductibility of certain types of losses.

1. Individual taxpayers are restricted to deducting losses incurred:
    (a)  In a trade or business.
    (b)  In a transaction entered into for profit that is not connected with a trade or business.
    (c)  As a result of a casualty or theft.

2. Losses incurred on the sale or exchange of personal assets are not deductible. Thus, the loss incurred on the sale of a personal residence or personal automobile is nondeductible. (Gains on these sales are taxed.)

3. Capital losses can be used to offset capital gains. Individual taxpayers can deduct at most $3,000 of capital losses that are not offset by capital gains.

4. Worthless stocks and securities are treated as capital losses and are deductible according to the rules in (3). Some worthless stocks and securities can provide ordinary loss treatment.

Some taxpayers may incur business losses and expenses that exceed the total amount of their gross income. The negative taxable income that results is known as a *net operating loss*. Net operating losses can be carried back to the third, second, and first preceding taxable years (in that order) to obtain a refund of taxes previously paid. Losses not used during the carryback period can be carried forward and reduce the taxable income (and, thus, the taxes) reported in the next fifteen taxable years. Losses not utilized by the end of the carryover period are lost forever. An election is available to forgo the three-year carryback and utilize the loss only as a carryover. Although such an election prevents the taxpayer from obtaining an immediate refund of taxes paid in prior years, the loss may be more valuable as a carryover if the taxpayer's anticipated marginal tax rates in the carryover period exceed the marginal tax rates previously encountered in the carryback period.

### Restrictions on
### Claiming Deductions
### and Losses

A number of restrictions in the tax laws may prevent a taxpayer from claiming a deduction or loss. Some of the more important ones are as follows:

1. *Section 265*—prohibits a deduction for interest and other expenses related to the earning of tax-exempt income.

2. *Section 267*—prohibits a deduction to be claimed by related

parties for interest or other expenses when (1) the expense has not been paid by the end of the payor's taxable year and (2) the payee has not reported the income in his taxable year during which the payor's taxable year ends because of the method of accounting used by the payee. Amounts paid by the payor after year end are deductible on the day they are included in the payee's income. Related parties include (1) family members, (2) an individual and a C corporation more than 50% owned by the individual, (3) a shareholder and an S corporation, (4) a partner and a partnership, and (5) two corporations (one of which is an S corporation and one which is a C corporation) more than 50% owned by the same persons. The stock ownership test is applied in terms of the value of the stock that is owned and requires the use of a set of constructive stock ownership rules which results in an individual being considered the owner of stock owned by other family members and certain related entities. The application of this rule, preventing a corporation from currently deducting a bonus paid to its controlling shareholder, is illustrated in the following example:

EXAMPLE 1-2.    Tax A. Voider owns all of the stock of TAV Corporation. She uses the cash method of accounting while her corporation uses the accrual method of accounting. Both taxpayers use the calendar year as their taxable year. On December 31, 19X5, TAV Corporation accrues for financial accounting purposes a $100,000 bonus payable to Tax A. Voider. The bonus is not paid until April 10, 19X6. Because under the cash method of accounting Tax A. Voider does not report the income until it is received in 19X6, the bonus cannot be deducted by TAV Corporation until 19X6.

3.   *Section 482*—permits the Internal Revenue Service (IRS) to distribute, apportion, or allocate income, deductions, losses, or credits between two incorporated or unincorporated businesses owned or controlled by the same interests in order to prevent tax avoidance. In making these adjustments, the IRS attempts to produce the result that would have been achieved had the related parties dealt with one another in an arm's-length transaction.

After this discussion of what constitutes a taxpayer's income and of allowable exclusions and deductions, it is important to consider the question of *when* an item should be included in income or reported as a deduction. The answer to timing questions lies with the taxpayer's choices of accounting periods and methods.

## ACCOUNTING PERIODS AND METHODS

The foundation of tax accounting is the annual reporting of income and deductions. Each tax reporting entity must elect a taxable year and accounting methods in order to properly determine its tax liability. This section examines the taxable year and some accounting method elections that are available. While this topic seems dry at first glance, a perceptive taxpayer will recognize that many opportunities for tax planning exist since tax provisions and tax rates can change from one period to another. In addition some of these accounting methods provide for a significant deferral of income.

### Accounting Periods

A tax reporting entity adopts its taxable year by filing its first tax return and reporting the income and expenses for the desired period. The taxable year that is adopted must coincide with the entity's annual accounting period; that is, the annual period that it regularly uses in keeping its books. For most taxpayers, this means that any taxable year can be selected as long as it coincides with the reporting period used for financial accounting purposes.

The most common taxable year is the calendar year. A fiscal year can be elected and is either a 12-month period that ends on the last day of a month other than December or a 52-53 week year. A 52-53 week year ends either (1) whatever date the same day of the week last occurs in a calendar month (e.g., the last Saturday in the month of August); or (2) whatever date the same day of the week falls that is the nearest to the last day of the month (e.g., the Saturday that falls the closest to the end of August).

Taxpayers generally have complete freedom in selecting the taxable year to be used. However, three restrictions can apply. First, a calendar year must be used if the taxpayer's records are inadequate or the taxpayer's accounting period does not meet the requirements for a fiscal year. Second, a proprietorship must use the same taxable year used for reporting the proprietor's individual income and deductions, because it is considered an extension of the individual taxpayer. Third, S corporations and partnerships have significant restrictions to their choice of a taxable year. The S corporation and partnership restrictions are explained in Chapters 5 and 6. Once an acceptable taxable year is selected, the entity must continue using that year until IRS approval is granted to make a change.

### Accounting Methods

Six primary accounting methods are discussed here. Three of the methods—the cash, accrual, and hybrid methods—act as overall accounting methods. The other three—the installment, percentage of completion, and completed contract methods—are specialized accounting methods that can be used to defer the recognition of income. If a taxpayer engages in more than one trade or business, a different overall method of accounting can be used for each trade or business. Once an overall method of accounting has been adopted it cannot be changed without IRS approval.

### *Cash Method*

In general under the cash method of accounting, income is recognized when it is collected and expenses are deducted when paid. Some restrictions are imposed on the use of the "pure" cash method of accounting: First, long-term prepayments such as rent or insurance premiums may have to be capitalized and amortized over the period of time covered by the contract. The general rule used by the IRS and the courts is that a prepayment can be deducted if the early payment is a customary industry practice and the period of time covered by the payment does not exceed 12 months. Second, capital expenditures such as purchase of depreciable properties cannot be deducted when acquired and paid for, but must be capitalized and depreciated or amortized over the time period designated in the law. Third, an expense cannot be deducted when paid if it results in a distortion of income. This requirement is subjective and depends on the facts and circumstances of the situation (e.g., the size of the payment, the frequency of the payments, etc.)

Three judicial doctrines have been established by the courts which modify the revenue recognition side of the cash method of accounting.

1.   The *cash equivalency doctrine* requires income to be recognized even though the property that has been received by the taxpayer is not cash. All that is needed for income recognition to occur is for the property that is received to have a fair market value. Thus, a note taken in exchange for the performance of services is counted as income provided it has a readily ascertainable market value. An accounts receivable that is not secured by a note, on the other hand, is generally considered to have no readily ascertainable market value and does not result in the recognition of income when taken in return for services.

2.   The *constructive receipt doctrine* restricts the ability of cash method taxpayers to arbitrarily shift income from one taxable year to another to minimize total taxes. Under this doctrine, income not actually in a taxpayer's possession is constructively received by him in the taxable year during which it is credited to his account or set apart for him so that he may draw upon it. Income is not constructively received if the taxpayer's control over its receipt is subject to substantial limitations or restrictions (e.g., the funds from a sale transaction are placed in an escrow account and can be released only when a certain contingency has passed). This doctrine can be applied to dividends, interest, compensation for personal services, and the proceeds resulting from the sale or exchange of property.

**EXAMPLE 1-3.**   Tax A. Voider, a cash method of accounting lawyer, was informed that her check for legal services rendered was available to be picked up on December 15, 19X3. She waited until January 15, 19X4 to pick up the check. Tax A. Voider must recognize the income in 19X3 under the "constructive receipt doctrine."

3.   The *claim of right doctrine* requires income to be recognized upon actual or constructive receipt if the taxpayer has an unre-

stricted claim to such an amount. The fact that the claim is subsequently found by a court to be invalid does not change the fact that the claim did exist. Should a taxpayer be required to repay income that was recognized under the claim of right doctrine, the repayment is deductible in the year that it is made.

**EXAMPLE 1-4.**   Tax A. Voider billed and collected $5,000 for legal services that he rendered. After the payment was received in 19X6, the fee charged became the subject of a dispute. The dispute was resolved in 19X7 by having Tax A. Voider refund $1,250 of the fee. The payment represents income to be reported in 19X6. The repayment fee is deductible in 19X7.

The primary advantages of the cash method of accounting are threefold. First, it is the simplest of the three overall methods of accounting. Second, it permits income to be earned by the taxpayer but not reported until the amount due is collected and the taxpayer has the ability to pay the taxes. Third, within limits it permits the taxpayer to accelerate or defer the reporting of the deductions merely by speeding up or slowing down the payment of the expenses.

### Accrual Method

The accrual method of accounting reports income when it is earned, whether or not the cash or property to be received in payment has been received. The income cannot be accrued if substantial contingencies exist or if the taxpayer is unable to make a reasonable estimate of the amount of income. The accrual method is modified in certain situations when the taxpayer receives prepaid income. Monies that represent prepaid interest and rents are taxable when received even though they have not yet been earned. Special exceptions do exist for prepayments received with respect to inventoriable goods and services that can permit the income recognition to be deferred until the amount is actually earned.

Expenses are deductible when they are incurred. To be deductible all of the events must have occurred to establish that a liability does exist *and* the amount of the liability must be determined with reasonable accuracy. The "all events" requirement prevents a deduction from being accrued until the activities producing the liability (known as economic performance) have occurred. Economic performance occurs for a taxpayer receiving goods and services at the time that the taxpayer receives such goods and services. For interest and rents economic performance occurs with the passage of time. A special exception to the economic performance requirement is available for recurring expenses of the taxpayer that are consistently treated for the taxable year. The "reasonable accuracy" requirement prevents accrual-method taxpayers from deducting some of the expenses that are estimated and accrued for financial accounting purposes (e.g., estimated warranty-service expenses that are accrued for financial accounting purposes cannot be deducted for tax purposes, until they are paid or incurred).

The accrual method can be used only if the taxpayer regularly uses this accounting method to compute his book income and the method clearly reflects his income. Normally, the IRS is reluctant to permit a taxpayer to change from the accrual to the cash method of accounting because of the potential income deferral that is available.

### Hybrid Method

This accounting method permits a taxpayer to use the accrual method for computing the income related to purchases and sales of inventory and the cash method to report all other income and expense items.

### Installment Method

The installment method of accounting can be used to report multiple-payment sales. If a taxpayer who sells personal property on a regular basis (a dealer) desires to report the profit from multiple-payment sales by using the installment method, he must make an election that applies for all future taxable years (unless IRS approval is obtained to change accounting methods).

Profitable sales of real or personal property made by a nondealer must be reported by using the installment method if multiple payments are to be received, or a single payment is to be received in a taxable year later than the year of sale. An election is available for the taxpayer not to use the installment method. Such an election might be advisable if the taxpayer desired to recognize income, so as to keep from losing the tax benefit of loss or credit carryovers that were about to expire. The installment method can not be applied to a transaction that results in a loss.

For dealers and nondealers the installment method determines the gain reported in any taxable year by using the following formula:

$$\begin{array}{c}\text{Income or gain} \\ \text{recognized in} \\ \text{taxable year}\end{array} = \frac{\begin{array}{c}\text{Payments received during} \\ \text{the taxable year}\end{array}}{\begin{array}{c}\text{Contract price (cash and} \\ \text{other property to be} \\ \text{received)}\end{array}} \times \begin{array}{c}\text{Realized gain on} \\ \text{sale of property}\end{array}$$

Note that the use of the installment method does not change the total amount of the gain to be reported or the character of the gain.

Interest income earned from an installment sale is ordinary income. The IRS has the power to impute interest income to a transaction where no interest, or a low rate of interest, is charged on a debt obligation. The imputing of the interest income prevents taxpayers from converting the interest income (ordinary income) into gain from a sale or exchange (capital gain). For most installment contracts entered into before July 1, 1985, if the contract does not provide for 9% simple interest, a 10% rate will be imputed. Starting July 1, 1985 the deferred payment sale will have to provide for an interest rate of at least 110% of the "applicable federal rate" for similar term obligations, or interest at 120% of such rate will be imputed.

### Percentage of Completion Method

Special accounting methods are available for long-term contracts. A taxpayer can report the profit or income from a long-term contract by using either the accrual or cash methods of accounting that he regularly uses in computing his income, or he can adopt the percentage of completion or the completed-contract methods of accounting.

The percentage of completion method requires the percentage of the gross contract price that corresponds to the percentage of the total contract which has been completed during the taxable year to be included in gross income. All costs incurred during the taxable year with respect to the contract are deducted in determining taxable income.

### Completed-Contract Method

The completed-contract method reports the gross contract price for a long-term contract in gross income in the taxable year in which the contract is completed. Direct and indirect costs that relate to the contract are capitalized during the project and deducted in the taxable year in which the contract is completed. Indirect costs that are not allocable to the contract (e.g., administrative expenses, interest, and taxes) are deductible according to the overall method of accounting employed by the taxpayer.

The major advantage of the completed-contract method is that it defers the recognition of income until the contract is completed. However, this deferral could result in a bunching of income in periods when a major contract is completed, and the reporting of small losses in other periods. The percentage of completion method, on the other hand, reports the income as the work is completed.

### NOTES

1. 159 F. 2d 848 (2nd Cir., 1947).
2. *Statistics of Income Bulletin,* Summer 1983, p. 80.
3. *Ibid.,* p. 83.
4. *Glenshaw Glass Co.* v. *CIR,* 348 U.S. 426 (1955).
5. 252 U.S. 189 (1920).

# 2

# BASIC TAX PLANNING CONCEPTS

Five basic tax planning concepts form the basis for many of the tax savings ideas illustrated throughout the remainder of this book. The illustrated concepts are:

1.  The conversion of taxable income into tax-exempt income.
2.  The deferral of income or gain from one taxable year to a later year.
3.  The acceleration of a deduction or loss from a later taxable year to an earlier year.
4.  The conversion of ordinary income into long-term capital gains.
5.  The conversion of long-term capital losses into short-term capital losses or ordinary losses.

## TAX EXEMPTION

A taxpayer may be able to convert taxable income into tax-exempt income and thereby increase his return merely by changing the nature of his investment activities. For example, a change from investing in corporate bonds to investing in state and local obligations can convert taxable interest income into tax-exempt interest income. This change in strategy can be advantageous only if the taxpayer's return on the state and local obligations exceeds his after-tax return on the corporate bonds.

**EXAMPLE 2-1.**    Tax A. Voider currently has a portfolio of corporate bonds providing a 12% pretax yield. Assuming a 40% marginal tax rate, Tax A. Voider's after-tax rate of return is 7.2% $[(1-0.40) \times 0.12]$. Ignoring any transaction cost on changing from corporate bonds to state and local obligations, Tax A. Voider can obtain a higher after-tax rate of return if she can invest in a portfolio of state and local obligations that provides a yield in excess of 7.2%.

The analysis of the two investment alternatives is not always so simple. First, a transaction cost (e.g., a broker's commission or an income tax levied on a sale) may be incurred when changing the investment portfolio. Second, some of the funds used to invest in the corporate bonds may be borrowed. The interest expense incurred when borrowing to purchase corporate bonds is deductible up to the taxpayer's investment-interest limitation. Interest expense associated with borrowing to purchase state and local obligations is not deductible. As such, a higher after-tax cost of borrowing may be incurred to acquire the tax-free interest income.

Certain gains can be made tax-exempt by restructuring or delaying a transaction. For example, an individual taxpayer who is at least 55 years of age can exclude from his gross income $125,000 of the gain realized from the sale or exchange of a personal residence. If an individual taxpayer is contemplating selling his residence at the age of 52, and he expects to realize a substantial profit on the disposition, the taxpayer might consider postponing the sale for three years in order to make the gain tax-exempt.

## TAX DEFERRAL

A tax exemption is a permanent exclusion of an income amount from taxation. A tax deferral, on the other hand, implies a postponement of the taxes for one or more years. Some tax deferrals result from the adoption of an accounting method. For example, reporting the gain from an asset sale by using the installment method of accounting permits the realized gain to be deferred until the sales proceeds are collected. The value of this tax deferral is a function of the amount and character of the gain that is deferred, the taxpayer's marginal tax rate, and the interest rate that can be earned by investing the deferred taxes.

**Example 2-2.** Tax A. Voider sells some land that produces a $240,000 profit. The sale is collected in three equal payments along with an appropriate interest charge. Tax A. Voider's marginal tax rate is 50%. Monies saved by deferring a tax liability can be invested and can earn a 12% after-tax return. The reporting of this gain under two alternative methods is summarized in the following manner:

| Year | Alternative Reporting Methods Accrual Sale | Installment Sale | Income Deferral | Tax Savings | Value of the Tax Savings |
|---|---|---|---|---|---|
|  | (1) | (2) | (3) = (1) − (2) | (4) = 0.50 × (3) |  |
| 1 | $240,000 | $ 80,000 | $160,000 | $80,000 | 0 |
| 2 | 0 | $ 80,000 | (80,000) | (40,000) | $ 9,600[a] |
| 3 | 0 | $ 80,000 | (80,000) | (40,000) | 4,800[b] |
| Total | $240,000 | $240,000 | $ 0 | $ 0 | $14,400 |

[a] $80,000 × 1 year × 0.12 = $9,600
[b] $40,000 × 1 year × 0.12 = $4,800

Tax A. Voider saves $80,000 in taxes in Year 1 by using the installment method to report the gain. In Years 2 and 3 the installment method requires the recognition of gain when the accrual method shows no further gain for these years. Because of his ability to invest the deferred taxes, Tax A. Voider realizes a total of $14,400 in additional interest income. Part or all of this savings would have been lost, however, if Tax A. Voider's marginal tax rate were higher in Years 2 and 3 than in Year 1.

A similar type of tax deferral is available for unrealized profits that accrue from the holding of assets. The holding gains are not taxed until realized through a sale or exchange transaction *in which a gain is recognized.* Thus, a taxpayer can sometimes realize a substantial savings merely by deferring the sale into a later year especially if a decline in the applicable marginal tax rate can be expected (from a legislated lowering of tax rates; expected losses from other sources; or retirement).

**EXAMPLE 2-3.**    Tax A. Voider holds undeveloped real estate that she purchased in 19X0 for $10,000. In December, 19X5, the real estate is worth $25,000. The undeveloped real estate can be exchanged for a different type of real estate in a like-kind exchange. This type of exchange postpones taxation of the $15,000 profit. Only when Tax A. Voider disposes of the second piece of real estate will the profit be taxed. Such an exchange, which is described in greater detail in Chapter 9, permits a long-term profit deferral along with a limited opportunity to change the nature of the investment.

## ACCELERATION OF TAX BENEFITS

Deductions and losses sometimes can provide a larger benefit if they are accelerated from a later taxable year into an earlier taxable year in order to take advantage of the time value of money. With the value of a deduction or a loss being a function of both the taxpayer's year of recognition and marginal tax rate, the acceleration of a deduction or a loss may, of course, be a disadvantage if the current-year's marginal tax rate is lower than the rate that is anticipated to be encountered in a future period.

One way to alter the timing of a deduction is through the accounting method that is selected. A cash method of accounting taxpayer can change the timing of a deduction merely by speeding up or slowing down the payment of expenses. A similar form of acceleration can also be used by an accrual method of accounting taxpayer. Because these taxpayers deduct an expense when it is accrued, a company can obtain a tax benefit for expenses that have been incurred, but have not yet been paid. Thus, a company can deduct a payroll that accrues as of the end-of-the-year, or a year-end bonus, or other operating expenses that have been incurred without being required to pay the expense until after year-end.

A similar type of acceleration can take place by altering the timing of a transaction. The selling of an asset prior to year-end can accelerate a tax loss into the current year.

EXAMPLE 2-4.    Tax A. Voider holds XYZ stock that was purchased in 19X0 for $10,000 and that is worth $1,000 in December, 19X1. The $9,000 unrealized loss can be recognized for tax purposes only if a sale or exchange occurs. Selling these stocks in December, 19X1, can make the loss available to be used on the 19X1 tax return. Deferring the sale until January, 19X2, however, could provide an additional advantage if Tax A. Voider felt that her 19X2 marginal tax rate would be sufficiently higher than her 19X1 rate, in order to offset the time value of the money used to pay the additional 19X1 taxes that are incurred.

The deductibility of a loss can also be accelerated by changing the nature of the transaction. Earlier, we saw that the gain realized on the disposition of a piece of real estate could be deferred by using a like-kind exchange (see Example 2-3). However, if the taxpayer has realized a loss on property and exchanges that property in a like-kind exchange, he *can not* deduct the loss. By selling an asset, instead of exchanging it in a like-kind exchange, the taxpayer can accelerate recognition of a loss.

EXAMPLE 2-5.    Assume the facts remain the same as in Example 2-4 except that the XYZ stock is instead undeveloped real estate. If the real estate is exchanged for a similar piece of real estate, the $9,000 loss is deferred until Tax A. Voider disposes of the second piece of real estate. An outright sale of the real estate would permit immediate recognition of the $9,000 loss. The tax benefits from this loss can be worth as much as $4,500 ($9,000 × 0.50).

## CONVERSION OF INCOME

Capital assets include all property, regardless of how long it is held, except for the following items:

1.  Inventory and stock in trade held primarily for sale to customers in the ordinary course of the taxpayer's conduct of a trade or business.
2.  Depreciable property used in a trade or business.
3.  Real property used in a trade or business.
4.  A copyright; a literary, musical, or artistic composition; a letter or memorandum, or similar property held by the taxpayer's whose efforts created such property.
5.  Accounts or notes receivable acquired in the conduct of a trade or business for services rendered or from the sale of property described in (1).
6.  Certain U.S. Government publications.

A limited number of other additions to this list can occur, but their discussion is deferred until Chapter 9.

The sale or exchange of property results in the taxpayer realizing a gain or loss. In general, this realized gain or loss is recognized for tax purposes and fully included in the taxpayer's tax computation. The realized gain or loss is determined in the following manner:

|          | Money received                                         |
|----------|--------------------------------------------------------|
| Plus:    | Fair market value of nonmoney property received        |
|          | Liabilities of the taxpayer assumed by the purchasing party |
| Equals:  | Amount realized                                        |
| Less:    | Adjusted basis of property sold or exchanged           |
| Equals:  | Realized gain                                          |

A taxpayer's basis is the amount that is treated for tax purposes as his investment in the property. Ordinarily, this amount begins as the taxpayer's acquisition cost for the property. Acquisition cost is the cash and the fair market value of the other property used to acquire the property, plus any liabilities incurred as part of the acquisition. Any subsequent capital improvements are added to this total and depreciation, depletion, amortization, or other capital recoveries are subtracted. The resulting amount is the taxpayer's adjusted basis.

A capital gain or loss is the gain or loss that is recognized when a capital asset is sold or exchanged. Capital gains and losses are characterized as short-term or long-term. A short-term capital gain (or loss) is a gain (or loss) derived from the sale or exchange of a capital asset held for 6 months or less. A long-term capital gain (or loss) is a gain or loss from the sale or exchange of a capital asset held more than 6 months. The six-month rule applies only to assets acquired after June 22, 1984. For other properties, a one-year dividing line is used to distinguish between short-term or long-term gains and losses.

Capital gains and losses are taxed differently from gains or losses realized from noncapital assets. To determine the tax treatment of a capital gain or loss, one must first divide all capital gains and losses into those that are short-term and those that are long-term (see Figure 2-1). All short-term capital gains and losses are summed into a net short-term capital gain or net short-term capital loss. Likewise, all long-term capital gains and losses are summed into a net long-term capital gain or net long-term capital loss (Step 1 of Figure 2-1). Then the net short-term gain (or loss) and net long-term gain (or loss) totals are summed, but *only if* one is a gain and one is a loss (Step 2 of Figure 2-1). As shown in Figure 2-1, one of four possible results can occur.

The tax treatment for each of the four results for an individual taxpayer is presented as follows: (Different rules apply for corporate capital gains and losses. See Chapter 4.)

1.   *Result No. 1.*   Both the net long-term capital gain and net short-term capital gain are included in gross income. A special FOR A.G.I. deduction can be claimed equal to 60 percent of the net long-

**FIGURE 2-1**   Combining of capital gains and losses.

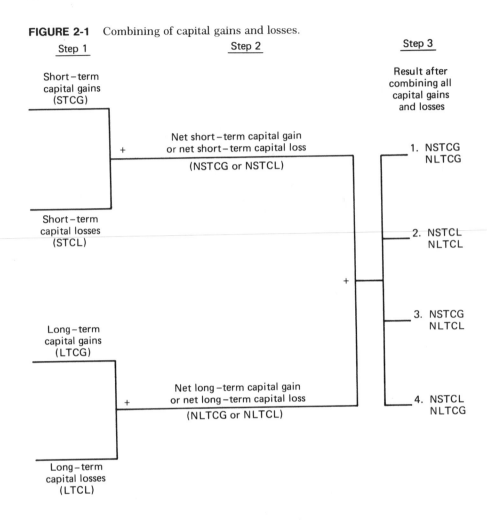

term capital gain. There is no special treatment for a net short-term capital gain.

2. *Result No. 2.* The net short-term capital loss is deductible but not in excess of the lesser of a $3,000 annual limitation ($1,500 if married and filing separate returns), or the taxpayer's taxable income. The net long-term capital loss is deductible after deducting any net short-term capital loss. Each dollar of long-term capital loss creates a 50 cent deductible loss. The long-term capital loss deduction cannot exceed (1) the lesser of $3,000 or the taxpayer's taxable

income, minus (2) any deduction claimed for the net short-term capital loss. Thus, the total of the two types of losses cannot exceed the lesser of $3,000 or taxable income. Capital losses that are not deductible can be carried over indefinitely.

3. *Result No. 3.* Two outcomes are possible here. First, if the net short-term capital gain exceeds the net long-term capital loss, the difference is treated like the net short-term capital gain in Result No. 1 and is includible in gross income. No special deduction is available. Alternatively, if the net long-term capital loss exceeds the net short-term capital gain, the difference is deductible like the net long-term capital loss in Result No. 2. The deduction equals one-half of the "excess" loss, but it cannot exceed the lesser of $3,000 or taxable income.

4. *Result No. 4.* Two outcomes are also possible here. First, if the net long-term capital gain exceeds the net short-term capital loss, the difference is includible in gross income. A special FOR A.G.I. deduction can be claimed equal to 60% of the "excess" gain. Alternatively, if the net short-term capital loss exceeds the net long-term capital gain, the difference is deductible. The deduction cannot exceed the lesser of $3,000 or taxable income.

The results are illustrated by the following example:

**EXAMPLE 2-6.**    Tax A. Voider realizes the short- and long-term capital gains and losses, as illustrated in the following four independent situations:

| Situation No. | Short-Term Capital | | Long-Term Capital | |
|---|---|---|---|---|
| | Gain | Loss | Gain | Loss |
| 1 | $4,000 | ($3,000) | $6,000 | ($5,000) |
| 2 | 4,000 | (6,000) | 6,000 | (10,000) |
| 3 | 6,000 | (3,000) | 6,000 | (8,000) |
| 4 | 4,000 | (6,000) | 6,000 | (2,000) |

These short- and long-term gains and losses are combined into net short-term and long-term gain or loss positions. These positions are reported on Tax A. Voider's tax return as shown below.

| Situation No. | Net Short-Term Gain (Loss) | Net Long-Term Gain (Loss) | Gross Income | Deductible Loss | Cap. Gain Deduction | Loss Carryover |
|---|---|---|---|---|---|---|
| 1 | $1,000 | $1,000 | $2,000 | | $ 600 | |
| 2 | (2,000) | (4,000) | | ($3,000) | | ($2,000) |
| 3 | 3,000 | (2,000) | 1,000 | | | |
| 4 | (2,000) | 4,000 | 2,000 | | 1,200 | |

In Situation No. 1, both net gain amounts are included in gross income, and a special deduction can be claimed equal to 60% of the net long-term capital gain. In Situation No. 2, both losses are deductible. The full $2,000 short-term capital loss is deducted first, and $2,000 of the long-term capital loss is then used to create an additional $1,000 deduction. The remaining $2,000 of loss can be carried over indefinitely. In Situation Nos. 3 and 4, the net gain exceeds the net loss and is includible in gross income. In the latter, the excess long-term gain qualifies for the special 60% deduction.

Example 2-6 illustrates the 60% tax savings that can accrue from converting ordinary income or short-term capital gains into long-term capital gains. Also illustrated, is the additional benefit that accrues from having a short-term capital loss instead of a long-term capital loss. However, both forms of capital losses suffer from a major disadvantage because they can only offset other capital gains, or be deducted up to the lesser of a $3,000 limitation or the taxpayer's taxable income. Excess losses can be used in future years to offset capital gains or be claimed as a deduction subject to the $3,000 limit. Losses from the sale or exchange of a noncapital asset can be deducted without limit. Noncapital losses that exceed a taxpayer's taxable income can be carried back 3 years to obtain a refund of taxes previously paid or carried over to reduce taxes to be paid in future years. Because of these differences, prudent tax planners do their best to ensure that capital gains are long-term, capital losses are short-term or, better still, ordinary losses. Further discussion of tax planning in connection with the capital gains rules is illustrated in Chapter 9.

# 3

# TAXATION OF INDIVIDUALS

Individual taxpayers are the backbone of the federal tax system. Calendar year 1981 brought the IRS 94 million individual federal income tax returns, or more than 70% of the total number of tax returns that were filed. Because of the sheer magnitude of the individual income taxes, they are an important part of our taxing system. This chapter examines the basics of the individual income tax rules by working through the basic income tax formula found in Figure 1-1. In addition, we will examine the benefits available from the use of income averaging.

## GROSS INCOME

Gross income equals the total of the taxpayer's income (from whatever source derived) minus all excluded income. The gross income discussion is divided into its two component parts—items specifically included in gross income and items specifically excluded from gross income.

## Includible Items

### Alimony

Alimony and separate maintenance payments are included in the income of the recipient. Because state law definitions of alimony vary widely from state-to-state, a uniform definition of alimony had to be developed for federal income tax purposes. The definition is beyond the scope of this book. Payments labeled for the support of a minor child under the terms of the written decree are never alimony, and therefore are not income to the recipient. Transfers of property between spouses (or former spouses) incident to a divorce usually do not result in the recognition of gain or loss. Instead, the basis of the property in the hands of the spouse making the transfer will carryover to the spouse receiving the property.

**EXAMPLE 3-1.**  Sam owns some X Corporation stock having a fair market value of $10,000 and an adjusted basis of $3,000 as his separate property. He transfers the property to Susan as part of the property settlement resulting from their divorce. Sam will not recognize any gain on the transfer. Susan's basis in the stock is $3,000.

### Annuities

Only the amount of an annuity payment that does not represent a return of the taxpayer's investment is income. The problem facing the taxpayer then is one of determining how much of a given annuity payment represents a return of his capital investment. A simple allocation of each annuity payment between income and capital is made.

The problem becomes more complex when the total annuity benefit is not specified in the annuity contract, as is the case when payments will be received for the taxpayer's remaining life. In this situation, the tax laws provide a table which specifies the period of time (based on the recipient's sex, age at which the annuity payments are first received, and the annuity's terms) over which the annuity payments can be expected to be received. The same portion of each periodic payment is excluded from gross income as a return of the annuitant's capital investment, regardless of the period of time that the annuity benefits are actually paid for.

One other rule can be important in determining the income to be recognized from an annuity that results from an employer–employee relationship when both the employer and employee have contributed to the annuity. In these cases the employee's contribution to the annuity may be insignificant in comparison to benefits to be received. If the taxpayer will receive payments equal to his investment during the first three-years the annuity payments are received, no allocation of payments into return of capital and income is made. Instead, the taxpayer claims no income until all his investment has been returned to him. After he receives all of his investment back, all future annuity payments are totally included in his income.

### Social Security Benefits

As a matter of administrative largess social security payments generally have not been taxed to the recipient at all. The Social Security Reform Act of 1983 made social security income taxable to taxpayers who have significant amounts of A.G.I. starting in 1984.

### Excludible Items

### Donative Intent Exclusions

Gifts and inheritances are totally excluded from the calculation of gross income. Any income earned from gifted or inherited property is, of course, taxable.

Scholarships and fellowships are excluded from gross income for degree candidates as long as the payment does not represent compensation for past, present, or future services and the scholarship or fellowship is not primarily for the benefit of the grantor. Non-degree candidates can exclude scholarships and fellowships for up to $300 per month for no more than 36 months under certain conditions.

Most prizes and awards represent compensation for a taxpayer's efforts, and therefore are taxed as income. However, prizes and awards in recognition of religious, charitable, scientific, educational, artistic, or civic achievements are not included in the winner's income as long as the recipient was chosen without any action on his part to enter the contest, and as long as no substantial future service is required of the winner. Two examples of prizes which are excluded from income are the Nobel and Pulitzer prizes.

### Personal Welfare Items

Proceeds from a life insurance policy received on the death of the insured are, in all but rare cases, excluded from the income of the recipient. Gross income does not include compensation for personal injuries and sickness received as workmen's compensation or by suit or agreement. Case law indicates that damages which are punitive damages to punish the defendant for gross negligence *are* taxable, as are damages which act as a substitute for lost wages or income (e.g., damages from a patent-infringement suit or insurance proceeds received from business interruption insurance).

### Investor Exclusions

Perhaps the most widely publicized of all exclusions is the exclusion of interest on state and local government obligations. Beginning in 1969, the interest exclusion is not available for arbitrage bonds—those for which the government unit invests the proceeds in higher yielding federal or corporate obligations. The exclusion is also unavailable if the proceeds are used to benefit directly or indirectly a particular business. These so-called "industrial development bonds" do, however, retain their interest exclusion if the bond issue is for $1,000,000 or less, or if it is used to finance public goods such as an industrial park, sports facilities, parks, convention or trade show facilities, or public housing projects. It should be noted, however, that only *interest* on these obligations is excluded; any gain on the sale of the securities is fully taxable.

A *very* small exclusion of dividend income received by individual shareholders of U.S. corporations is available. The rationale for the exclusion is to provide relief from double taxation. (The corporation pays tax on its income and the shareholder also pays tax on any amounts the corporation distributes as dividends.) However, the annual exclusion of $100 in dividend income for an individual taxpayer (or $200 for a married couple filing jointly) is so small that its relief value is questionable.

In 1981, a new dividend exclusion was instituted specifically to encourage continued investment in public utility corporations. In recent years, many public utilities have developed a plan which allows each shareholder to choose cash dividends or to choose additional shares of the utility stock in lieu of cash dividends. If an individual taxpayer elects, dividends which are reinvested in such a plan can be excluded for amounts up to $750 per year ($1,500 for a married couple filing jointly). The tax consequences of receiving the dividend shares depends on how long the shareholder holds these shares. If the stock is sold within 1 year after receipt of the dividend, the shareholder will recognize ordinary income. If the stock is held more than 1 year, the entire sale proceeds are taxed as a long-term capital gain.

In addition to the exclusions discussed here, there are numerous exclusions for employee fringe benefits. These exclusions are discussed in Chapter 10 along with other information on employee compensation.

## OTHER DEDUCTIONS FOR INDIVIDUAL TAXPAYERS

First, it is necessary to remember that deductions for individual taxpayers, unlike those for corporations, must be classified into deductions FOR A.G.I. or deductions FROM A.G.I. A review of Figure 1-1 will be useful at this stage to help you see how the two categories are treated in the calculation of the tax liability. Deductions FOR A.G.I. will first be briefly discussed followed by deductions FROM A.G.I.

### Deductions FOR A.G.I.

A sole proprietor reports all the ordinary and necessary expenses of his trade or business as deductions FOR A.G.I. on his personal tax return. In addition, partners and S corporation shareholders report the losses and ordinary and necessary expenses of these business entities as FOR A.G.I. deductions. Section 62 of the Code also authorizes a variety of other deductions at this stage of the calculation.

## Employee Deductions

Five kinds of employee expenses are deductible FOR A.G.I.:

1.  Expenses of outside salesmen.
2.  Expenses for travel away from home.
3.  Transportation expenses.
4.  Reimbursed expenses.
5.  Moving expenses.

All other employee expenses must be deducted FROM A.G.I., if they can be deducted at all.

All expenses incurred by an outside salesman in the performance of his job are deductions FOR A.G.I. This is true whether or not the expenses are reimbursed by the employer. Congress, in fact, has chosen to treat this particular category of employee in many ways as if he were self-employed and accordingly allow a FOR A.G.I. deduction for his ordinary and necessary business expenses.

Employee expenses for travel away from home include the cost of transportation, reasonable amounts for meals and lodging, and incidental expenses such as laundry and valet services incurred while traveling away from home as part of employment. Travel generally constitutes "travel away from home" when it is a business trip that is long enough to require a rest period or an overnight stay.

If a business trip within the United States is used to combine business and pleasure, a more stringent set of rules apply. Transportation costs are deductible only if the trip is primarily for business. The determination of whether a trip is primarily for business or for pleasure is based on relative time spent on the two activities. Even if the trip is determined to be primarily for pleasure, the meals, lodging and incidental expenses for time actually spent on business remain deductible. When the business-pleasure trip is outside the United States, a much more complex set of rules apply and a tax advisor should be consulted.

Transportation expenses are the second category of employee expenses which are deductible FOR A.G.I. Transportation expenses include the costs of taxis, buses, auto travel, tolls, and parking incurred in a trade or business or as an employee. Qualified transportation expenses do not include the costs of commuting to and from work, but it does include the costs of transportation from your regular job location to a customer or client's office, or of making a delivery away from your regular job location.

All employee expenses which are reimbursed by the employer qualify as deductions FOR A.G.I. In theory, all reimbursements are gross income and all reimbursed expenses result in deductions FOR A.G.I. As a matter of administrative ease, if the employee has to give the employer an accounting of expenses, the reporting requirements are simpler. In this case, if reimbursements equal expenses, neither amount is reported on the taxpayer's return. If reimbursements exceed expenses, only the excess reimbursement is reported as income. If expenses exceed reimbursements, the employee must report reimbursements as gross income, the portion of the expenses that were reimbursed as a FOR A.G.I. deduction and the unreimbursed portion of the expenses as a FOR or FROM A.G.I. deduction depending upon their nature. (If the taxpayer uses only the zero bracket amount, the unreimbursed employee expenses provide him with no tax benefit at all.)

While entertainment expenses are common employee expenses, their treatment is more restrictive. Entertainment expenses are deductible only if directly related to the conduct of a trade or business, the production of income, or are associated with such activities by having the entertainment take place immediately before or after a substantial and bona fide business discussion. If the entertainment expense is incurred by a self-employed individual it is a FOR A.G.I. deduction. Employees are permitted to deduct unreimbursed entertainment expenses as a FROM A.G.I. deduction. If the employee is reimbursed for his entertainment expenses, then the deduction rules outlined below for reimbursed expenses apply. The tax laws restrict the deduction for entertainment facilities (e.g., country club and social club membership) and business gifts. Dues paid to civic or professional clubs are deductible. Dues paid to country clubs or social clubs are deductible only if the membership is used more than 50% of the time for business. Business gifts are restricted to $25 per person each year.

Special rules are also found in Section 274 regarding documentation of the expenses. Starting in 1985 a taxpayer must maintain *contemporaneous* records for traveling expenses (including local and away from home travel), expenses incurred for entertainment, amusement, or recreation facilities, and business gifts that are trade or business expenses or related to the production of income. For travel and entertainment expenses and expenses for a recreation facility, the records must include the date, time, location, and business purpose of the expense; the business relationship of the individuals who were entertained; and the amount of the expenditures. For business gifts the records must include the date and description, amount, and business purpose of the gift, and business relationship of the individual receiving the gift. The deduction will be denied for improperly substantiated travel and entertainment expenses and business gifts.

The three major kinds of employee expenses and their effect on the taxpayer's return can be best shown by an example.

**EXAMPLE 3-2.** Tax A. Voider, an employee of the Cleveland office of Big Firm, Inc., incurred the following expenses related to his job:

| | |
|---|---:|
| Expenses of a 3-day business meeting in Miami | $ 428 |
| Hotels and meals in Miami | 375 |
| Rental car in Miami | 140 |
| Laundry and valet service in Miami | 22 |
| Auto expenses related to calling on clients in Cleveland | 155 |
| Meals with clients in Cleveland | 400 |
| Subscription to trade magazine closely related to job | 80 |
| Total | $1,600 |

His total reimbursements were $1,200. No breakdown of the amounts being reimbursed was given to Tax A. Voider.

FOR A.G.I.

| | |
|---|---:|
| Travel away from home ($428 + $375 + $140 + $22) | $ 965 |
| Transportation | 155 |
| Other reimbursed employee expenses: | |

$$\frac{\text{Other employee expenses (\$480)}}{\text{Total employee expenses (\$1,600)}} \times \$1,200 \text{ reimbursement} \quad 360$$

FROM A.G.I. deductions

| | |
|---|---:|
| Other employee expenses ($480) − FOR A.G.I. | |
| deduction ($360) | 120 |
| Total | $1,600 |

Note that all travel and transportation expenses are deductible FOR A.G.I. whether or not they are reimbursed. Other employee expenses are deductible FOR A.G.I. only to the extent they are reimbursed. If reimbursements are not clearly identified as to what they represent, the amounts must be prorated among all three categories of employee expenses.

The final category of employee expenses which generates FOR A.G.I. deductions is moving expenses. For a taxpayer to be able to deduct any moving expenses he must be accepting a new job and meet a distance and a time test. The distance test requires that the taxpayer's new job be at least 35 miles farther from his old home than his old job was from his old home. (Notice there is no requirement related to the distance from the new job to the new home.)

The time test requires that the taxpayer work 39 weeks on a full-time basis in his new job location during the 12 months following the move. (Self-employed taxpayers must work in the new job location for 78 weeks in the first 24 months following the move, as well as work 39 weeks in the first 12 months.) If the employee is transferred, disabled, or discharged through no fault of his own, the time test is waived.

Once the time and distance tests are met, the taxpayer must determine the amount of deductible moving expenses. All direct moving expenses are deductible without limit. These direct expenses include all the costs of getting the taxpayer, the members of his household, and his household goods and personal belongings from the old residence to the new residence. These direct expenses include reasonable costs incurred for packing, moving, and storing household goods as well as the actual costs of travel (including reasonable amounts for meals and lodging along the way) for the taxpayer and his household.

In addition to the fully-deductible direct moving expenses, the taxpayer may deduct limited amounts of three kinds of indirect moving expenses. First, the taxpayer may deduct up to $1,500 in total for house-hunting trips to the new location and temporary living expenses incurred during the first 30 days in the new location. Qualified house-hunting trip expenses include transportation, meals, and lodging for any number of trips to the new work location to find housing. However, no trip qualifies as a house-hunting trip until after a job is accepted.

**EXAMPLE 3-3.**   Tax A. Voider knows that she wants to relocate in Houston, Texas. She makes a trip from Richmond, Virginia to Houston to look for housing and to interview with several companies about a job. None of the expenses of the trip can be deducted as a moving expense since Tax A. Voider had not accepted a job in Houston before beginning the trip.

Temporary living expenses include meals and lodging in temporary quarters in the new work location during any period of 30 consecutive days after accepting employment in the new location (i.e. the costs of meals and hotel rooms in the new job location while waiting to close on a new house or while waiting for the new apartment to be ready for occupancy).

The other item of deductible indirect moving expenses is the "qualified residence sale, purchase, or lease expense." This expense when added to temporary living expenses and house-hunting trip expenses cannot exceed $3,000. Sales, purchase, or lease expenses include the costs of selling the old residence (such as broker's commissions, attorney's fees, title fees, escrow fees, and points paid by the seller) and the costs of purchasing the new residence (such as attorney's fees, escrow fees, appraisal fees, title costs, points paid by the buyer which do not represent prepayment of interest).

### Offices Located in the Home

The tax laws have also placed substantial restrictions on a taxpayer's ability to deduct expenses related to the maintenance of an office located in his personal residence. No deduction can be claimed for a portion of a residence used as an office unless it is *exclusively* used on a *regular* basis as (1) the principal place of business for any trade or business, or (2) a place of business that is used by the taxpayer regularly in the normal course of business to meet with patients, clients, or customers.

These rules do not restrict the deduction that can be claimed for expenses that are otherwise deductible by the taxpayer either as a

FOR A.G.I. or FROM A.G.I deduction (e.g., business expenses other than those related to the office, interest, and taxes). Office-in-home operating expenses such as maintenance, utilities, insurance premiums, and depreciation are restricted to the lesser of (1) the actual expense incurred or (2) the amount of gross income earned from the business activity minus the interest, property taxes, etc. that are otherwise deductible.

**Example 3-4.** Tax A. Voider uses an office in his personal residence on a regular basis for operating a consulting practice. He makes no other use of the office during the year, and uses no other premises for the consulting activity. His gross income from the consulting activities is $2,900. Expenses for part-time secretarial help, telephone service, and supplies amount to $1,850. Interest and property taxes total $7,000 of which $700 are allocable to the office space. Utilities, maintenance, and depreciation allocable to the office space are $100, $200, and $300, respectively. The deductible office expenses are determined as follows:

|         |                                                 |          |
| ------- | ----------------------------------------------- | -------- |
|         | Gross income                                    | $2,900   |
| Less:   | Secretarial help, telephone, supplies           | (1,850)  |
| Equals: | Gross income derived from the use of the unit   | $1,050   |
| Less:   | Allocable portion of interest and taxes         | ( 700)   |
| Equals: | Limitation on further deductions                | $ 350)   |
| Less:   | Allocable portion of utilities and maintenance  | ( 300)   |
| Equals: | Limitation on depreciation                      | $ 50     |

The limitation on the deductions prevents $250 of the depreciation from being deducted. All of these expenses are deductible FOR A.G.I. The $6,300 of interest and taxes that apply to the remainder of the personal residence are deductible FROM A.G.I.

### Hobby Losses

The hobby loss rules are intended to prevent a taxpayer from deducting losses from an activity that is not "engaged in for profit." If the taxpayer can show that the activity was engaged in with an intent to earn a profit, then the losses that are incurred can be deducted without restriction. The hobby loss rules establish a basic presumption that an activity is engaged in for profit if the gross income exceeds its deductions for two or more taxable years out of a period of five consecutive taxable years (seven consecutive taxable years for horse breeding and racing).

Hobby-related expenses, which are deductible under the tax laws even if a profit-making motive is not present (e.g., interest, taxes, and casualty losses), remain deductible without limit even if the activity is determined to be a hobby. Other expenses can be deducted only to the extent of the taxpayer's gross income from the activity.

### Other FOR A.G.I. Deductions

Individuals are allowed numerous other deductions FOR A.G.I. but only three others will be discussed briefly here: alimony paid, contributions to an I.R.A., and bad debts. The general rule for alimony paid is that the payor can deduct what the payee must include in income.

Contributions to an Individual Retirement Account (IRA) are limited by numerous rules which will be discussed in detail in Chapter 10. At this point, it is sufficient to know that qualifying contributions to an IRA will result in deductions FOR A.G.I. Similarly, contributions to a self-employed individual (H.R.10) pension plan are also deductible as a FOR A.G.I. deduction.

Business and nonbusiness bad debts of an individual taxpayer are deductible FOR A.G.I. A business bad debt is an ordinary loss that is deductible without limitation. A nonbusiness bad debt is treated as a short-term capital loss and is deductible according to the capital loss rules.

### Deductions FROM A.G.I.

As noted earlier in this chapter, each individual taxpayer can deduct FROM A.G.I. the sum of: (1) the taxpayer's itemized deductions that exceed a zero bracket amount; and (2) the taxpayer's personal and dependency exemptions. A taxpayer's itemized deductions include deductions for medical expenses, interest, taxes, charitable contributions, certain casualty losses and other miscellaneous expenses. These items are briefly discussed in the proceeding sections.

### Medical Expenses

Deductible medical expenses are the unreimbused amounts *paid* during the year by the taxpayer for doctors, dentists, hospitals, and other medical treatments and procedures for himself, his spouse, and his dependents. The deduction is allowed only to the extent the expenses exceed 5% of A.G.I.

### Taxes

Nonbusiness taxes paid by the individual taxpayer can be deducted FROM A.G.I. These deductible taxes include state, local, and foreign income and excess profits taxes; foreign, state, and local real property taxes; state and local personal property taxes; state and local general sales taxes; and the windfall profits tax. (The taxpayer may choose either to deduct or credit foreign income taxes, but a larger benefit is usually obtained if such taxes are credited.) Remember that *all* taxes paid as part of the ordinary and necessary expenses of a trade or business, or that relate to rental or royalty income, are deductible FOR A.G.I.

### Interest

Interest paid on the taxpayer's personal obligations is deductible FROM A.G.I. Any interest expense that is incurred in connection with a trade or business activity, or that relates to rental or royalty income, is deductible FOR A.G.I. Interest that relates to other income-producing activities is deductible only as a FROM A.G.I. deduction.

Interest is deductible by a cash-basis taxpayer only in the year in which it is paid. Interest can be deducted by an accrual-basis taxpayer when it accrues and economic performance has occurred (by the passage of time), even if not yet paid. However, prepayments of interest expense can be deducted by either a cash or accrual-basis taxpayer only when they accrue.

One other limit exists on the deductibility of interest expense. Formerly, taxpayers could borrow without limit monies to invest in property which generated little or no current income (e.g., land held for appreciation). Since the interest expense was currently deductible and any gain was deferred and possibly taxed at preferential capital gains rates, such investments effectively functioned as tax shelters. To limit such investments, Congress restricted the annual deduction for interest incurred by a noncorporate taxpayer on borrowings used to purchase or carry investment property to the sum of $10,000 plus the net investment income for the year. Net investment income equals the gross income from interest, dividends, rents, royalties, short-term capital gains and other passive income items minus related expenses. Any interest not deductible because of the "investment interest limitation" can be carried over and deducted in later years.

### Charitable Contributions

Charitable contributions are deductible FROM A.G.I. for the individual taxpayer. To qualify as a charitable contribution the gift must be made to an organization that meets any one of the following requirements:

1. A state, a possession of the United States, or a political subdivision.
2. A domestic organization operated exclusively for a religious, charitable, scientific, literary, or educational purpose or for the prevention of cruelty to children or animals.
3. A veterans organization, a cemetery company, or a fraternal organization operating under the lodge system.

Each year a taxpayer can deduct the amount of cash plus the fair market value of the noncash property actually contributed (rather than pledged to qualifying charitable organizations). The amount of the deduction for a property contribution is reduced by the amount of ordinary income or short-term capital gain that would have been reported had the property been sold. Tangible personal property donated (1) to a public charity for a use that is unrelated to the organization's tax exempt function or (2) to a private nonoperating (grantmaking) foundation must be reduced by 40% of the long-term capital gain that would have been reported had the property been sold. [An exception to the private nonoperating foundation reduction requirement is available for appreciated stock (that does not exceed 10% of a corporation's outstanding stock) for which a market quotation is available.] Advice should be sought from a tax professional as to the valuation of such items.

A significant advantage can accrue from contributing appreciated property to a charity, instead of selling it and donating the cash proceeds from the sale.

**EXAMPLE 3-5.**   Tax A. Voider, a 50% tax bracket taxpayer, has appreciated XYZ stocks that are worth $200,000. These stocks originally cost $50,000 and have been held 5 years. A donation of the stocks to a public charity results in a $100,000 tax benefit (assuming that the individual limitations on contribution deductions do not apply). None of the appreciation accruing to Tax A. Voider is taxed at the time of the donation. A sale of the stocks would result in a $30,000 tax on the capital gain ($150,000 × 0.40 × 0.50). This leaves $170,000 of cash to be donated, thus resulting in a tax benefit of $85,000. The donation of the appreciation stock increases Tax A. Voider's tax benefit by $45,000.

Some charitable contribution deductions can be claimed by a taxpayer even if he uses the zero bracket amount. The amount of this deduction equals a specified percentage time the lesser of the actual amount of the charitable contributions made or a dollar limitation. The percentages, dollar limitation, and maximum deductible contribution for the period from 1984 to 1986 are as follows:

| Year | Percentage | Dollar Limitation[a] | Maximum Contribution |
|------|-----------|---------------------|----------------------|
| 1984 | 25 | $300 | $75 |
| 1985 | 50 | None | None |
| 1986 | 100 | None | None |

[a] The limitation is halved for married taxpayers filing separately.

### Casualty Losses

A taxpayer can deduct a casualty or theft loss for trade or business property, property held for the production of income, and nonbusiness property. For tax purposes, a casualty is a sudden, unexpected, or unusual event that results in the destruction of, or damage to, property. Common examples of casualties include storms, shipwrecks, floods, fires, thefts and similar events. The casualty loss for a business property which is partially destroyed, and nonbusiness property which is partially or totally destroyed, is calculated as the lesser of (1) the decline in fair market value of the property immediately before and after the casualty event, or (2) the basis of the property. This tentative loss is reduced by any insurance reimbursements received. If the business property is totally destroyed or stolen, the casualty loss is the basis of the property less any insurance reimbursement. [It is, of course, possible that these calculations could result in a casualty or theft gain (rather than a loss). This gain must be reported as a part of gross income. The gain can be deferred if the insurance proceeds are reinvested in qualifying property. (See Chapter 9.)]

**EXAMPLE 3-6.** TAV Corporation owned a machine having a fair market value of $10,000 and a basis of $6,000. After the machine was damaged in a fire, it was appraised at a fair market value of $5,500. Insurance proceeds of $3,000 were received. TAV reports a casualty loss of $1,500 calculated as follows:

| | | | |
|---|---|---|---|
| Lesser of: | Decline in fair market value, or | $4,500 | |
| | basis before casualty | 6,000 | $4,500 |
| Less: | Insurance reimbursement | | (3,000) |
| Equals: | Casualty loss | | $1,500 |

If TAV's machine was totally destroyed, the deductible casualty loss would be $3,000 ($6,000 basis minus $3,000 insurance proceeds).

Individual taxpayers suffering a casualty or theft loss to nonbusiness property can deduct the loss only to the extent that the loss exceeds $100 for each casualty event, and the total of all casualty and theft losses sustained by the taxpayer during the year (after reduction for the $100 nondeductible amount) exceeds 10% of A.G.I.

**EXAMPLE 3-7.**   Assume the same facts as in the preceding example except that TAV Corporation is instead Tax A. Voider who has an A.G.I. of $10,000, the loss relates instead to a personal automobile, and the loss is the only casualty and theft loss incurred for the year. The $1,500 loss for the partially destroyed automobile must be reduced by the $100 nondeductible amount, by 10% of A.G.I. and then can be claimed as a $400 itemized deduction [$400 = $1,400 − (0.10 × $10,000)].

For purposes of applying the 10% rule, all gains and losses from nonbusiness casualties and thefts are combined. If the recognized gains exceed the recognized losses (after reduction for the $100 nondeductible amount), then the "net" gain is treated as a capital gain. The 10% rule does not apply to any portion of these recognized losses. If the recognized losses exceed the recognized gains, then the "net" loss is treated as an ordinary loss. The "net" loss is deductible only to the extent that it exceeds 10% of the taxpayer's A.G.I.

### Miscellaneous Deductions

In addition to the five categories of itemized deductions discussed above there are numerous miscellaneous deductions. Nonreimbursed employee expenses which cannot be deducted FOR A.G.I. can be deducted FROM A.G.I. The cost of items such as uniforms and hard hats required for employment, union and professional dues, and subscriptions for professional magazines and newsletters can be deducted. Other items which can be deducted are all costs of determining one's tax liability and the preparation of tax forms.

As noted previously, deductions FROM A.G.I. reduce taxable income only to the extent they exceed the zero bracket amount (ZBA). The ZBA is $1,700 ($1,770 for 1985) for each person who is married filing separately, $3,400 ($3,540 for 1985) for a couple who are married filing jointly, and $2,300 ($2,390 for 1985) for other taxpayers. (The ZBA is annually adjusted for inflation beginning in 1985.) If the taxpayer's total deductions FROM A.G.I. are less than the applicable ZBA, the taxpayer gets the benefit of the entire ZBA.

### Personal and Dependency Exemptions

Each taxpayer is eligible for one $1,000 ($1,041 for 1985) personal exemption for himself, and an additional $1,000 ($1,041 for 1985) exemption for a spouse when a joint return is filed. Additional $1,000 ($1,041 for 1985) personal exemptions are available for the taxpayer and spouse if either is 65 years of age or older or blind.

A $1,000 ($1,041 for 1985) dependency exemption is also available for each individual who is a dependent of the taxpayer. To qualify as a dependent the Code provides 5 requirements must be met. Your tax adviser can answer questions on this sometimes complex analysis.

## FILING STATUSES AND TAX RATES

Six filing statuses are available in the tax laws. Each of these filing statuses is outlined below. The tax schedules for all six filing statuses are presented in Appendix A.

### Single Taxpayers

A taxpayer is single if he/she is not married on the last day of the taxable year, or does not qualify for one of the other special filing statuses. This category of taxpayer includes those individuals that are legally separated from their spouse under a decree of divorce or separate maintenance on the last day of the taxable year.

### Married Filing Joint Return

A husband and wife who are married on the last day of the taxable year can elect to file a joint tax return. This tax return includes the combined income, deductions, and exemptions of both spouses. The two spouses are jointly and severally liable for any taxes, interest, and penalties that may come due for the year. The tax liability for a married couple filing a joint return is lower than the tax due for a single individual reporting a similar amount of taxable income. If the total income pool is earned by both the husband and wife, the tax liability incurred by filing a joint return may exceed that incurred by the two individuals filing separately. This additional tax is known as the "marriage penalty."

A FOR A.G.I. deduction now reduces this "marriage penalty." Two-wage-earner couples filing joint returns are eligible for this special "two-wage-earner deduction." The deduction equals 10% of the earned income (but not in excess of $30,000) reported by the spouse having the smaller earned income.

**EXAMPLE 3-8.** Tax A. Voider and spouse earn salaries of $67,000 and $54,000, respectively, during 1984. If they file a joint return, they can claim a two-wage-earner deduction of $3,000 (10% of the lesser of the actual earned income ($54,000) or the $30,000 ceiling).

### Married Filing Separate Returns

If a couple so chooses, each spouse may report his/her income, deductions, and exemptions on a separate tax return. Normally, no tax savings accrues to a married couple by electing to file two separate returns since the zero bracket amount and each rate bracket for separate return filers is exactly one-half of that used by those married taxpayers that elect to file a joint return. A tax savings can occur when one spouse has large medical deductions or casualty losses and a small A.G.I.

### Head of Household

To qualify as a head of household, the taxpayer must:

1.  Be unmarried; and
2.  (a)  Provide over one-half of the cost of maintaining a home in which the taxpayer and an individual listed below reside:

    (i)  Unmarried child or stepchild of the taxpayer or an unmarried descendant of the taxpayer's child or stepchild even if that person does not qualify as the taxpayer's dependent.

(ii)  A dependent of the taxpayer.

(b)  Provide over one-half of the cost of maintaining a home in which a dependent father or mother reside.

For 1984 and earlier years the individual was required to reside in the taxpayer's home for the entire year. Starting in 1985 the individual only must reside in the home for more than one-half of the taxable year to qualify for head of household status. The father or mother does not have to reside with the taxpayer, but may instead reside in a facility such as a nursing home.

### Surviving Spouse

In the year that a married taxpayer dies, a joint return can be filed by the decedent and his spouse provided the spouse has not remarried by year-end. This joint return privilege is extended to the surviving spouse for the two taxable years following the year of death (or a total of 3 years) if the spouse: (1) has not remarried; (2) maintains a home that is the principal place of residence for a dependent child or stepchild; and (3) provides over one-half of the cost of maintaining the household.

A comparison of the relative 1984 tax liabilities of an individual taxpayer for selected taxable-income amounts under the various filing statuses is indicated as follows:

Filing Status

| Taxable Income | Single | Married Filing Jointly/ Surviving Spouse | Married Filing Separately | Head of Household |
|---|---|---|---|---|
| $10,000 | $ 1,075 | $   819 | $ 1,230 | $ 1,012 |
| 20,000 | 3,205 | 2,461 | 3,929 | 2,966 |
| 40,000 | 9,749 | 7,858 | 11,784 | 9,051 |
| 60,000 | 18,371 | 15,168 | 20,912 | 17,122 |
| 100,000 | 37,935 | 32,400 | 40,700 | 35,650 |
| 200,000 | 87,935 | 81,400 | 90,700 | 85,484 |

## INCOME AVERAGING

Because the federal income tax system applies progressively higher rates, a taxpayer who has large income in a single year, fluctuating income, or even a substantial increase in income from one year to the next, is disproportionately taxed relative to a taxpayer with a fairly even taxable income. Income averaging provides substantial relief in these circumstances. Income averaging permits a taxpayer to treat his current year income as if it had been earned over a 4-year period. The following requirements must be satisfied in order to use income averaging:

1.  The taxpayer's current-year taxable income must exceed his averageable income by at least $3,000. "Averageable income" means the taxpayer's current-year taxable income minus 140% of his average taxable income for the three preceding tax years.

2.  The taxpayer must be a U.S. citizen or resident alien during the current year and the three preceding taxable years.

3.  The taxpayer (and spouse) must have provided at least one-half of their support for the current year and the three preceding taxable years.

There are three exceptions to the support requirement which your tax adviser can explain.

The income averaging tax computation is illustrated in the following example.

EXAMPLE 3-9.    Tax A. Voider is married and reports taxable income in 19X5 of $100,000. His taxable income for the period 19X2–19X4 is as follows: 19X2, $30,000; 19X3, $40,000; and 19X4, $50,000. He files a joint return for the current year and meets all income averaging requirements. Tax A. Voider's averageable income is $44,000 [$100,000 − (1.4 × average 19X2–19X4 income of $40,000)].

| | | | |
|---|---|---|---|
| 1. | Tax on nonaverageable income of $56,000 ($100,000 − $44,000) | | $13,648 |
| 2. | Tax on averageable income | | |
| | Tax on sum of nonaverageable income ($56,000) plus ¼ of averageable income ($11,000), or $67,000 | $18,108 | |
| | Less: tax on nonaverageable income (see above) | (13,648) | |
| | Equals: tax on ¼ of averageable income | $ 4,460 | |
| | | × 4 | |
| | Total tax on averageable income | | 17,840 |
| 3. | Tax using income averaging [(3) = (1) + (2)] | | $31,488 |
| 4. | Tax using regular married-filing-jointly rate schedules and taxable income of $100,000 | | $32,400 |
| 5. | Tax savings by using income averaging [(5) = (4) − (3)] | | $ 912 |

Different income averaging rules applied to 1983 and earlier taxable years. These rules provided for averaging the income over a 5-year period and averageable income being current year income in excess of 120% (instead of 140%) of the average base period income. The changes for 1984 and later years have substantially reduced the number of taxpayers that are eligible to use income averaging and the savings available to eligible taxpayers.

## TAX CREDITS AND PREPAYMENTS

### Tax Credits

Individual taxpayers are able to claim a variety of nonbusiness tax credits. Some of the more common credits are as follows:

1. Political contribution credit.
2. Earned income credit.
3. Credit for the elderly.
4. Child and dependent care credit.
5. Residential energy credit.

6.   Foreign income taxes.

7.   Nonhighway gasoline usage.

The child care credit, credit for the elderly, residential energy credit, and political contributions credit are restricted in total to the taxpayer's tax liability. Excess credits can not be refunded or carried over. Taxes withheld or paid as an estimated tax payment, the earned income credit, and the nonhighway gasoline usage credit can be used to fully offset the taxpayer's tax liability. Excess taxes withheld or paid and these final two credits can be refunded to the taxpayer.

### Withholding and Estimated Taxes

The federal income tax system does not permit a taxpayer to pay his entire tax bill for the year at the time he files his return. Taxpayers who work as employees have federal income taxes withheld from the compensation they receive for their personal services. The amount withheld is based upon the taxpayer's filing status and number of personal and dependency exemptions claimed. Taxpayers who anticipate itemizing their deductions can reduce the amount of their withholding by claiming an additional exemption for withholding purposes for each $1,000 of deductible payments including, for example, itemized deductions, pension contributions, and business and investment losses. Claiming these additional withholding exemptions reduces the income taxes withheld from the taxpayer's wages.

Many taxpayers earn income that is not subject to withholding such as self-employment income, interest, dividends, rents, royalties, pensions, and capital gains. The income taxes due on these amounts must be paid throughout the year in the form of estimated tax payments.

All taxpayers are potentially subject to an underpayment of estimated taxes penalty starting in 1985. The underpayment penalty is not imposed for the entire year if the tax shown on the return (less any credits) is less than $500. The underpayment penalty is not imposed on the January 15th payment if the taxpayer files his tax return on or before the January 31st following the payment due date. The quarterly payment exceptions to the underpayment penalty have been changed. No penalty is imposed if the payments made by the quarterly payment date exceed the amount of the quarterly payment (25%, 50%, etc.) required or if the annual estimated tax amount was the smaller of: (1) the tax liability shown on the tax return for the immediately preceding taxable year; (2) an amount equal to 80% of the tax due on the taxpayer's annualized current year income; or (3) an amount equal to 80% of the tax shown as being due on the taxpayer's tax return for the current taxable year.

Individual taxpayers pay social security taxes on the income they earn as employees. The 1984 rate is 6.7% (a 7.0% tax rate applies to the employer for his social security tax contribution). It is imposed on a maximum of $37,800 of earned income. [The employee and employer rates increase to 7.05% in 1985 with an income ceiling of $39,600.] Self-employed individuals do not pay social security taxes on their self-employment income, but instead pay a self-employment tax. The 1984 rate is 11.3% (14.0% tax reduced by a 2.7% credit). It is imposed on a maximum of $37,800 of self-employment income minus the amount of income the taxpayer has had subject to the social security taxes. The self-employment tax rate increases to 14.1% in 1985 with a 2.3% credit, or a 11.8% "net" tax. The 1985 income ceiling is $39,600. Self-employment income includes the net business profit from self-employment activities and the distributive share of any S corporation or partnership business profits. It does not include dividends, interest, or gain from the disposition of assets.

# 4

# TAXATION
# OF REGULAR
# CORPORATIONS

The corporate form is the dominant means by which business activities are conducted. Some reasons for using the corporate form are not related to the tax laws—limited liability for the shareholders, unlimited life for the entity, and ease of transferability for the ownership interests. Other reasons are directly related to the tax laws—the ability to accumulate earnings at the lower corporate tax rates, the availability of fringe benefits for the shareholder-employees, and the ability to exchange interests in the corporate stock or the corporate assets through the use of tax-free reorganizations.

## TYPES OF CORPORATIONS

A number of different types of corporate entities are found in the tax laws. The most common type is the *regular corporation* or C corporation. The regular corporation's income is taxed at a series of progressive rates from 15 to 46%. Distributions made by a regular corporation out of current or accumulated earnings are taxed to the recipients as dividend income. A special tax election is available to closely held corporations. This election creates a special corporation form known as the S *corporation,* and results in the entity being taxed like a partnership. (See Chapter 5.) A number of other special tax exemptions are also available for qualifying corporations. These include:

1. *Domestic International Sales Corporations (DISC).* A corporate income tax exemption is available for qualifying corporations conducting primarily export-related activities. [The DISC benefits have been repealed (except for "small" DISCs) starting in 1985.]

2. *U.S. Possessions Corporation.* A special tax credit can be claimed by a corporation that conducts a majority of its activities in Puerto Rico or a U.S. possession. This credit exempts from U.S. taxation any foreign trade or business income and certain foreign investment income forms.

3. *Real Estate Investment Trusts (REIT).* A corporate income tax exemption is available for qualifying corporations engaged primarily in real estate activities.

4. *Regulated Investment Companies.* A corporate income tax exemption is available for qualifying corporations engaged primarily in investment activities.

5. *Tax-exempt Organizations.* A corporate taxpayer that meets certain requirements regarding the tax-exempt activities it conducts receives a partial tax-exemption. These corporations are taxed only on the business income earned, which is unrelated to exempt activities.

The earnings of the Domestic International Sales Corporation, Real Estate Investment Trust, and Regulated Investment Company are taxed only to the entity's shareholders.

All corporations are classified as either *domestic corporations* or *foreign corporations.* A domestic corporation is a corporation incorporated under the laws of the United States, one of the 50 states, or the District of Columbia. All other corporations are foreign corporations. Domestic corporations are taxed on their worldwide taxable income according to the rules outlined below. They may also qualify for any of the five special tax statuses described above. Foreign corporations are exempt from U.S. taxation unless they earn investment income in the United States, or they conduct a U.S. trade or business. The investment income is taxed at a 30%-rate. No deductions are permitted to reduce the gross investment income. The trade or business income is taxed at the regular corporate income tax rates.

The earnings of a foreign corporation that is owned by a domestic corporation, or a group of U.S. citizens, is exempt from U.S. taxation unless it earns income from U.S. investment or trade or business activities. This income is not taxed to its U.S. owners until it is brought back to the United States as a dividend. This tax exemption is known as the "deferral privilege." Certain forms of "tainted" income are constructively distributed to the U.S. shareholders in the year in which it is earned (instead of the year in which it is received as a dividend) under the Subpart F rules and the Foreign Personal Holding Company rules. These rules prevent U.S. shareholders from using foreign corporations to shelter the income derived from certain kinds of overseas activities.

The 1984 Tax Act created a new category of foreign corporation— the Foreign Sales Corporation (FSC). Starting in 1985, these entities replace the Domestic International Sales Corporation. The FSCs are primarily foreign incorporated subsidiaries of a U.S. parent corporation that are engaged in exporting activities. Qualifying FSCs will have part or all of their profits exempted from the U.S. corporate income tax when earned.

## DETERMINATION OF CORPORATE TAX LIABILITY

The corporate tax liability is calculated following the general income tax formula outlined in Figure 1-1. The corporate formula is illustrated in Figure 4-1. Each of its components is examined in the proceeding sections.

**FIGURE 4-1**   Determination of the corporate tax liability.

|          |                                                                                                    |
| -------- | -------------------------------------------------------------------------------------------------- |
|          | Income broadly conceived                                                                           |
| Less:    | Exclusions                                                                                         |
| Equals:  | Gross income                                                                                       |
| Less:    | Trade or business (regular) deductions                                                             |
|          | Special deductions (dividends-received and dividends-paid deductions)                              |
| Equals:  | Taxable income                                                                                     |
| Times:   | Corporate tax rates                                                                                |
|          |    1.  Ordinary income rates                                              |
|          |    2.  Alternative tax rate on long-term capital gains                    |
| Equals:  | Gross tax liability                                                                                |
| Less:    | Tax credits                                                                                        |
|          | Estimated tax payments                                                                             |
| Plus:    | Recapture of previously claimed tax credits                                                        |
| Equals:  | Net tax liability (or net refund due the corporation)                                              |

## Gross Income

The regular corporation elects its own taxable year. The taxable year can be either a fiscal year or a calendar year, and can be different from that of its shareholders. Similarly, the regular corporation can adopt its own accounting methods independent of those used by its shareholders.

The gross income rules for the corporate taxpayer generally follow those that apply to an individual taxpayer. The basic exclusions for tax-exempt bond interest, proceeds of life insurance policies, recovery of previously claimed deductions which provided no tax benefit to the taxpayer, income derived from the discharge of an indebtedness and so on are also available to the corporate taxpayer.

A number of exclusions are available only to corporations because of their treatment as a separate entity independent from its shareholders. For example, corporations can exclude capital contributions received from shareholders and nonshareholders, and gains realized on certain dividend and liquidating distributions.

## Deductions

All of a regular corporation's activities are considered to be connected with the conduct of a trade or business. Therefore, its expenses are deductible under Code Section 162. Compare this result to the individual taxpayer who is subject to separate rules relating to (1) trade or business expenses and (2) transactions entered into with a profit motive.

A number of special deduction and loss rules apply to corporate taxpayers. Differences between the taxation of individual and corporate taxpayers are pointed out in the pages that follow.

### Charitable Contributions

As discussed in Chapter 3, a charitable contribution deduction is normally claimed in the taxable year in which it is paid. The amount of the deduction for a corporation generally follows the rules for individual taxpayers but there are some minor modifications. First, contributions of inventory used to care for the ill, the needy, or infants and contributions of scientific property to an educational institution to be used for research activities are eligible for increased contribution deductions when donated by a corporation. The amount of the deduction in these situations equals their basis plus one-half of the excess of the property's fair market value over its basis. The deduction, however, may not exceed two times their basis. (Normally a deduction for the contribution of inventory property would be valued at its basis.) Second, the deduction for capital gain properties contributed to private nonoperating foundations (other than certain appreciated stocks), or to public charities for a purpose unrelated to its tax exemption, equals the property's fair market value minus $28/46$th of the amount of long-term capital gain that would be reported if the property were instead sold.

A corporation that uses the accrual method of accounting can accrue part or all of its contributions and deduct them in the year of the accrual. To do this, the contribution must be approved by the board of directors prior to year-end, and be paid in the first 2½ months following year-end. Deducting contributions (up to the dollar limitation described below) in the year that they are pledged accelerates the tax savings provided by the contribution by one year.

The deduction for corporate charitable contributions are restricted to 10% of taxable income (as computed by excluding charitable contributions, dividends-received deductions, and net operating loss or capital loss carrybacks). This limitation is separate from the limitation that applies to the corporation's shareholders. In the case of a closely held corporation, contributions made by the corporation can be used to increase the giving that the shareholder(s) is able to carry out under the tax laws. Excess contributions can be carried over for five years and deducted against any unused limitation.

### Dividends-Received Deductions

A domestic corporation can claim a dividends-received deduction for dividends received from other domestic corporations. The amount of the deduction equals 85% of the gross income reported as a result of receiving the dividend. Thus, if a $100 dividend is received, only $15 of the dividend is included in taxable income. If the dividend is received from a distributing corporation whose stock is more than 80% owned by the distributee corporation, then the dividends-received deduction percentage is increased from 85 to 100. Such an increase permits a property distribution to be received tax-free from a "related" corporation. (A further discussion on the dividends-received deduction can be found in Chapter 11.).

### Net Operating Losses

These losses can be carried back three years, and forward fifteen years. As with an individual taxpayer, an election can be made to forgo the carryback and only carryover the loss to the succeeding fifteen years.

The losses of a regular corporation are presumed to be incurred as a result of conducting a trade or business. As such, they are not subject to the "hobby loss" rules. They are subject to the "at risk" rules only when the regular corporation is closely held and satisfies the stock ownership requirement for personal holding companies.

### Bad Debts

All of the activities of a corporate taxpayer are considered to be related to the conduct of a trade or business. As a result, all bad debts incurred by the corporation are business-related and can be used to offset the ordinary income derived by the corporation.

A taxpayer can use the reserve method or the specific charge-off method to report its bad debt deductions. The specific charge-off method results in a bad debt being deducted at the time that it becomes partially or totally worthless. Use of the reserve method permits the taxpayer to claim a deduction each year for the amount of the reasonable addition to the bad debt reserve (even though the specific debt has not yet been written off). Partially or totally worthless bad debts are then written off against the balance of the bad debt reserve. The IRS and the courts have accepted a formula to define the taxpayer's bad debt experience which is a 6-year weighted average of the ratio of bad debts (less any recoveries) to accounts and notes receivable. The bad debt deduction is the amount of the addition to the reserve that is needed to bring its balance up to the amount calculated by applying the formula to the current year and preceding 5 years' bad debt information.

**EXAMPLE 4-1.** TAV Corporation uses the accrual method of accounting along with the specific charge-off method for reporting its bad debts. In early 19X6 it sells inventory to individual X for $10,000. In June, 19X7 X files for bankruptcy and it is estimated that TAV will receive 30 cents for each dollar owed it by X. In December, 19X8 TAV collects $2,000 from X. The sales revenue is reported in the 19X6 tax return because TAV uses the accrual method of accounting. A $7,000 bad debt deduction (($10,000 − $3,000) can be claimed in 19X7 for the partial worthlessness of the debt that X owes TAV. An additional $1,000 bad debt deduction can be claimed in 19X8 because the final payment of $2,000 is $1,000 less than what was expected to be collected. Alternatively, TAV could have taken an $8,000 deduction when the final payment was received in 19X8.

**EXAMPLE 4-2.** Assume that TAV uses the reserve method to account for its bad debts. Each year TAV would claim a deduction for a reasonable addition to its bad debt reserve that is based upon its "experience" with uncollectible accounts. The $8,000 bad debt, resulting from the sale to X, is charged off against the bad debt reserve in 19X7 and 19X8; this does not directly affect TAV's taxable income.

*Inventories*

The use of the accrual method of accounting for inventories is required whenever the production, purchase, or sale of merchandise is an income-producing factor. The tax laws permit a taxpayer to use either the cost or lower of cost or market (LCM) method to value the inventories. Certain inventory practices used in financial accounting are prohibited by the tax laws—such as deducting a reserve for price changes, or using a base stock concept. Write-downs are permitted for goods that are unsalable at normal prices because of damages, imperfections, broken lots, and so on.

The determination of an inventory's "cost" follows detailed rules found in the tax laws. Manufacturers must use the full-absorption inventory costing method. Full-absorption costing requires that direct material, direct labor, and fixed and variable overhead costs be included in determining the inventory's cost. Other alternatives such as direct costing or prime costing are not acceptable.

Taxpayers can elect to use the specific identification, First-in, first-out (FIFO) or last-in, first-out (LIFO) inventory flow method. If a taxpayer uses the LIFO method for tax purposes, it must also use the LIFO method for reporting to its owners and creditors. The LIFO method carries with it the advantage that the most recently incurred inventory costs are offset first against the sales revenues to determine the taxpayer's gross profit. In inflationary times this means that the most expensive inventory items are considered to have been sold, thus providing the largest reduction to taxable income and the lowest tax liability. The LIFO election may not suit all taxpayers. Taxpayers in industries where prices are declining, or where inventory quantities fluctuate widely, may be able to minimize their taxable income by using the FIFO or LCM method.

The lower of cost or market method permits a taxpayer to account for each inventory item at the lower of its cost or market value. Market value for purchased goods is the bid price for the commodity or good on the inventory date. Market value for manufactured goods is its reproduction cost. Some taxpayers may find that the use of the lower market value permits greater tax savings than does the LIFO method, particularly where an item's reproduction cost is declining (e.g., calculators or computers).

### Capital Losses

Corporate capital losses cannot be deducted as an offset to ordinary income in the year that they are incurred. These losses must first offset the current year's capital gains. Then any unused losses are carried back to the three preceding taxable years and carried forward to the succeeding five taxable years to offset capital gains in those years. All capital losses are carried back and forward as short-term capital losses regardless of their original character. Thus, a long-term capital loss is carried back as a short-term capital loss and is first used to offset the short-term capital gains (if any) in the third preceding taxable year. The advantage of properly timing the recognition of a capital loss can be illustrated by the following example:

**EXAMPLE 4-3.** TAV Corporation has reported the following capital gains and losses:

| Year | Long-Term Capital Gain (Loss) | Short-Term Capital Gain (Loss) |
|------|-------------------------------|--------------------------------|
| 19X1 | $35,000 | |
| 19X2 | | $15,000 |
| 19X3 | 25,000 | 40,000 |
| 19X4 | 10,000 | |

In each year the long-term capital gains were taxed at the 28% alternative tax rate (explained later in this chapter), and the short-term capital gains were taxed at the 46% rate. TAV would like to realize a $50,000 short-term capital loss. If a 19X4 transaction is entered into, the loss offsets the following gains: 19X4, $10,000 long-term capital gain; 19X1, $35,000 long-term capital gain; and 19X2, $5,000 short-term capital gain. A 19X5 transaction would offset short-term capital gains recognized in 19X2 and 19X3 of $15,000 and $35,000, respectively. The delayed transaction, which offsets only short-term capital losses, creates a larger tax benefit since short-term capital gains have been taxed at a rate 18 percentage points above that applying to the long-term capital gains.

## Credits

The following credits relate to business activities and are the ones most likely to be encountered by corporate taxpayers. (See also the investment tax credit and business energy tax credit in Chapter 8.)

### Foreign Tax Credit

In order to mitigate the effects of double taxation of income by the United States and foreign jurisdictions, income taxes paid or accrued to a foreign country or U.S. possession can be claimed as a tax credit or a tax deduction. Except in very limited circumstances, a taxpayer generally will choose the credit alternative. Domestic corporations that own at least ten percent of the voting stock of a foreign corporation, and who receive a dividend from such corporation, can also claim a foreign tax credit for a proportionate amount (based upon the portion of the after-tax profits that are received) of the income taxes that are paid by the foreign corporation.

### Targeted Jobs Credit

A special credit is available equal to a portion of the first-year or second-year wages paid to eligible employees. Eligible employees include members of various economically disadvantaged groups, students participating in certain cooperative education programs, and certain summer jobholders.

### Nonhighway Use of Gasoline Credit

A credit is available to refund the amount of the federal excise taxes levied on gasoline and oils used for nonhighway uses such as farming and certain transportation activities.

### Alcohol Fuels Credit

A credit of 60 cents (50 cents for 1984 and earlier years) is permitted for each gallon of alcohol or alcohol mixture fuel that is sold or used in connection with the conduct of a trade or business.

### Research and Experimental
### Expense Credit

A credit is available for 25% of the amount by which the taxpayer's research expenditures for the current taxable year exceed the average of the taxpayer's annual research expenditures during the three preceding taxable years. This credit is intended to encourage increased research activities by making the credit available in addition to the deductions that are otherwise available for such expenditures.

### Credit Limitation

Business tax credits—the investment tax credit, the targeted jobs credit, the alcohol fuels credit, and the employee stock ownership credit are lumped together for purposes of determining the taxpayer's credit limitation. These credits can offset 100% of the taxpayer's income tax liability up to $25,000 and 85% of the liability in excess of $25,000. Excess credits can be carried back 3 years and forward 15 years. In applying the excess credits, any credit carryover to a taxable year is used before the credits that are earned in the taxable year are used. After the current year credits have been used, then credit carrybacks to the taxable year can be used. Any credits which are not utilized by the end of the 15-year carryover period can be deducted in the next taxable year.

## TAX CALCULATION

### Basic Corporate Tax Rates

The first $100,000 of taxable income is taxed by using a series of four progressive tax rates. A flat 46% marginal tax rate applies to all taxable income in excess of $100,000. The corporate tax rates are as follows:

| Taxable Income | Tax Rate |
|---|---|
| First $25,000 | 15% |
| Second $25,000 | 18 |
| Third $25,000 | 30 |
| Fourth $25,000 | 40 |
| $100,000 – up | 46 |

The reduced tax rates applying to the first $100,000 of taxable income produce a tax savings of $20,250 over the liability that would be incurred if the corporate tax rate were a flat 46 percent on all income.

The $20,250 tax savings is phased-out for any corporation having taxable income in excess of $1,000,000 by imposing an additional 5% tax. Regular corporations will thus end up paying a marginal tax rate of 51% for all of their taxable income from $1,000,000 to $1,-405,000 ($20,250 = $405,000 × 0.05).

The computation of the corporate tax liability is illustrated by the following example:

**Example 4-4.** TAV Corporation reports taxable income of $150,000. Using the current tax rates, the $48,750 corporate tax liability can be calculated in one of two ways:

| Alternative Number 1 | | Alternative Number 2 | |
|---|---|---|---|
| Tax on: | | Taxable income | $150,000 |
| First $25,000 of taxable income | $ 3,750 | Times: Highest marginal tax rate | ×     0.46 |
| Second $25,000 of taxable income | 4,500 | | $ 69,000 |
| Third $25,000 of taxable income | 7,500 | Less: Tax savings | (20,250) |
| Fourth $25,000 of taxable income | 10,000 | Equals: Gross tax liability | $ 48,750 |
| Remaining taxable income ($50,000) | 23,000 | | |
| Equals: Gross tax liability | $48,750 | | |

**FIGURE 4-2**   Tax savings from the use of a regular corporation.

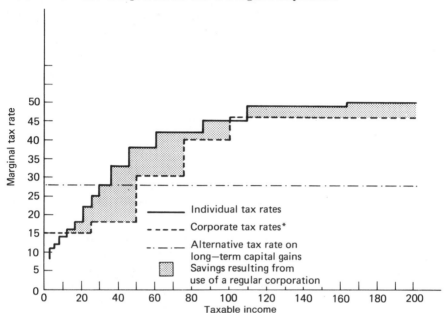

Individual tax rates

Corporate tax rates*

Alternative tax rate on long—term capital gains

Savings resulting from use of a regular corporation

*A special 5% surtax applies to corporate taxable income from $1,000,000 to $1,405,000.

The corporate tax rates offer three tax savings advantages over being taxed as an individual. The first two of these advantages are illustrated in Figure 4-2. First, the marginal tax rates that apply to the first $100,000 of corporate taxable income are generally lower than the rates applying to a similar dollar amount of taxable income earned by an individual taxpayer. Second, the maximum marginal tax rate that applies to a corporation (in all cases except when taxable income is between $1,000,000 and $1,405,000) [46%] is four percentage points below the maximum marginal tax rate that applies to an individual [50%]. These two differences can permit a corporate taxpayer to pay a lower dollar amount of taxes and accumulate a larger amount of after-tax income for reinvestment or debt service purposes.

**EXAMPLE 4-5.**   Tax A. Voider, a married taxpayer who files jointly with his wife, operates a sole proprietorship that earns $200,000 of profits annually. Assuming that no other income is earned and the personal deductions can not be itemized, Tax A. Voider incurs an $80,400 tax liability ($198,000 of taxable income, 1984 tax rates) by operating the business as a sole proprietorship. This leaves $119,600 ($200,000 − $80,400) of after-tax income available for reinvestment. Had Tax A. Voider elected to use a regular corporation instead of a sole proprietorship, the corporate tax liability would be $71,750 ($92,000 − $20,250). No tax liability is incurred by Tax A. Voider until the corporate profits are withdrawn from the business. The funds available for reinvestment would now be $128,250, or an increase of $8,650 over the sole proprietorship alternative.

The tax savings derived from the use of the corporate entity may or may not be permanent. A second income tax levy is encountered if the earnings are distributed to the shareholder or the stock is sold or exchanged in a taxable transaction. This second tax levy can be deferred for a number of years and the present value of the future liability may be quite small. Alternatively, the shareholder might exchange his stock as part of a tax-free reorganization, or hold the stock until his death. If the stock is held until death, the heirs will take a basis equal to the fair market value at the time of the shareholder's death for computing any gain or loss recognized on a subsequent sale or exchange. Thus, all appreciation accruing prior to the shareholder's death completely escapes the income tax.

The third tax advantage from the corporate form accrues because the corporation is an entity separate from its shareholders. Both the shareholder and the corporation can avail themselves of the progression in the individual and corporate tax rates. As a result, a total of $211,400 can be accumulated by a married taxpayer, who files a joint return, and by his wholly owned corporation before any income is taxed at the 46% marginal tax rate. Such an advantage is illustrated by the following example:

**EXAMPLE 4-6.**    Tax A. Voider, a married taxpayer who files a joint tax return, owns all of the stock of TAV Corporation. TAV Corporation earns $211,400 in 19X6. The tax liability for the corporation and its sole shareholder is illustrated in Figure 4-3 (using the 1984 rates) for the following three alternatives: (1) retention of all of

**FIGURE 4-3** Use of the corporation as an income-splitting device.

| | Situation Numbers | | |
| --- | --- | --- | --- |
| | 1 | 2 | 3 |
| | Retention of all income by the corporation | Payment of a $111,400 dividend to Tax A. Voider | Payment of a $111,400 salary to Tax A. Voider |
| Corporate tax liability: | | | |
| Income (1) | $211,400 | $211,400 | $211,400 |
| Less: salary to shareholder | ( 0) | ( 0) | (111,400) |
| Equals: taxable income | $211,400 | $211,400 | $100,000 |
| Corporate tax liability (2) | $ 76,994 | $ 76,994 | $ 25,750 |
| Shareholder tax liability: | | | |
| Income | 0 | $111,400 | $111,400 |
| Less: dividend exclusion | | (200) | |
| personal exemptions | | (2,000) | (2,000) |
| Equals: taxable income | 0 | $109,200 | $109,400 |
| Shareholder tax liability (3) | 0 | $ 36,540 | $ 36,630 |
| Total tax liability (4) = (2) + (3) | $ 76,994 | $113,534 | $ 62,380 |
| Funds available for reinvestment or debt service (5) = (1) − (4) | $134,406 | $ 97,866 | $149,020 |

the income by the corporation; (2) payment of $111,400 in dividends to Tax A. Voider; and (3) payment of $111,400 in salary to Tax A. Voider. Payment of the dividend to the shareholder is the most costly alternative since it results in substantial double taxation. Retention of all of the income in the corporation eliminates the double taxation, but does not permit the income splitting effects that are available by making the deductible salary payment. The two advantages of the salary payment alternative—avoidance of double taxation and income-splitting—increases the funds available for reinvestment by $14,614 ($149,020 − $134,406). This increase results from the fact that full advantage is taken of the 11 to 45% marginal tax rates for the individual taxpayer and the 15 to 40% marginal tax rates for the corporate taxpayer. Some additional costs might be incurred with the salary payment because of the payroll tax liability that is owed by the employee and the corporation.

### Capital Gains

Unlike individual taxpayers, a corporation's long-term capital gains do not receive the special 60% deduction. Thus, both short- and long-term capital gains are fully included in taxable income. Two alternatives do exist for taxing a corporation's "net capital gain" (defined as the excess of net long-term capital gains over net short-term capital losses). These "net capital gains" are taxed at the lower of (1) the regular tax rates or (2) a special alternative tax rate of 28%. No special rate reduction applies to short-term capital gains. The first alternative requires the corporation's taxable income (ordinary income, short-term capital gains, and long-term capital gains) to be taxed at the applicable 15 to 46% marginal tax rates. The second alternative taxes the corporation's taxable income (other than the net capital gain) at the regular tax rates and taxes the net capital gain at a 28% alternative tax rate. The total tax liability using the second alternative is the sum of the two separate calculations. The second alternative ensures that no long-term capital gains are taxed in excess of a 28% effective tax rate.

Rather than calculate both alternatives each time, two simple decision rules can be used.

1.  If the corporation's taxable income (other than its net capital gain) is in excess of $50,000, then use the alternative tax rate. (The marginal tax rate(s) applying to the net capital gain is reduced from 30, 40, or 46% to 28%.)
2.  If the corporation's taxable income is less than $50,000, then use the regular tax rates. (The marginal tax rate(s) applying to the net capital gain is no higher than 15 or 18%.)

In all other situations the tax liability must be calculated using both of the alternatives and the alternative resulting in the smaller tax liability is then selected.

**EXAMPLE 4-7.** TAV Corporation reports the following:

|  | Situation Numbers | | |
|---|---|---|---|
|  | 1 | 2 | 3 |
| Ordinary income (excluding property transactions) | $30,000 | $100,000 | $25,000 |
| Long-term capital gain | 10,000 | 60,000 | 30,000 |
| Short-term capital gain (loss) |  | (10,000) | 10,000 |
| Taxable income | $40,000 | $150,000 | $65,000 |
| Tax liability using: |  |  |  |
| Regular tax rates | $ 6,450 | $ 48,750 | $12,750 |
| Alternative tax rates | 7,450 | 39,750 | 13,950 |

In Situation Nos. 1 and 2 the two decision rules can be used and one can easily see which of the two alternatives would produce the smaller tax liability. The short-term capital loss in Situation No. 2, permits only the $50,000 net capital gain to be taxed at the alternative tax rate. The decision rules cannot provide the optimal solution to Situation No. 3. The regular tax rates produce the lowest tax liability because the tax savings resulting from part of the long-term capital gain being taxed at the 18% marginal tax rate outweighs the added cost of having the portion of the taxable income in excess of $50,000 taxed at the 30% marginal tax rate.

## Controlled Group Restrictions

The $20,250 tax savings that results from the progression in the corporate tax rates can offer an incentive to establish many separate corporations under common control, so that the income earned by any single corporation is no more than $100,000. If five additional corporations were created, the total tax savings that could result from such a plan could be as much as $101,250 ($20,250 × 5). In an attempt to control such tax planning, Congress created the controlled group provisions which require certain tax benefits to be allocated among the members of a controlled group. If a corporation can avoid being included as a member of a controlled group of corporations, it can obtain substantial additional benfits. Some of the tax provisions limited to a single tax benefit for a controlled group of corporations are:

1. The reduced tax rates (15 to 40%) available to a corporation.
2. The $150,000 or $250,000 lifetime exemption for the accumulated earnings tax.
3. The $10,000 exemption for the corporate minimum tax.
4. The $25,000 tax liability amount eligible for a 100% business tax credit offset.
5. The $125,000 limit on used property acquisitions that are eligible for the investment tax credit.
6. The $5,000 limitation on the asset acquisitions that are eligible to be expensed in the year of acquisition.

A controlled group must allocate the reduced tax rate benefit equally among its members, unless a different method of allocation is elected. Thus, if two corporations were part of a controlled group, each corporation would be limited to only $12,500 ($25,000 ÷ 2) of income that could be taxed at each of the four marginal tax rates that apply to the first $100,000 of taxable income, unless a different allocation method were selected.

There are three types of controlled groups subject to these rules: a brother-sister controlled group, a parent-subsidiary controlled group, and a combined controlled group. Each of these groups is illustrated in Figure 4-4. A series of stock attribution rules apply for purposes of all three definitions, which results in an individual being considered to own any shares actually owned plus shares owned by family members or related entities, as well as stock on which he holds a purchase option.

The "brother-sister" rules are illustrated by the following two examples:

**FIGURE 4-4**  Types of controlled groups.

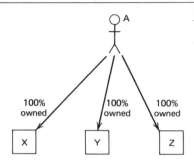

Brother-Sister Controlled Group:
Five or fewer individuals, trusts or estates own:
(1)   At least 80% of the voting power of all classes of voting stock, or at least 80% of the value of all classes of stock of each corporation; and
(2)   More than 50% of the total voting power of all classes of voting stock, or at least 50% of the total value of all classes of stock of each corporation when taking into account only each person's "identical" stock ownership.

Parent-Subsidiary Controlled Group:
A parent corporation (X) owns at least 80% of the voting power of all classes of voting stock, or at least 80% of the value of all classes of stock of a second, subsidiary corporation (Y).

Combined Controlled Group: Each corporation is a member of a brother-sister or parent-subsidiary controlled group, *and* one or more corporations (X) is a parent corporation of a parent-subsidiary controlled group and a member of a brother-sister controlled group.

**EXAMPLE 4-8.** Individuals X and Y own all of the stock of the P and S Corporations. Their stock ownership percentages are as follows:

| | Stock Ownership in: | | Identical |
|---|---|---|---|
| Individual | P Corporation | S Corporation | Ownership |
| X | 80% | 50% | 50% |
| Y | 20 | 50 | 20 |
| Total | 100% | 100% | 70% |

Since both tests are met, P and S Corporations are a brother-sister controlled group. If the stock ownership in S Corporation were changed so X and Y owned 20 and 80%, respectively, then the identical ownership would be only 40% (20 + 20) and the two corporations would not be part of a controlled group.

**EXAMPLE 4-9.** Individuals X, Y, and Z own all of the stock of P and S Corporations. Their stock ownership percentages are as follows:

| | Stock Ownership in: | | Identical |
|---|---|---|---|
| Individual | P Corporation | S Corporation | Ownership |
| X | 70% | 80% | 70% |
| Y | 25 | 0 | 0 |
| Z | 5 | 20 | 5 |
| Total | 100% | 100% | 75% |

The P and S Corporations are not controlled corporations since only the identical ownership test is satisfied. Only individuals X and Z who own stock in *each* of the corporations are counted for purposes of the "80% test." As a result, only 75% of P Corporation's stock is owned by a group of five or fewer shareholders. Thus, P and S Corporations are not members of a controlled group and each can utilize the $20,250 of savings from their first $100,000 of taxable income.

## Separate Versus Consolidated
## Tax Returns

A parent corporation and its subsidiary corporations can elect to file a single consolidated tax return that reports the results for the entire affiliated group. The affiliated group definition requires a group of corporations to be related through a common parent corporation whereby:

1.  The common parent corporation owns at least 80% of the voting stock and at least 80% of each class of nonvoting stock of one corporation.

2.  At least 80% of the voting stock and at least 80% of each class of the nonvoting stock of the remaining members of the affiliated group is owned by corporations included in the affiliated group. (Starting in 1985 the nonvoting stock test is changed to 80% of the value of the outstanding stock for each of the two requirements.)

While some large affiliated groups contain more than 250 corporations, an election to file a consolidated tax return can be made by as few as two corporations. Some of the advantages of filing a consolidated tax return include:

1.  Offsetting in the current year the losses of unprofitable group members against the profits of profitable group members.
2.  Deferring gains realized on intercompany transactions.
3.  Receiving tax-free dividends from other group members.

## SPECIAL TAX LEVIES

Three special tax levies—the corporate minimum tax, the accumulated earnings tax, and the personal holding company tax—can be imposed on a regular corporation.

## Corporate Minimum Tax

The corporate minimum tax is a tax levied on a corporation in addition to its regular federal income tax liability. This levy is determined in the following manner:

|         | Total tax preferences |
|---------|------------------------|
| Less:   | Greater of statutory exemption ($10,000) or the regular tax deduction |
| Equals: | Tax base |
| Times:  | Tax rate (0.15) |
| Equals: | Corporate minimum tax |

The regular tax deduction equals the federal income tax liability minus all corporate tax credits, except the ones claimed for non-highway use of gasoline and for employee stock ownership plans.

Not all items that receive preferential treatment in the tax laws are considered tax preference items. Tax preference items under the corporate minimum tax include:

1.  The "excess" of the depreciation or capital recovery deduction actually claimed on real property over the amount determined by using a hypothetical straight-line calculation.
2.  The "excess" of the amortization deduction claimed on a certified pollution control facility over a hypothetical depreciation calculation.
3.  The amount of the percentage depletion deduction claimed in excess of the basis of the depletable property.
4.  39.13% of the corporation's net capital gain (excess of the net long-term capital gains over net short-term capital losses).

Additional tax preference items can apply to corporations that are characterized as personal holding companies.

## Accumulated Earnings Tax

The accumulated earnings tax is a penalty surtax that can be imposed on any corporation that accumulates an unreasonable amount of earnings. Generally this tax is imposed on only closely-held corporations. The tax is intended to discourage the use of a corporation to shelter income from taxation by imposing a penalty tax on any earnings that are accumulated for a tax avoidance purpose (e.g., avoiding the tax imposed on a dividend distribution). Transactions that can be indicative of a tax avoidance purpose include: (1) dealings between a corporation and its shareholders—such as loans made to the shareholders that have not been repaid; (2) corporate investments that have no reasonable connection with current business activities; and (3) a low level of dividend distributions.

Corporations, other than those engaged in service activities, can accumulate $250,000 over their lifetime without incurring this penalty tax. Service companies (including professional corporations) in the fields such as health, law, engineering, and accounting are limited to a $150,000 exemption. Additional earnings are exempted from the penalty tax if they are accumulated to meet the reasonable needs of the business. Such needs include providing for: (1) the expansion or replacement of plant, (2) the acquisition of the assets or stock of a business, (3) the retirement of debt, (4) the maintenance of working capital levels, and (5) the making of loans to suppliers or customers.

The penalty tax is imposed on a corporation's current year earnings that are retained in the business in excess of the greater of (1) the unused portion of its $150,000/$250,000 lifetime exemption or (2) the current year's addition to the earnings accumulated for the reasonable needs of the business. The first $100,000 of the unreasonably accumulated earnings is taxed at a 27½% rate; the remainder at a 38½% rate.

## Personal Holding Company Tax

The penalty surtax on a personal holding company is intended to discourage a corporation from accumulating certain forms of passive income. Corporations that are closely held and earn predominately passive income are subject to the personal holding company tax on the portion of their current year earnings that are not distributed to their shareholders. The penalty tax is levied at a 50% rate, and is imposed in addition to the corporate income tax. A corporation that is characterized as a personal holding company cannot also be liable for the accumulated earnings tax.

A personal holding company is a corporation that (1) has more than 50% of the value of its outstanding stock owned by five or fewer individuals at any time during the last half of its taxable year, and (2) has at least 60% of its income being personal holding company income. In determining if the stock ownership requirement has been satisfied, an individual is considered to own not only his own shares but also any shares owned by other family members and related entities, and stock for which he holds a purchase option. Personal holding company income includes: dividends; interest; royalties; annuities; rents; mineral, oil, and gas royalties; copyright royalties; produced film rents; income from personal services contracts; and amounts received from an estate or trust. Exclusions are available which, if satisfied, can eliminate some of these income forms from the personal holding company income definition.

## ESTIMATED TAX PAYMENTS

Every corporation must make estimated tax payments if it expects its estimated taxes for the taxable year to be 40 dollars or more. A corporation's estimated tax liability equals its gross federal income tax liability (excluding the corporate minimum tax) minus any tax credits that can be claimed.

## TAX RETURN

A regular corporation must file its corporate income tax return (Form 1120) within 2½ months of the end of its taxable year. For a calendar-year corporation, the Form 1120 is due on March 15. A 6-month extension in which to file the return is available upon request.

# 5

# TAXATION OF S CORPORATIONS

S corporations are rapidly increasing in popularity. These corporations are in no way different from any other regular corporation for state law purposes. An S corporation has a special status only for purposes of calculating and paying income taxes.

The S corporation tax provisions, known as Subchapter S in the Internal Revenue Code, were enacted in order to permit "small corporations that are essentially partnerships to enjoy the corporate form of organization without being made subject to the possible tax disadvantages of the corporation." Three major advantages are obtained by having the corporate entity taxed like a partnership. First, the corporation's income is taxed to the shareholders who may enjoy a lower marginal tax rate than the corporation. Second, the corporation's losses are passed-through to the shareholders and are deducted on their individual tax returns. This permits the losses to provide an immediate tax benefit where they might otherwise only be available as a carryover. Third, the corporation can distribute its earnings as a tax-free return of the shareholder's capital investment and avoid the double taxation associated with regular corporations.

## REQUIREMENTS

Two types of requirements must be satisfied in order to be taxed under Subchapter S—the corporate requirements and the shareholder requirements.

### Corporate Requirements

Five corporate requirements must be satisfied to have a small business corporation taxed under Subchapter S. These are:

1.  The corporation must be a domestic corporation.
2.  The corporation must not be characterized as an ineligible corporation.
3.  The corporation must have only a single class of stock outstanding.
4.  The corporation must make the appropriate election.
5.  The corporation must not fail the Passive Investment Income test for each of three consecutive taxable years.

The ineligible corporation requirement prevents an S corporation from making certain kinds of investments or acquiring certain special tax statuses. A small business corporation cannot acquire directly, or in combination with other related corporations, 80% or more of the stock of another domestic or foreign corporation. Banks, certain financial institutions, and insurance companies can not be Subchapter S corporations.

The corporation must elect to be taxed under the Subchapter S rules. The election can be filed by an existing corporation at any time during the taxable year preceding the year for which the election is effective, or during the first 2½ months of the taxable year for which the election is effective. In order to have a valid election all of the requirements must be satisfied on the date the election is made. A late election, or an election made in a taxable year where one or more of the requirements are failed at some time between the first day of the year and the election date, is invalid for that year and results in the election becoming effective with the first day of the next taxable year.

**EXAMPLE 5-1.**   TAV Corporation has been in existence for 3 years and uses the calendar year as its taxable year. It desires to be taxed under the Subchapter S rules commencing in 19X5. A valid election can be made by the corporation at any time during 19X4, or during the period January 1 through March 15, 19X5. An election made after March 15, 19X5 becomes effective for 19X6.

**EXAMPLE 5-2.**   Assume the same facts as above except that TAV Corporation had a corporate shareholder in 19X4. The sale of the corporate shareholder's stock must take place before January 1, 19X5 in order to permit a valid election to be made during the first 2½ months of 19X5. A sale of the stock after December 31, 19X4 results in the election starting in 19X6. This rule prevents the allocation of income or loss to ineligible shareholders who hold the stock during the pre-election period of 19X5.

A new corporation can only make the election during the first 2½ months of its initial taxable year. An election made after this date becomes effective with the next taxable year.

### Shareholder Requirements

Four shareholder requirements must also be satisfied in order to permit a corporation to be taxed under the Subchapter S rules. These are:

1.  The corporation must not have more than 35 shareholders.
2.  All shareholders must be individuals, estates, and certain kinds of trusts.
3.  Individual shareholders must be either U.S. citizens or resident aliens.

4.  All shareholders at the time of the election must file the appropriate consent.

The shareholder restrictions prohibit nonresident alien individuals, corporations and partnerships from owning any S corporation's stock. Only a few trusts (grantor trusts, voting trusts, those trusts that distribute all of their income to a sole income beneficiary who is treated as the owner of the trust, and certain Qualified Subchapter S Trusts) can be an S corporation shareholder. In the case of each of these trusts, the grantor, deemed-owner, or beneficiary must also be eligible to be a shareholder. An estate can hold S corporation stock only for 60 days. At the end of the 60-day period the election terminates, unless a special exception for grantor trusts, or trusts where the sole income beneficiary is treated as the owner of the trust, applies. This exception permits the estate to hold the stock for a total of 2 years.

Each shareholder owing stock on the election date must consent to the election. This consent is binding on all future years unless the shareholder, or a group of shareholders, revokes the election, or the election terminates because one or more of the corporate or shareholder requirements have been failed. Shareholders who acquire the S corporation stock after the date the election is made do not have to consent to the election. Minority shareholders are therefore automatically bound by the election, and can revoke the election only if they join with additional shareholders to form a group that owns more than 50% of the outstanding stock *and* they file the necessary revocation statement.

## EFFECT OF THE ELECTION

Making an election to be taxed under the Subchapter S provisions causes the following changes to the corporate rules that were outlined in Chapter 4:

1.  S corporations are exempt from the corporate income tax, the accumulated earnings tax, and the personal holding company tax. Limited taxes may be levied on "excess" net passive in-

come amounts and long-term capital gains that have been earned by the S corporation.

2. The shareholder is taxed on his ratable share of the corporation's ordinary income[1] and a number of separately stated income items.

3. The shareholder can deduct his ratable share of the corporation's ordinary loss[2] and a number of separately stated deduction and loss items.

4. The shareholder can claim a credit for his prorata share of the tax credits earned by the corporation.

5. Distributions made by the corporation are generally tax-exempt as a return of the shareholder's capital investment. Distributions are taxable only to the extent that they represent earnings accruing prior to the election's effective date, or to the extent that they exceed the shareholder's basis for his stock investment.

6. The shareholder's basis for his stock investment is increased for his share of the ordinary income and separately stated income items. The basis amount is decreased for any tax-free distributions as well as the pass-through of the ordinary loss and the separately stated deduction and loss items.

Each of these effects of electing to be taxed under the Subchapter S rules is explored in the following sections of this chapter.

## TERMINATION OF THE ELECTION

A number of events can cause the termination of the S corporation election. These include:

1. The corporation electing to be taxed under a special provision, which causes it to be characterized as an "ineligible corporation."

2. The corporation having more than 25% of its gross income as passive investment income in each of three consecutive tax-

able years *and* having accumulated Subchapter C earnings
and profits at the end of each of the three taxable years.

3. The corporation exceeding the 35-shareholder limitation.
4. The corporation or a shareholder transferring stock to an ineligible shareholder.
5. The corporation issuing a second class of stock.
6. The corporation acquiring an 80% or more interest in a subsidiary corporation.

When one of these events occurs, the S corporation election is terminated effective the day preceding the day on which the terminating event occurs. This results in the corporation having to file two
short-period tax returns for the year. The first return covers the time
period from the beginning of the taxable year through the day preceding the day on which the terminating event occurs. The second
return covers the remainder of the corporation's taxable year. The
income for the entire year is allocated to the two return periods on a
daily basis. The income included in the first return is passed-through
to the shareholders under the Subchapter S rules. The income included in the second return is taxed to the corporation using the regular corporation rules. As an alternative to the daily allocation, all of
the shareholders on the last day of the S corporation taxable year and
the first day of the C corporation taxable year can elect to allocate the
income to the two time periods by using the corporation's regular tax
accounting records. Under this election, the actual income or loss
reported prior to the termination is passed-through to the shareholders under the Subchapter S rules. If a 50% or more change in stock
ownership occurs, then only the "tax accounting" allocation method
can be used.

EXAMPLE **5-3.** TAV Corporation has been taxed under the Sub-
    chapter S rules for a number of years. The corporation purchases
    all of the stock of a second corporation on August 1, 19X5. This
    purchase causes the S Corporation election to be terminated as of
    the close of business on July 31, 19X5. If the necessary election is
    made, the actual 19X5 income for the period from January 1
    through July 31, 19X5 is reported using the S corporation rules.

The remainder of the income is taxed to the corporation. Otherwise, the income is allocated on a daily basis.

The passive investment income test only applies to corporations that have accumulated "Subchapter C" earnings and profits at the end of a taxable year. "Subchapter C" earnings and profits are those earnings that have accumulated during a taxable year in which a Subchapter S election was *not* in effect. A corporation having such earnings and profits must be careful not to have its passive investment income exceed 25% of its gross receipts for each of three consecutive taxable years in which the Subchapter S election is in effect. If the test "is failed" for three consecutive taxable years, the election is terminated effective the first day of the next taxable year. In addition to the termination of the S corporation election, each individual failure will trigger the imposition of a special tax on the corporation's "excess" net passive income. An S corporation that does not have any accumulated Subchapter C earnings and profits can earn an unlimited amount of passive income without having the special tax levy imposed, being a personal holding company, or losing its S Corporation election. A special election is available which permits a corporation to distribute its Subchapter C earnings and profits. The distribution is taxable to its shareholders and eliminates any potential disqualification that could occur because of excess passive investment income. Passive investment income includes royalties, rents, dividends, interest, annuities and gains from the sale or exchange of stocks and securities. Rental income is not passive income if the corporation renders significant services to the occupant.

## REVOCATION OF THE ELECTION

The Subchapter S election can be revoked by the corporation at any time. The revocation statement must contain the consent of shareholders that own more than one-half of the stock on the day the revocation statement is filed. A revocation statement filed in the first 2½ months of the corporation's taxable year takes effect at the beginning of the taxable year. A revocation statement filed after the first 2½ months have passed takes effect at the beginning of the next taxable year. Alternatively, the corporation and the shareholders can designate a prospective revocation date which is on or after the date the revocation statement is filed. When the revocation date is other than the first day of the taxable year, the corporation's taxable year is divided into two short-period taxable years. Allocation of income between the two short-period years, and taxation of the income to the shareholders or the corporation, occur according to the rules outlined earlier for a termination.

Once an S corporation election has been terminated or revoked, the corporation cannot make a new election until the fifth taxable year which follows the taxable year in which the termination or revocation is effective. An earlier reelection is permitted only with IRS consent. Sometimes an S corporation may inadvertently terminate its election through no apparent fault of its own. The IRS has the power to ignore such an inadvertent termination when it occurs and treat the Subchapter S election as having continued without any break. Such a situation could occur, for example, when a corporation exceeded the 25% passive investment income limit in three consecutive years and was not concerned with a termination because it thought that it had no accumulated Subchapter C earnings and profits at any point during that time period. A later discovery of Subchapter C earnings and profits by the IRS during the conduct of an audit probably will not result in a termination of the S corporation election, because it most likely can be proven that the termination was inadvertent.

## TAXABLE YEAR

S corporations that were in existence prior to 1983 were permitted unlimited use of a calendar year or fiscal year as their taxable year. Many of these corporations elected to use a taxable year that differed from that of their shareholders and which could permit a tax deferral for the corporation's income.

This type of tax planning is no longer available to a corporation that desires to (1) make an election to be taxed as an S corporation or (2) change its taxable year. These corporations are restricted to using the calendar year as their taxable year unless they choose to use one of the following taxable years:

1.  A taxable year that is the same as the taxable year used by shareholders owning more than one-half of the corporation's stock.

2.  A taxable year that results in a deferral of income by shareholders owning more than one-half of the corporation's stock of no more than 3 months (e.g., September 30, October 31, or November 30 for shareholders using a calendar year as their taxable year).

3.  A taxable year that coincides with the corporation's natural business year.

4.  A taxable year for which a business purpose exists that meets with IRS approval.

Corporations having made a Subchapter S election prior to October 19, 1982 can retain their existing taxable year until a cumulative 50% stock ownership change occurs. If such a change occurs, then the corporation must adopt a calendar year, or one of the four permitted taxable years indicated above, or have its Subchapter S election terminated. Stock ownership changes that are not counted for purposes of determining if the 50% minimum has been exceeded include transfers at death, gifts made to other family members, and certain intra-family buy-sell agreements.

## CALCULATION OF ORDINARY INCOME

### Elections

All accounting method elections are made by the S corporation, other than four which relate to—the calculation of the investment interest limitation, the deduction for mining exploration expenditures, depletion of oil and gas properties, and the credit for foreign income taxes.

## The Ordinary Income Computation

The S corporation is treated as an individual taxpayer and all income, deduction, and loss items are either included in the ordinary income (or ordinary loss) computation or are separately stated and passed-through to the shareholders. Although the S corporation is treated as an individual, it is denied the following deductions:

1. Personal and dependency exemptions.
2. Foreign income taxes.
3. Charitable contributions.
4. Net operating loss carrybacks or carryovers.
5. Additional itemized deductions (e.g., deductions related to profit-making transactions, medical expenses, and alimony).
6. Depletion claimed on oil and gas wells.

Organizational expenditures incurred in forming the corporation can be amortized over the 60 (or more) month period of time selected by the corporation. The S corporation is treated as a noncorporate shareholder for purposes of reporting its dividend income and can not take advantage of any dividends-received deduction.

An S corporation must separately state any item of income, loss, deduction, or credit whose separate treatment could affect the tax liability of *any* of its shareholders. By being separately stated, these items do not enter into the corporation's ordinary income computation, but are instead passed-through directly to the individual shareholders. Some of the items that must be separately stated are:

1. Short-term capital gains and losses.
2. Long-term capital gains and losses.
3. Section 1231 gains and losses.
4. Charitable contributions.
5. Tax-exempt interest.
6. Dividends eligible for exclusion by noncorporate shareholders.

7. Foreign income taxes.
8. Property qualifying for the investment tax credit.
9. Tax preference items.

The pass-through of these items to the shareholders can permit a number of different advantages. One advantage is the avoidance of double taxation. For example, the long-term capital gains are exempt from tax at the corporate level and are eligible for the special 60% capital gains deduction at the shareholder level. A second advantage is the avoidance of the corporate limitation for a deduction or credit item. For example, charitable contributions are passed-through to the individual shareholder and subject to only the individual limitations. A similar advantage applies to the investment tax credit, because the limitation on the amount of the credit is calculated only at the shareholder level. Thus, an investment tax credit can be claimed by each of the shareholders even though the S corporation is operating at a loss. A regular corporation operating at a loss must carryback or carryforward its unused investment tax credits.

Two special restrictions are imposed on payments to shareholders of the S corporation. First, expenses owed to the shareholder can be deducted by the corporation only in the year in which they are paid. Thus, an accrual method of accounting corporation cannot deduct these expenses when they are incurred but must defer them until they are paid. Second, shareholder-employees of an S corporation that own at least 2% of the outstanding stock are not treated as employees for fringe benefit purposes (e.g., group-term life insurance, accident and health benefit plans, etc.). This rule prevents such amounts from being deducted by the corporation and excluded from the shareholder's gross income. Instead, they must be treated as a distribution made by the corporation to a shareholder. A special exception that is available through 1987 permits the payment to be deducted by the S corporation and excluded by the shareholder if the S corporation election was made before 1983, has not been revoked or terminated, and a more than 50% cumulative stock ownership change has not taken place.

## INCOME TAXABLE TO SHAREHOLDER

### Ordinary Income and Separately Stated Income Items

Each shareholder receives a pro rata share of the S corporation's ordinary income (or ordinary loss) and each separately stated income, deduction, loss, or credit item. These items are included in the shareholder's tax return for the taxable year, which includes the last day of the S corporation's taxable year. Each shareholder's allocable share of these items is determined as follows:

1. Determine the daily amount for the income, deduction, loss or credit item by dividing the item by the number of days in the corporation's taxable year.
2. Allocate the item to each shareholder by dividing the daily amount by the number of shares outstanding on a given day and multiplying it by the number of shares of stock owned by the shareholder on that day.
3. Total the daily amounts for the time period that the shareholder held the stock during the corporation's taxable year.

The allocation process is illustrated by the following examples:

EXAMPLE 5-4. TAV Corporation is owned by Tax A. Voider and individuals A and B. These three individuals own 100, 60, and 40 shares of the S corporation's stock, respectively. In 19X3, TAV earned $140,000 of ordinary income and $50,000 of long-term capital gains. Tax A. Voider, A, and B will report the following ordinary income and long-term capital gains:

|  | Ordinary Income | Long-Term Capital Gain |
|---|---|---|
| Tax A. Voider ($\frac{100}{200}$ × Income amount) | $ 70,000 | $25,000 |
| A ($\frac{60}{200}$ × Income amount) | 42,000 | 15,000 |
| B ($\frac{40}{200}$ × Income amount) | 28,000 | 10,000 |
| Total | $140,000 | $50,000 |

**EXAMPLE 5-5.**   Assume the same facts as in the preceding example except that A sold his TAV stock to individual C on July 2, 19X4 (the 184th day of a leap year). Under the general rules A would report $21,000 of ordinary income [$140,000 × (60 ÷ 200) × (183 ÷ 366)] and $7,500 of long-term capital gain [$50,000 × (60 ÷ 200) × (183 ÷ 366)]. C would report an identical amount of income, since she also owned the 60 shares of TAV stock for one-half of the year. Alternatively, because A terminated his stock ownership, A and the other shareholders could have made an election to allocate the income based upon the accounting methods used by TAV. If such an election were made, A would report only 60/200th of the actual income reported during the period January 1, 19X4 through July 1, 19X4.

The daily allocation of the income reduces the effectiveness of dividing an S corporation's income among family members. Prior to 1983, the Subchapter S rules allocated all of the profits to the shareholder who owned the stock on the last day of the corporation's taxable year. This rule permitted a stock transfer (e.g., a gift) to transfer an interest in the corporation's income to the shareholder's children, who were in low-tax brackets. The income transfer was retroactive to the first day of the taxable year, no matter when during the year the transfer took place. No longer can such retroactive tax planning take place. Taxpayers should be cautious when making such transfers to ensure that the children (or the appropriate guardian) has control over the stock. If a parent transfers the stock and then retains post-transfer control over the stock, the IRS may disregard the transfer and attribute the income back to the transferor. Such an action negates the income-splitting advantage associated with the gift.

Some taxpayers attempt to take advantage of the division of taxable income among the shareholders by reducing the salary income paid to a "key" shareholder-employee, and thereby increasing the income allocated to the other shareholders. The IRS has the power to adjust the amount of the income, loss, deduction, and credit items taken into account by family members to reflect the amount of services rendered or capital furnished by the individuals to the corporation. This ability to reallocate income prevents a wealthy taxpayer from (1) making a gift of part of his stock in an S corporation to his children, (2) maintaining the salary that he receives from the corporation at a level below that paid similar individuals in comparable businesses, and (3) causing part of the corporation's income to be allocated to the children and reported on their tax returns.

### Ordinary Loss and Separately Stated Loss and Deduction Items

Each shareholder receives an allocable share of the corporation's ordinary loss and the separately stated loss and deduction items. These items are allocated to each shareholder according to the rules outlined above for ordinary income and the separately stated income items. The pass-through of losses permits them to be deducted on the shareholders' individual tax returns and allows them to provide an immediate tax benefit. The availability of the loss pass-through can be used to deduct the corporation's start-up losses.

EXAMPLE 5-6.   TAV Corporation owns a franchise for a fast food restaurant that has enormous profit potential. Its sole shareholder is in the 50% marginal tax bracket. The restaurant operation is expected to incur losses associated with its start-up costs for its first 5 months and then become profitable. The restaurant commences operations on July 1, 19X3. An election to be taxed under Subchapter S, that is in effect for the first 5 months of operation, would permit the loss to be passed-through to the shareholder. A revocation of the election that becomes effective at the point in time (December 1, 19X3) when the business becomes profitable, may be advisable so that the subsequent profits can be taxed at the lower regular corporation tax rates.

A revocation of the S corporation election might also be advisable at the time when the business has passed out of the "start-up" phase and earns a sufficient amount of income so that an advantage accrues to having the income taxed at the regular corporate tax rates.

A corporation may also find it advantageous to make the Subchapter S election in order to pass-through a one-time loss to its shareholder for an immediate tax benefit and prevent a large loss from being "trapped" in the corporation and available only as a carryforward to subsequent taxable years.

Four limitations restrict the availability of loss pass-throughs. First, net operating losses or capital losses incurred by a regular corporation cannot be carried over to a taxable year in which an S Corporation election is in effect and passed-through to its shareholders. Second, an ordinary loss or a separately stated deduction or loss incurred by an S corporation cannot be carried back or forward to a taxable year in which the Subchapter S election was not in effect. Third, an S corporation, or its shareholders, may be subject to the "at-risk" loss limitation, the investment interest limitation, and the hobby loss restrictions. The "at-risk" rules restrict a shareholder's deduction for the loss pass-through to the amount the shareholder has "at risk" (generally, any capital contributions and debts for which a personal liability exists) in the corporation at the end of the taxable year. The investment interest limitation for each individual shareholder includes both the net investment income and investment interest deduction passed-through from the S corporation. Each shareholder's individual limitation may restrict the availability of the deduction for the passed-through investment interest expense.

Finally, each shareholder's deduction for his allocable share of the ordinary loss and separately stated loss and deduction items is limited to the sum of (1) the shareholder's basis for his stock, plus (2) the basis of any corporate indebtedness to the shareholder. The basis for the stock is determined as of the beginning of the taxable year and is increased by the amount of any separately stated income items passed-through to the shareholder. Any portion of the ordinary loss or separately-stated deduction and loss items that are passed-through and which exceed the above limitation can be carried over to subsequent taxable years when the shareholder again has a basis for his stock or a corporate indebtedness.

**EXAMPLE 5-7.** Tax A. Voider owns 60% of the stock of TAV Corporation. The remaining stock is owned equally by X and Y. During 19X5 the corporation incurs a $120,000 ordinary loss and a

$30,000 long-term capital loss. TAV's liabilities at the close of 19X5 are as follows:

| Accounts payable | $ 75,000 |
|---|---|
| Liability to: | |
| Tax A. Voider | 35,000 |
| X | 15,000 |
| Total liabilities | $125,000 |

The basis for Tax A. Voider's stock is $45,000. Tax A. Voider's portion of the ordinary loss and long-term capital loss are $72,000 and $18,000, respectively. Tax A. Voider's loss limitation is $80,000 ($45,000 + $35,000). This limitation prevents deduction of $10,000 of the loss passed-through to Tax A. Voider. The nondeductible portion of the loss is allocated ratably between the two types of losses—$8,000 of ordinary loss and $2,000 of long-term capital loss. These losses can be carried over to later taxable years.

The losses that are deducted by the shareholder first reduce his basis in the stock. Once the basis of the stock has been reduced to zero, the basis of any corporate indebtedness to the shareholder is reduced. Subsequent profits and separately stated income items first restore the basis of the corporate indebtedness to the shareholder for any prior reductions. As soon as the basis of the corporate indebtedness has been fully restored, subsequent positive basis adjustments increase the shareholder's basis for his stock.

**EXAMPLE 5-8.**   Assume the facts are the same as in the preceding example. The $80,000 of deductible loss first reduces the basis of the stock to zero, and then reduces the basis of the corporate indebtedness to zero.

**EXAMPLE 5-9.**   Assume the facts are the same as in the preceding example except that TAV Corporation reports $50,000 of ordinary income in 19X6. Tax A. Voider is allocated $30,000 of the ordinary income. The income pass-through permits all $10,000 of the loss carryovers to be deducted by Tax A. Voider. Since the shareholder reports both the income and loss, or a net amount of $20,000, the basis of the corporate indebtedness can only be increased from zero to $20,000. Had TAV Corporation instead reported $100,000 of ordinary income, Tax A. Voider would receive a $60,000 allocation of the income, report a "net" amount of $50,000, restore the basis of the indebtedness to $35,000, and increase the basis of the stock from zero to $15,000.

Shareholders that want to use the loss pass-throughs immediately can increase the basis of their stock, or lend additional funds to the corporation, prior to the end of the corporation's taxable year. The increased basis for the stock can come by making additional capital contributions with respect to shares that are already outstanding, purchasing additional shares from the corporation, or purchasing additional shares from the other shareholders. The additional capital contributions or additional loans need only be made prior to the end of the taxable year in order to provide the increased basis necessary to currently deduct the "excess" losses.

Taxpayers may desire to delay the making of the loan or the capital contribution in order to increase the value of the deduction that can be claimed for the loss. For example, assume that Tax A. Voider was in the 20% marginal tax bracket in 19X5 when the S corporation incurred an $80,000 loss. This loss exceeds by $50,000 his loss limitation. Tax A. Voider projects that he will be in the 50% marginal tax bracket in 19X6. A delay in the making of the additional capital contribution or loan from 19X5 to 19X6 can increase the value of each dollar of loss that exceeds his loss limitation from 20 cents to 50 cents, or a $15,000 increased tax savings. A similar type of tax savings can result from the shareholder taking no action in 19X5 and offsetting the loss against 19X6 profits passed-through from the S corporation.

Loss carryovers that remain unused on the day a Subchapter S election is terminated or revoked can be deducted on the last day of the post-termination transition period. The post-termination transition period generally means the one-year period of time commencing on the day following the last day of the last taxable year as an S corporation. The post-termination transition period is reduced to 120 days if the termination occurs as a result of a determination (e.g., a court decision indicating that a termination had occurred). The loss carryover can be deducted only to the extent that the shareholder has a basis in his stock. Losses that are not deducted on the last day of the post-termination transition period are lost. Shareholders should attempt to increase the basis of their stock by the end of the post-termination transition period so as to avoid losing their loss deductions.

If an S corporation incurs substantial losses, the stock may be sold or exchanged at a loss, or the stock may become worthless. The loss incurred on the sale, exchange, or worthlessness of the stock may be an ordinary loss (instead of a capital loss) if the stock qualifies as Section 1244 stock.

## DISTRIBUTIONS BY AN S CORPORATION

Distributions made by an S corporation are generally not taxable to its shareholders. These distributions reduce the shareholder's basis in his stock by the amount of cash or the fair market value of the property distributed. Only if the total distribution exceeds the basis of the shareholder's stock is the distribution taxable. The amount received in excess of the basis of the shareholder's stock is taxable as gain from the sale or exchange of the stock. S corporations with accumulated earnings and profits which accrued prior to making the S corporation election, or in a pre–1983 taxable year in which a Subchapter S election was in effect, can make dividend distributions that are taxable. Further discussions of the S corporation distribution rules are contained in Chapter 11.

Avoiding double taxation on a distribution can be a significant S corporation advantage when the business activities require only a small portion of the annual profits be retained. Such an advantage is illustrated by the following example:

EXAMPLE 5-10.    Tax A. Voider owns all of the stock of TAV Corporation. In 19X6 the corporation earned $500,000 of ordinary income. A comparison of the regular corporation and S corporation tax results is illustrated for the three situations below. Assume in each situation that Tax A. Voider is in the 50% marginal tax bracket.

|  | Situation Numbers | | |
| --- | --- | --- | --- |
|  | 1 | 2 | 3 |
| Percent of after-tax earnings distributed (1) | 100% | 50% | 0% |
| TAXATION AS A REGULAR CORPORATION |  |  |  |
| Regular corporation taxable income (2) | $500,000 | $500,000 | $500,000 |
| Regular corporation tax liability (3) | 209,750 | 209,750 | 209,750 |
| Shareholder's taxable income (4) = [(2) − (3)] × (1)] | 290,250 | 145,125 | 0 |
| Shareholder tax liability (5) = (4) × 0.50 | 145,125 | 72,562 | 0 |
| Total corporate and shareholder tax liability (6) = (3) + (5) | 354,875 | 282,312 | 209,750 |
| TAXATION AS AN S CORPORATION |  |  |  |
| S Corporation (and shareholder's) ordinary income (7) | $500,000 | $500,000 | $500,000 |
| Shareholder tax liability (8) = (7) × 0.50 | 250,000 | 250,000 | 250,000 |
| S CORPORATION TAX SAVINGS (TAX COST) (9) = (6) − (8) | 104,875 | 32,312 | (40,250) |

The S corporation provides a substantial tax savings in Situation Nos. 1 and 2 because double taxation is avoided on at least one-half of the income. The savings that results from regular corporation status is illustrated in Situation No. 3 where the lower regular corporation tax rates save $40,250. This savings is reduced in later periods as double taxation occurs when the earnings are distributed or the stock is sold.

The results in Situation No. 3 do not reflect the tax planning illustrated in Figure 4-3 using two tax entities—the individual taxpayer and a regular corporation. By dividing the income-producing activities between an S corporation and a regular corporation, one can obtain the same income-splitting benefits, avoid the employment taxes associated with a large salary payment, and also obtain the other tax and nontax benefits of the S corporation form of doing business.

## BASIS OF THE
## SHAREHOLDER'S STOCK

The basis of the shareholder's stock is affected by three events: (1) the pass-through of ordinary income and separately stated income items; (2) the pass-through of an ordinary loss or separately stated deduction or loss items; and (3) tax-free distributions. The formula for computing the basis of the shareholder's stock (other than adjustments for oil and gas related items) is as follows:

|        | Initial investment (basis) |
|--------|----------------------------|
| Plus:  | Additional capital contributions |
|        | Allocable share of: |
|        |    ordinary income |
|        |    separately-stated income items (including tax exempt income) |
| Less:  | Tax-free distributions |
|        | Allocable share of: |
|        |    ordinary loss |
|        |    separately stated loss and deduction items (including nondeductible expenses that cannot be charged against the capital account) |
| Equals: | Adjusted basis for the stock |

This calculation needs to be performed annually. Once the initial year of stock ownership has passed, the initial investment amount in the formula becomes the basis of the stock at the beginning of the taxable year.

## TAX LIABILITIES OF THE
## S CORPORATION

The four types of tax levies imposed on the S corporation are the excessive net passive income tax, the capital gains tax, the corporation minimum tax on the preference portion of certain long-term capital gains, and the recapture of previously claimed investment tax credits.

### Excess Net Passive Income Tax

A tax can be incurred when for a year an S corporation has passive investment income in excess of 25% of its gross receipts *and* has "Subchapter C" earnings and profits at the end of the year. No tax is levied if the corporation fails to have Subchapter C earnings and profits at the end of the taxable year, even though its passive income exceeds the 25% maximum. Passive income is defined in the same manner as it was for purposes of the passive income test above. The tax levy is determined by the following calculation:

$$
\begin{matrix} \text{Excess} \\ \text{net} \\ \text{passive} \\ \text{income} \\ \text{tax} \end{matrix} = 46\% \times \left[ \begin{matrix} \text{Passive income} \\ \text{(less any} \\ \text{related deduc-} \\ \text{tions)} \end{matrix} - \frac{\text{Passive income—25\% of gross receipts}}{\text{Passive income}} \right]
$$

The amount of the tax levy reduces the passive income passed-through to the shareholders.

### Capital Gains Tax

A capital gains tax is imposed at the corporate level in order to discourage regular corporations from making an S Corporation election for the purpose of passing a capital gain through to the shareholders with a tax being levied only at the shareholder level.

To prevent this tax avoidance maneuver, an S corporation is subject to the capital gains tax if for a taxable year its: (1) taxable income exceeds $25,000; (2) net capital gain (excess of net long-term capital gains over net short-term capital losses) exceeds $25,000; and (3) net capital gain exceeds 50% of taxable income. A corporation meeting these three requirements is exempt from the tax if the S corporation election has been in effect for the shorter of the three immediately preceding taxable years or the corporation's entire existence. The tax equals the lesser of (1) 28% times the amount by which the net capital gain exceeds $25,000, or (2) the tax imposed upon the corporation's taxable income (if it were not an S corporation) using the regular tax rates.

## Corporate Minimum Tax

An S corporation's tax preference items are generally passed-through to each shareholder on a daily basis. Whether a shareholder is subject to the alternative minimum tax thus will depend upon his total tax preference items and his tax liability. An S corporation is liable for the corporate minimum tax only on the preference portion of the long-term capital gains that are subject to the capital gains tax. Special rules determine the preference portion of the capital gain that is subject to the corporate minimum tax.

## Investment Tax Credit Recapture

An S corporation allocates all of its property acquisitions to its shareholders thus permitting them to claim the investment tax credit. Each shareholder receives a pro-rata share of the 3-year and 5-year recovery property as well as each of the properties eligible for a special credit. Used property is subject to the $125,000 limitation at both the corporate and shareholder levels. If the property is disposed of before the end of the recovery period, or ceases to be qualifying property in the corporation's hands, then the previously claimed investment tax credits are recaptured at the shareholder level. A reduction of more than one-third in a shareholder's interest in the stock of an S corporation can also trigger a recapture of part or all of the shareholder's previously claimed investment tax credits.

The making of an S corporation election does not precipitate the application of the recapture rules. The corporation remains liable for taxes due as a result of a disposition of property acquired prior to the making of the S corporation election.

## TAX RETURNS AND TAX PAYMENTS

An S corporation must file a special corporate tax return (Form 1120S) within 2½ months of the end of its taxable year. For a calendar-year corporation, Form 1120S is due on March 15. A 6-month extension in which to file the return is available upon request.

Estimated tax payments are not required of an S Corporation. Any taxes due must be paid within 2½ months of the end of the taxable year.

## ADVANTAGES/DISADVANTAGES OF AN S CORPORATION ELECTION

Some of the advantages and disadvantages of the S corporation election are as follows:

### Advantages

1. The S corporation's income is exempt from tax, except for a limited tax on capital gains and excess net passive income and the corporate minimum tax.

2. The corporate income is taxed at the shareholder level which can produce a tax liability lower than the corporate tax liability.

3. Ordinary losses and separately stated losses pass-through to the shareholders and are deducted on their personal tax returns.

4. Distributions are treated as tax-free returns of the shareholder's capital investment and are not subject to double taxation.

5. Long-term capital gains retain their character as they pass-through to the shareholders, rather than being taxed as dividend income.

6. The investment tax credit (and other credit) benefits pass-through to the shareholders and can be claimed even when the corporation is operating at a loss.

7. S corporations are not subject to the accumulated earnings tax or the personal holding company tax.

8. S corporation shareholders can participate in a qualified retirement plan that provides the same dollar limit on the de-

ductibility of contributions as is available for a regular corporation.

### Disadvantages

1.   The corporate tax rates may be lower than the rates applicable to individual shareholders, and thereby permit a greater after-tax earnings accumulation.

2.   The S corporation is subject to the "at-risk" rules and the "hobby loss" rules. Regular corporations are not generally subject to these loss restrictions.

3.   The loss limitation of an S corporation's shareholders is smaller than for the partners in a partnership since only corporate debt owed to the shareholder is included in the loss limitation.

4.   Fringe benefits paid to a shareholder-employee owning at least 2% of the stock are restricted. Similar restrictions do not apply to a regular corporation.

5.   Expenses owed to an S corporation shareholder cannot be deducted until paid. Similar restrictions do not apply to a regular corporation.

6.   Restrictions exist as to type and number of shareholders, type of income, investments in subsidiaries, and capital structure.

7.   S corporations are restricted in the taxable year that they can adopt.

8.   Special allocations of income, deductions, loss, or credit items are not permitted as with a partnership.

9.   Dividends that are received by an S corporation are not eligible for the dividends-received deduction.

10.   Earnings are taxed to the shareholders whether they are distributed or not. This may necessitate quarterly advances to the shareholders to pay estimated taxes on undistributed corporate profits.

## **NOTES**

1.  Ordinary income represents the excess of total income over total deductions. This is different from taxable income because excluded from total income and total deductions are any separately stated income, gain, deduction and loss items.

2.  An ordinary loss occurs when the total deductions exceed total income. This is different from a net operating loss because excluded from total income and total deductions are any separately stated income, gain, deduction and loss items.

# 6

# TAXATION OF PARTNERSHIPS

Partnerships can be found in a wide variety of forms and involved in a wide variety of activities. At one end of the spectrum of partnership forms is the general partnership that results from two or more individuals working with only an oral partnership agreement in a mom and pop business venture. At the other extreme is the syndicated limited partnership made up of a corporate general partner and hundreds of limited partners who purchase one or more investment units in a partnership offering. The legal and tax structure for partnerships are sufficiently flexible to accommodate this wide variety of groups and activities.

## GENERAL AND LIMITED PARTNERSHIPS

### General Partnerships

The more common and simpler of the two partnership types is the General Partnership. Each owner of the partnership is a general partner and has the right to participate in partnership management. Each general partner also has the ability to make binding commitments for the partnership. (This ability logically leads to partnership agreement provisions which allow existing partners to determine whether a purchaser of an ownership interest in the partnership's business will be admitted as a formal partner.)

Each general partner has full personal liability for all partnership recourse liabilities. If the partnership fails to pay the liability, the partner is liable for the payment even if the debt is far greater than the entire value of the partnership. A general partner's liability extends to his personal as well as business assets. It should be noted that some partnerships incur nonrecourse liabilities. These are debts where the lenders' recourse in case of nonpayment is limited to the property put up as security for the debt. Clearly, even a general partner has no liability for partnership nonrecourse debt.

### Limited Partnerships

A partnership form that has become a common vehicle for structuring tax shelters is the limited partnership. A limited partnership is comprised of one or more limited partners and a general partner. A limited partner's risk of loss is limited to the amount of his partnership investment and any additional amounts that he is obligated to contribute under the partnership agreement. The general partner is personally liable for the partnership's liabilities, as he would be in the case of a general partnership. Not surprisingly, corporate general partners with minimal assets are common.

The limited partners "pool" their capital resources into a fund which gives them greater purchasing power and, in many cases, greater diversity of risk than would be available if each partner had invested on his own. The limited partner can not participate in the day-to-day management activities of the partnership without losing his limited liability. The operating activities are managed by the general partner.

## NONTAX ADVANTAGES/DISADVANTAGES OF A PARTNERSHIP

While we are primarily interested in the tax implications of various business forms, it is also important to keep some of the nontax attributes of the entities firmly in mind. A number of nontax advantages (and disadvantages) can be found when comparing a partnership with a corporation. Some of the nontax advantages of the partnership form include the following:

1.   The ability to attract the capital or skills of other individuals who become partners in the activity in return for a "piece of the action."
2.   Greater flexibility to distribute disproportionate benefits to the partners through special allocations of profits, losses, and cash flows in the partnership agreement. Corporate allocations of these benefits are based upon stock ownership.
3.   The ability to function without the requirement for formal documentation. A corporation can not exist until the corporate charter and bylaws are drawn up, signed, and filed. A partnership can function indefinitely with no more than a verbal agreement between the partners. (Nevertheless, it is better to have a written partnership agreement for tax purposes.)

Some of the nontax disadvantages of the partnership form include the following:

1.   Frequent needs to transfer ownership interests and raise capital can make use of the partnership form cumbersome.
2.   A corporation shields personal assets from the business liabilities. An investor's loss is limited to his capital contributions. Limited liability is available for a limited partner, but the general partner retains the potential for personal liability for business debts.

3.   Corporations have an unlimited existence. Partnerships may, under state law or the partnership agreement, terminate upon the death, insanity, bankruptcy, retirement, resignation, or expulsion of an individual partner.

## TAX ADVANTAGES/DISADVANTAGES OF A PARTNERSHIP

After considering the nontax comparison of partnerships and corporations, it's time to consider some of the tax law advantages of the partnership form. The following overview of these concepts will help keep them in perspective during our later, more detailed discussion:

1.   A partnership is not subject to any federal income tax since all items of income and loss are taxed directly to the partners.

2.   Income, gains, losses, deductions and credits are passed through the partnership and taxed to the partners. The partner can obtain an immediate tax benefit for the losses, deductions, and credits that might have to be carried over to other years if a regular corporation were used to conduct the activities.

3.   Partnership losses can be deducted up to the amount of the partner's basis for his partnership interest. This basis includes the partner's share of *all* partnership liabilities.

4.   The allocation of partnership income, losses, deductions, and other tax benefits occurs according to the partnership agreement. Special allocations of these tax benefits (which have substantial economic effect) are permitted and can increase the value of these tax benefits to the partners.

5.   Distributions of earnings made to partners are generally tax-exempt.

6.   Liquidation of a partnership generally does not result in the recognition of gain or loss by the partner.

7.   The partnership is not subject to the personal holding company and accumulated earnings penalty taxes as is a regular corporation.

While these tax advantages of the partnership form are substantial, there are also significant tax disadvantages of the partnership form, which are as follows:

1. Tax rates of a regular corporation may be lower than those of a partner. This may permit a greater capital accumulation by the corporation for reinvestment purposes and debt reduction.

2. The partnership's taxable year generally must coincide with that of its principal partners unless a business purpose is established. This prevents the adoption of many fiscal years.

3. Partners are generally not considered to be employees of the partnership. While they may be eligible for meals and lodging exclusions, they are ineligible for many fringe benefits available to a shareholder-employee of a regular corporation. They can not be employees for purposes of a qualified pension plan, for example.

4. Partnerships are restricted in the form of deferred compensation plans that can be offered to the partners. Compensation forms unavailable to a partner (that are available to a shareholder-employee of a corporation) include qualified profit sharing plans, incentive stock options, employee stock ownership plans, stock options, and so on.

5. A partnership's taxable year terminates when within a 12-month period there is a sale or exchange of 50% or more of the total interests in partnership capital and profits. Such a change my result in a "bunching" of the income from two partnership taxable-years within a single taxable year of a partner.

6. Tax-free reorganizations involving the assets or stock of a corporation can be accomplished more easily than can similar exchanges involving a partnership.

7. The deductibility of partnership losses may be limited by the "at-risk" rules. The at-risk rules do not apply to a regular corporation unless it is closely held.

8. The income of a regular or S corporation can be assigned to a minor child through the transfer of the corporation's stock. Such a transfer of a partnership interest is available only if the child receives a capital interest in a partnership where capital is a material factor in the partnership's activities.

## CALCULATING PARTNERSHIP INCOME

### Partnership Taxable Year

Calculating partnership income for tax purposes first requires the selection of a taxable year. Unlike a regular corporation, the partnership is restricted in the taxable year that it may adopt. These restrictions largely prevent the partnership and partners from deferring the partnership income from taxation through the selection of their taxable year. A partnership may not change to, or adopt, a taxable year other than that of *all* of its princpial partners unless it obtains IRS approval. (A principal partner is a partner having an interest of at least 5% in the partnership's capital or profits.) The partnership must use a calendar year as its taxable year if all of its principal partners do not use the same taxable year, or it must obtain IRS approval to use a different taxable year. A partner may not change to, or adopt, a taxable year other than that of a partnership in which he is a principal partner, unless he obtains IRS approval. All requests to use a taxable year different from its principal partners must be supported by a business purpose. The taxable-year restrictions prevent the use of a combination of calendar and fiscal years to defer the taxation of partnership profits. Fiscal years are normally permitted for a partnership only if they result in a deferral of income of three months or less (e.g., a September 30, October 31, or November 30 year-end is acceptable for a partnership when the partners use a calendar year-end). To choose such a fiscal year requires the permission of the IRS.

### Partnership Accounting Methods

Any election affecting the computation of the partnership's taxable income or loss must be made by the partnership, except for six limited exceptions that are made separately by each partner. These exceptions are in general the same ones that were indicated earlier for an S corporation. Because the partnership is a separate entity, it can elect to use the accrual method of accounting, even though each of its partners use the cash method.

### Partnership Ordinary Income Computation

Partnership ordinary income[1] is generally computed as if the partnership were an individual taxpayer. However, a number of deductions that can be claimed by an individual taxpayer can not be deducted in computing partnership ordinary income. These include the following:

1. Personal and dependency exemptions.
2. Foreign income taxes.
3. Charitable contributions.
4. Net operating losses.
5. Expenses related to the production of income (Section 212).
6. Medical and dental expenses.
7. Alimony.
8. IRA contributions.
9. Percentage depletion.

In addition, a number of deductions and losses must be separately stated and passed-through to the partner independent of the partnership ordinary income computation. Any item that can affect the tax liability of *any* partner must be separately stated on the information return filed by the partnership and provided to each partner. For example, separately stated items include those which are eligible for a special exclusion, subject to a special limitation, or subject to a special election. Items receiving a separate allocation include:

1. Net short-term capital gain (loss).
2. Net long-term capital gain (loss).
3. Net Section 1231 gain (loss).
4. Dividends eligible for exclusion or a dividends-received deduction.
5. Tax-exempt interest.
6. Guaranteed payments made by the partnership.
7. Charitable contributions.

8.  Asset costs expensed in the year of acquisition.

9.  Payments made by the partnership to IRAs, H.R. 10 plans, or Simplified Employee Pensions.

10. Property qualifying for the investment tax credit.

11. Property subject to investment-tax-credit recapture.

12. Tax preference items.

13. Investment interest expense.

14. Foreign income taxes.

The calculation of partnership ordinary income is illustrated in Figure 6-1. A brief explanation of selected items is presented. The Sec-

**FIGURE 6-1**    A sample calculation of partnership ordinary income.

|  | | Partnership | |
|---|---|---|---|
|  | Total Income | Ordinary Income | Separately Stated Items |
| Gross margin from sales | $400,000 | $400,000 | |
| Long-term capital gain | 20,000 | | $20,000 |
| Short-term capital loss | (7,000) | | (7,000) |
| Section 1231 gain | 16,000 | | 16,000 |
| Section 1245 gain | 9,000 | 9,000 | |
| Interest: | | | |
|   Corporate bonds | 11,000 | 11,000 | |
|   Municipal bonds | 8,000 | | 8,000 |
| Dividends from domestic | | | |
|   corporation | 12,000 | | 12,000 |
| | $469,000 | $420,000 | |
| Operating expenses | (275,000) | (275,000) | |
| Charitable contributions | (15,000) | | (15,000) |
| Foreign income taxes | (3,000) | | (3,000) |
| Depreciation—total | (27,000) | (27,000) | |
| Amortization of organization costs | (3,000) | (3,000) | |
| Investment interest expense | (10,000) | | (10,000) |
| Net investment income | | | 32,000 |
| Tax preferences: | | | |
|   Excess depreciation on real | | | |
|     property | | | (7,500) |
|   Intangible drilling costs | | | ( 11,000) |
| Total | $136,000 | $115,000 | xxx |

tion 1245 (depreciation recapture) gain is included in the partnership ordinary income calculation because it can not receive any special treatment for any partner since it is always ordinary income. The other gains and losses are separately stated and combined with each partner's capital gains and losses and Section 1231 gains and losses from his other activities, to determine the partner's overall gain or loss position. Charitable contributions are passed-through to the partner and are subject to the contribution limitation applicable to that partner. The foreign income taxes are passed-through to the partner and he makes the election to deduct or credit these taxes. The investment interest expense and net investment income are passed-through to the partner and combined with similar items from other investment activities at the partner level, in order to determine the partner's investment interest deduction and carryover. The tax preference items are passed-through to the partner and combined with his other preference items to determine the taxpayer's alternative minimum tax liability or corporate minimum tax liability (if any).

## ALLOCATION OF PARTNERSHIP ITEMS

### Recognition of Income and Loss

A partner's taxable income includes his distributive share of the partnership income, gain, loss, or deductions for any taxable year of the partnership ending within or with the partner's taxable year.

**EXAMPLE 6-1.** The MNO Partnership uses a fiscal year ending September 30 as its taxable year. MNO's three partners, individuals, M, N, and O, use the calendar year as their taxable years. Each partner includes the partnership's results for the fiscal year covering October 1, 19X6 through September 30, 19X7 in her 19X7 individual tax return, because the pass-throughs are treated as if they occur on the last day of the partnership's taxable year.

The use of the end of the partnership's taxable year as the reference point for determining the time to recognize its income or loss can result in the recognition of more than 12 months of partnership income in a single taxable year of a partner.

**EXAMPLE 6-2.**    Assume the facts remain the same as in the preceding example except that the MNO Partnership terminates its existence on December 15, 19X7. The termination closes MNO's taxable year. The results from both taxable years—the one ending September 30, 19X7 and the one ending on December 15, 19X7—are included in each partner's 19X7 individual tax return.

### Distributive Share

The term "distributive share" refers to a partner's allocated portion of the partnership ordinary income or loss and the separately stated items. A partner's distributive share of the ordinary income or loss and separately stated items is normally determined by the partnership agreement. A simple partnership agreement may use the same allocation percentage to determine the distributive share of partnership ordinary income and loss as well as each separately stated item. A more complex agreement may provide for the distributive share of one or more separately stated items to be determined differently from the distributive share for other separately stated items, or for different ratios to be employed to allocate partnership profits and losses. If the partnership agreement contains no special provision for allocating a separately stated item, a partner's distributive share of the item is determined in accordance with the partnership's ordinary income or loss. If no such allocation is specified or there is no written agreement, an allocation consistent with all the available facts is presumed.

A partner's distributive share of items of income and loss is controlled by the partnership agreement if the allocation has substantial economic effect. If an allocation does not have the necessary economic effect, the IRS can require that the allocation be based upon the partner's interest in the partnership. A partner's interest in the partnership is based on the facts and circumstances, including the partners relative interests in profits and losses, cash flow, and liquidating distributions. In essence, an allocation has an economic effect if the allocation can actually affect the dollar amount received by the partner. For the allocation to affect the dollar amount received by the partner there must be an adjustment to the partner's capital account for the allocation, any liquidation proceeds must be based on the capital account balances, and any capital account deficits which exist at the time of liquidation must be repaid. Even if the allocation has an economic effect, it must also be substantial when weighed against the tax consequences of the allocation in order to be accepted by the IRS. An allocation that would not be accepted by the IRS would be one where the partnership's tax-exempt income is allocated to a partner with a higher tax rate while allocating an equal amount of taxable income to a partner having a much lower marginal tax rate.

Calculation of a partner's distributive share of the partnership's income or loss is simple when the partnership agreement does not change during the taxable year and when the partner's interest in the partnership remains constant. However, a change in a partner's relative interest during the taxable year requires that the partner's distributive share of the partnership income or loss be determined separately for each of the two periods. The partner's distributive share for the entire year is the sum of the pre- and post–change distributive share calculations. The partners may agree to use either one or two methods to make the calculation. The first method involves a daily allocation of the income or loss to each day in the taxable year based upon the partner's interest on that day. The second method involves closing the partnership's books on the date of the change. The pre- and post–change partnership income or loss amounts are then allocated based upon the partner's interest in each period.

A new partner entering the partnership during the taxable year is allocated partnership's income or loss only for the days that he is a partner. This prevents a partner from being allocated a portion of the partnership income or loss for a period of time prior to the acquisition of the partnership interest, except to the extent that the annual income or loss can be allocated to him on a daily basis.

**EXAMPLE 6-3.** Tax A. Voider invests in the DEF Partnership on December 1, 19X7 and acquires a 20% interest. DEF uses the calendar year as its taxable year and reports a $73,000 loss during 19X7. $65,000 of the loss is attributable to the results of activities occurring prior to the Tax A. Voider's investment. Using the daily allocation method, Tax A. Voider's distributive share of the loss is $1,240 [$73,000 × (31 ÷ 365) × 0.2). Using the interim allocation method, Tax A. Voider's distributive share of the loss is $1,600 ($8,000 × 0.2).

These rules prevent individuals from purchasing tax losses by having the partnership make retroactive allocations of losses to a partner. This technique was used in certain tax sheltered limited partnerships to allocate losses to a partner that were incurred during the portion of the partnership's taxable year preceding the acquisition of the partnership interest.

The sale or exchange of a partner's entire interest in the partnership closes the partnership's taxable year with respect to that partner. The partner reports his distributive share of the partnership income or loss for the period beginning with the first day of the partnership's taxable year and ending with the day the partnership interest is disposed of.

**EXAMPLE 6-4.**  The XYZ Partnership uses the calender year as its taxable year. X, Y, and Z were equal partners until X sold her entire interest to Z at the close of business on August 31, 19X5. XYZ reported the following ordinary income for 19X5.

| | |
|---|---|
| January 1 through August 31 | $40,000 |
| September 1 through December 31 | 48,000 |
| Total | $88,000 |

X reports, as her distributive share of the XYZ income, either $13,333 ($40,000 × 1/3) if there is an interim closing of the books, or $19,529 ($88,000 × 243/365 × 1/3) if income is allocated on a daily basis.

## BASIS OF THE PARTNERSHIP INTEREST

Unlike basis in corporate stock, a partner's basis is constantly changing. The basis calculation is crucial since basis determines the extent to which losses can be deducted and the tax consequences of a distribution. The basis of a partnership interest is determined in the following manner:

|        | Basis of partnership interest following formation of the partnership or acquisition of the interest |
|--------|-----|
| Plus:  | Distributive share of: |
|        | 1. Partnership ordinary income |
|        | 2. Separately stated income or gain items (including tax-exempt income) |
|        | 3. Depletion deductions claimed in excess of the partnership's basis in the depletable property |
|        | Additional capital contributions |
|        | Payments made for additional partnership interests acquired |
|        | Allocable share of any increase in partnership liabilities |
| Less:  | Distributive share of: |
|        | 1. Partnership ordinary loss |
|        | 2. Separately stated loss or deduction items |
|        | 3. Nondeductible expenditures that are not chargeable against the capital account |
|        | 4. Percentage depletion claimed on oil and gas wells |
|        | Cash or property distributions |
|        | Allocable share of any decrease in partnership liabilities |
| Equals: | Basis of partnership interest at year-end |

This calculation must be updated at each year-end in order to determine the amount of the losses that can be deducted by a partner (subject to the "at-risk" rules) or the taxability of partnership distributions. Interim events such as the sale or exchange of part or all of a partnership interest, or the liquidation of a partner's entire interest, may also require such a determination.

At the time an individual acquires his initial interest in the partnership—either by making a capital contribution, by purchasing another individual's interest, or by any other means—he is permitted to increase his basis in the partnership interest by his share of the partnership's liabilities. A subsequent increase in the partnership's liabilities increases the amount of the liabilities allocated to the partner and is treated as a contribution made by the partner to the partnership. A subsequent decrease in the partnership's liabilities decreases the amount of the liabilities allocated to the partner and is treated as a distribution of money made by the partnership to the partner. Recourse liabilities are allocated to the individual partners and included in their basis by using the ratio for sharing losses stated in the partnership agreement. If none of the partners are personally liable for any part of the liability (e.g., a nonrecourse mortgage on real estate), the allocation uses the ratio for sharing profits stated in the partnership agreement. Limited partners can increase their basis in the partnership interest by their allocable share of the partnership's nonrecourse liabilities. Recourse liabilities are allocated to a limited partner, only to the extent that the limited partner is obligated under the partnership agreement to make additional investments in the partnership.

**EXAMPLE 6-5.** T purchases a one-third interest in the AB Partnership for $40,000. At the time of purchase, AB had $150,000 in liabilities. By the end of the year, its liabilities had increased to $180,000. T's basis for the partnership interest at the time of its acquisition is $90,000 [$40,000 + (⅓ × $150,000) ]. At year-end, T's basis must be increased by $10,000 since the increase in his share of AB's liabilities is treated as a capital contribution [⅓ × ($180,000 − $150,000)]. If the liabilities had instead decreased to $120,000, T's basis would be decreased by $10,000 [⅓ × ($150,000 − $120,000)] since the decrease in his share of AB's liabilities is treated as a distribution of money.

Changes in the basis are also made each year to reflect partnership income and loss. The application of these rules is illustrated in the following example.

**EXAMPLE 6-6.** Tax A. Voider has a one-half interest in the JKL Partnership whose results were illustrated in Figure 6-1. The basis for her partnership interest on January 1, 19X3 was $160,000 which included her share of $60,000 of partnership liabilities. Partnership liabilities increased by $32,000 during 19X3. The change in the basis for Tax A. Voider's partnership interest for 19X3's activities (assuming all items are divided equally in the partnership agreement) occurs as follows:

|  |  |  |
|---|---|---:|
|  | Basis, 1/1/19X3 | $160,000 |
| Plus: | Distributive share of: |  |
|  | 1.  Partnership ordinary income | 57,500 |
|  | 2.  Long-term capital gain | 10,000 |
|  | 3.  Section 1231 gain | 8,000 |
|  | 4.  Municipal bond interest | 4,000 |
|  | 5.  Dividends | 6,000 |
|  | Allocable share of increase in partnership liabilities | 16,000 |
|  |  | $261,500 |

| Less: | Distributive share of: | |
|---|---|---|
| | 1. Short-term capital loss | (3,500) |
| | 2. Charitable contributions | (7,500) |
| | 3. Foreign income taxes | (1,500) |
| | 4. Investment interest expense | (5,000) |
| Equals: | Basis, 12/31/19X3 | $244,000 |

When a partnership interest is sold or exchanged, the partner is treated as being released from a liability, and includes the amount of such a liability in his proceeds from the sale or exchange.

EXAMPLE 6-7.  Assume the facts remain the same as in the preceding example, except that Tax A. Voider sells her partnership interest at the close of business on December 31 for $250,000. She realizes a $52,000 gain on the sale [($250,000 + ½ ($60,000 + $32,000) amount realized − $244,000 adjusted basis].

## PASS-THROUGH OF PARTNERSHIP LOSSES

A partner's distributive share of the partnership's losses is deductible only to the extent of the partner's basis in the partnership interest at the end of the partnership's taxable year. (The "at-risk" rules which modify this result are discussed later in this chapter.) If a partner's distributive share of the partnership losses (including losses disallowed in earlier years) exceeds his year-end basis, the excess losses are disallowed. These losses are carried over to future taxable years, combined with prior year disallowed losses, and deducted when the partner again has positive basis for his partnership interest.

EXAMPLE 6-8.  C's basis for his interest in the ABC Partnership at the beginning of 19X7 was $5,000. At the end of 19X7 partner C had the following distributive share of partnership items: tax-exempt income, $500; ordinary loss, $6,000; and long-term capital loss, $2,000. His share of partnership liabilities increased by $1,500 during the partnership's taxable year. Assuming that C is "at risk" for partnership liabilities, C's limitation on deducting the losses is $7,000 ($5,000 + $500 + $1,500). The limitation prevents $1,000 of the $8,000 ($6,000 + $2,000) total loss from being deducted. The nondeductible loss consists of $750 of ordinary loss [$1,000 × ($6,000 ÷ ($6,000 + $2,000))] and $250 of long-term capital loss [$1,000 × ($2,000 ÷ ($6,000 + $2,000))]. These losses can be carried over indefinitely until C has a sufficient positive basis to absorb the losses.

Carryover losses can be avoided by increasing the partner's basis in his partnership interest. One way to accomplish this is by having the partner make additional capital contributions or to make loans to the partnership by year-end. Alternatively, the partnership can increase its liabilities and an allocable share of these liabilities will increase each partner's basis for his partnership interest. If there is a strong reason to claim partnership losses in a particular year, some partnerships have been known to take out a loan from a bank, place the loan proceeds in a CD or similar account at the lending institution, and pledge that account as security for the loan. While this meets the technical requirements for an increase in the partners' bases, it is probably vulnerable to attack from the IRS unless there is a *business* (rather than tax avoidance) purpose for the borrowing.

If the individual partner(s) anticipates being in a higher marginal tax bracket in the following year, a taxpayer might want to delay any controllable increase in basis beyond year-end. By delaying the deduction for the losses, the value of the losses would be increased.

If a partnership has used nonrecourse financing, the deduction of the losses may be subject to the "at-risk" limitations. The "at-risk" rules restrict a partner from deducting losses in excess of what he has at risk in the activity at the end of the taxable year. These rules apply to all activities, other than real estate, that are engaged in by a partnership. Further discussion on this limitation is included with the tax shelter discussion in Chapter 13.

## SPECIAL RULES FOR PARTNER-PARTNERSHIP PAYMENTS

Although the partnership is considered to be an extension of the individual partner in many cases, a partner can engage in certain transactions with the partnership as if they were unrelated parties. If the partner is acting "not in his capacity as a partner," transactions between the partner and his partnership will be taxed as if the two are unrelated parties. Both the partner and the partnership will report these transactions under their normal methods of accounting. The major difficulty with use of this tax provision is determining when an owner is not acting in his capacity as a partner. An example may help clarify this idea. A partner who makes her living as a doctor may be hired to do physical examinations, for life insurance purchases, on the employees of a citrus grove partnership in which she has a 15% ownership interest. She is dealing with the partnership "not in her capacity as a partner." In this setting, the doctor will report her fees using her normal method of accounting for her medical practice. The partnership will deduct the expense of her fee as it would the fee of *any* doctor they would hire to do the examination. In addition, two kinds of transactions between partners and partners that have special rules—guaranteed payments and sales and exchanges—are examined in detail next.

### Guaranteed Payments

Guaranteed payments are payments made to a partner acting in his capacity as a partner (i.e. a partner's payment for managing a real estate partnership's real property). Payments made by a partnership to a partner for services or for the use of capital will be treated as guaranteed payments if the payments are determined without regard to partnership income. The partner must report these payments as ordinary income in his taxable year, which includes the end of the partnership's taxable year in which the partnership deducted the payment under its method of accounting. Guaranteed payments for services are treated as self-employment income and subject to the self-employment tax and estimated tax requirements. Guaranteed payments that constitute a trade or business expense are deductible in determining partnership ordinary income. These guaranteed payments, just like salary to outsiders, are deductions regardless of the amount of ordinary income the partnership has and can create or increase a partnership loss. Guaranteed payments that represent a capital expenditure (e.g., organization or syndication fees) must be capitalized, and if allowable under the normal rules of partnership taxation can be amortized or depreciated.

**EXAMPLE 6-9.** Tax A. Voider has a 20% interest in the ABC Partnership. ABC and Tax A. Voider both use the calendar year as their taxable year. ABC reports $200,000 of ordinary income (before any guaranteed partnership payments). Under ABC's partnership agreement, Tax A. Voider receives a $25,000 annual payment for his services plus his 20% distributive share of income reported by the partnership. Tax A. Voider reports $60,000 of ordinary income in 19X7 as a result of the partnership's activities [$25,000 guaranteed payment + 0.20 ($200,000 − $25,000) distributive share].

### Transactions Involving the Partner and the Partnership

Sales and exchanges of property between the partner and the partnership also can take place as if they involved unrelated parties. However, two sets of special rules must be discussed which restrict some tax planning opportunities under these circumstances. Under the first set of rules, a loss cannot be deducted on the sale or exchange of property between:

1. A partnership and a partner owning more than 50% of either the capital or profits interests in the partnership.

2. Two partnerships in which the same persons own more than 50% of either the capital or profits interests.

A set of constructive ownership rules are used to determine if the 50% threshold has been exceeded. The constructive ownership rules establish an individual to be the deemed owner of partnership interests owned by other family members and by certain related entities, such as trusts and corporations. Losses that are disallowed under this rule can be used by the purchaser to offset gains that would otherwise be recognized on a subsequent sale of the property.

**EXAMPLE 6-10.** Tax A. Voider sold land for its fair market value of $18,000 to the ABC Partnership in which she is a 60% owner. Tax

A. Voider had a basis in the land of $20,000 at the time of sale. Tax A. Voider can not recognize her $2,000 loss from this sale ($18,000 sales price − $20,000 basis). If ABC later sells this land for $21,000, the partnership has a realized gain of $3,000 ($21,000 sales price − $18,000 basis) but only reports a $1,000 gain ($3,000 actual partnership gain − $2,000 loss previously disallowed to Tax A. Voider).

The second set of rules can apply to the sale or exchange of property, which, in the hands of the transferee, is a noncapital asset. The sales and exchanges involved are those which occur between:

1.  A partnership and a partner owning more than 80% of either the capital or profits interests in the partnership.
2.  Two partnerships in which the same persons own more than 80% of either the capital or profits interests.

These rules cause any gain recognized by the selling party to be ordinary income regardless of the asset's use in the transferor's hands. As with the first set of rules above, a set of constructive ownership rules are used to determine if the 80% threshold has been exceeded.

EXAMPLE **6-11.**    Tax A. Voider holds a large tract of land as an investment (a capital asset to Tax A. Voider). The land which has a $30,000 basis to Tax A. Voider is sold for its $100,000 fair market value to the LMN Partnership in which Tax A. Voider has an 85% interest. LMN, a real estate development partnership, plans to develop this tract into a new subdivision so the land is inventory (not a capital asset) to the partnership. Even though Tax A. Voider sold an asset which was a capital asset in his hands, he must recognize $70,000 ($100,000–$30,000 basis) of ordinary income on the sale.

## FILING REQUIREMENTS

A partnership must file a Form 1065 to report its income, deductions, and so on. Each partner receives a Schedule K–1 (Form 1065) to report his distributive share of the partnership income, loss, and so on. The partnership return is due on or before the 15th day of the fourth month after the partnership's year-end unless an extension is obtained.

### NOTES

1.  Because certain tax attributes are segregated and passed-through separately to the partners, the "bottom-line" income amount is not the partnership's taxable income, but is instead called ordinary income (or ordinary loss).

# 7

# FORMATION OF A BUSINESS ENTITY

The tax consequences of operating as a sole proprietorship, a regular corporation, an S corporation and a partnership have been discussed. The formation of a sole proprietorship has very few tax difficulties, since a proprietorship represents nothing more than an extension of the individual taxpayer. The formation of a corporation or a partnership, on the other hand, represents the creation of a separate legal entity. An exchange of a direct ownership interest in property or services for an indirect interest in a business entity occurs in the formation. Such an exchange can be either a taxable or tax-free event, depending on the circumstances. If the exchange is tax free, part or all of the gain or loss realized on the transfer may be tax exempt.

This chapter examines the formation of both the corporate and partnership entities. There is no difference in the formation of a regular corporation and an S corporation, so we shall simply discuss corporate formations as a single topic. Included is a discussion of the basic tax questions that are fundamental to the owners of the business and the business entity itself. Each question is answered separately for the corporate entity and the partnership entity.

## AN OVERVIEW

The formation of a business entity is illustrated by Figure 7-1. The transferor(s) passes property and services to the partnership or corporation in exchange for an ownership interest. The entity provides the transferor with either a partnership interest or some of its stock. In addition, it may provide the transferor with cash, noncash property, or some of its debt obligations. A partner in a partnership is also considered to receive his share of the partnership's liabilities.

## TRANSFERS TO CORPORATION

### Recognition of Gain or Loss by the Transferor

A transfer of property by a transferor to a corporation in exchange for its stock is a taxable event. As a general rule, the gain or loss that is realized on the exchange is included in gross income or deducted. The realized gain or loss equals:

> Fair market value of stocks and securities received
> Amount of money received
> Fair market value of other property received
> Liabilities of the transferor assumed by the transferee

|        |                                              |
|--------|----------------------------------------------|
| Equals: | Amount realized                             |
| Less:   | Adjusted basis of the properties transferred |
| Equals: | Realized gain or loss                       |

The adjusted basis of the properties that are transferred equals the taxpayer's book value for tax purposes. Ordinarily, this equals the

**FIGURE 7-1**  Formation of a business entity.

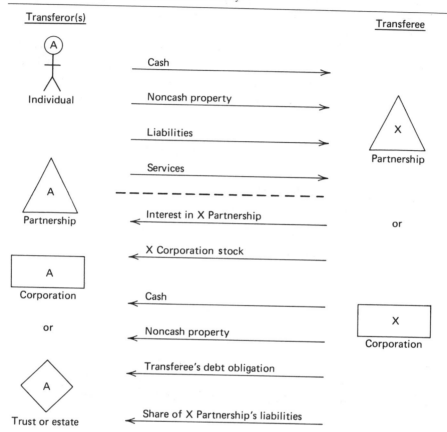

*Transfer to Corporation*
General Rule: Tax-free event for the shareholders and transferee corporation, if six requirements are met

Exceptions:
Receipt of boot
Liabilities assumed or acquired by transferer corporation for tax avoidance purpose or in excess of basis of transferred properties

*Transfer to Partnership*
General Rule: Tax-free event for the partners and the partnership

Exceptions:
Assumption of liabilities by the partnership may result in cash distribution to partner in excess of basis
Transfer is made to an "investment company"

taxpayer's cost for the property adjusted downward for any depreciation, depletion or amortization that has been claimed.

To eliminate the possiblity that an individual might be prohibited from incorporating his business because of the tax costs that are involved, an exception to the general rule outlined above has been created which requires that the gain or loss realized upon the formation of a corporation be deferred. The taxpayer's gain or loss must be deferred if six requirements found in the tax laws are satisfied. These requirements, which apply equally to a transfer to a newly created or to an existing corporation, are the following:

1. Property must be involved.
2. A transfer that qualifies as an "exchange" must occur.
3. One or more transferors must be involved.
4. Control of the corporation must be held by the transferor(s).
5. The control requirement must be satisfied immediately after the exchange.
6. Stock and securities must be received by the transferor(s).

If one or more of these requirements is failed, then the entire realized gain or loss must be recognized. Recognition of the loss may be denied under the rules on related-party transactions (e.g., when the transferor owns more than 50% of the transferee's stock).

### Property Requirement

The nonrecognition rules apply only to property that is transferred to a corporation in exchange for stock and securities. Property includes money, tangible property, and intangible property. Excluded from the property definition are three items: (1) an indebtedness of the transferee corporation that is not evidenced by a security; (2) interest on an indebtedness of the transferee corporation that accrued on or after the beginning of the transferor's holding period for the debt; and (3) services. The services exception prevents a transferor from performing services for a corporation, being compensated for the services by receiving stock and securities, and avoiding taxation on the fair market value of the stock and securities that are received until they are sold or exchanged. The fair market value of the stocks, securities and other nonmoney property received, plus the amount of money received, for the performance of services is taken into the transferor's gross income at the time of receipt.

### Exchange Requirement

The nonrecognition rules do not apply unless an exchange of property for stock and securities occurs. Normally this does not present a problem. Occasionally, a question arises whether a transfer of a patent or other intangible to a transferee corporation constitutes an exchange or a licensing agreement. If it is a licensing agreement, the proceeds are treated as royalty income and taxed as a capital gain or ordinary income.

### One-or-More-Transferor Requirement

The nonrecognition rules apply to situations involving single or multiple transferors. As illustrated in Figure 7-1, a transferor can be an individual, a corporation, a partnership, a trust, or an estate. When more than one transferor is involved, the transfers need not take place at a single point in time. In such a case, the control requirement is tested after completion of all the transfers, provided they take place as part of a single plan.

### Control Requirement

The nonrecognition rules require the transferors as a group to own 80% of the total voting power of the transferee corporation's stock, plus 80% of each class of nonvoting stock immediately after the exchange. There is no specific time period for which the minimum stock ownership requirement must be maintained. Generally, the requirement is met when the transferors hold title to the stock and are able to engage in whatever actions they desire with respect to the transferee corporation's stock. A prearranged plan to transfer the property for stock and securities *and* then to relinquish control through a sale or exchange of some or all of the stock will destroy the tax-free nature of the transaction. Stock issued for services is not counted for purposes of satisfying the control tests unless the transferor transfers both property and services to the corporation in exchange for the stock or securities.

The control requirement ordinarily will not be satisfied when a new shareholder is brought into an existing corporation, since it is unlikely that the new transferor will acquire sufficient stock to "control" the transferee corporation. When a transfer of additional property to the corporation is made by the original shareholder group, their original stock can be counted for purposes of the control test only when the value of their additional property contribution equals at least ten percent of the value of the stocks and securities that are already held.

**EXAMPLE 7-1.** Tax A. Voider has a patent worth $1,000,000 and which was developed at a cost of $100,000. The Hi-Flyer Corporation approaches Tax A. Voider about marketing the product covered by the patent. Tax A. Voider is offered a 50% interest in Hi-Flyer (worth $1,000,000) in exchange for the patent. If the exchange takes place as planned, Tax A. Voider is taxed on her $900,000 gain. A deferral of this gain is possible only if Hi-Flyer's original shareholder group transfers sufficient additional property to the corporation to be counted as transferors, and thereby permit Tax A. Voider and the other transferors to "control" Hi-Flyer immediately after the exchange.

### Stock and Securities Requirement

The tax deferral is available only when stock and securities are received by the transferor. Stock includes both common and preferred stock but does not include stock rights or stock warrants. The stock does not need to have voting rights so long as the control requirement is satisfied. Securities are debt obligations of the transferee corporation, but not all debt obligations qualify as securities. The test of whether a debt obligation qualifies as a security is based upon the nature of the debt, the duration of the obligation, the degree of continuing interest in the business provided by the obligation, and the purpose of the obligation. Ordinarily, debt obligations having a duration of less than 5 years do not qualify as securities, while obligations having a duration of more than 10 years do qualify as securities. For debt obligation with a life between 5 and 10 years, the characterization depends on the facts and circumstances.

Property other than stock and securities that is received by the transferors triggers the recognition of gain. The recognized gain equals the lesser of (1) the transferor's realized gain or (2) the sum of the money received and the fair market value of the nonmoney property other than stocks or securities ("boot" property) received. No losses are recognized, even when boot property is received by the transferor. When multiple assets are transferred to a corporation, the gain or loss is computed separately for each property using the above rule. A pro rata share of each form of consideration received is allocated to the various properties transferred based upon each property's relative fair market value.

The deferral of gain or loss that accompanies the receipt of stock or securities permits a corporation to select its capital structure without being constrained by tax laws. The corporation can take advantage of the tax provisions that favor the use of debt capital without causing the transferor to be taxed on part or all of his realized gain, provided the debt capital can be characterized as a security.

### Transfer of Liabilities

The transferee corporation generally can assume the transferor's liabilities, or acquire the transferor's property subject to a liability, and not have these liabilities be considered as money or other property. By treating the assumption of the liabilities in this way, a transferor can transfer the accounts payable and long-term liabilities of a trade or business to a new corporation without having to recognize any gain on the exchange.

Two exceptions to this general rule apply. The first exception applies when the principal purpose for the assumption or acquisition of the transferor's liability by the transferee corporation was the avoidance of federal income taxes, or no business purpose existed for the assumption or acquisition of the liability. In this case, all liabilities that are assumed or acquired by the transferee corporation in the exchange are treated as money by the transferor. The second exception taxes the net economic gain that accrues to the taxpayer by being released from liabilities that are in excess of his investment in the assets for tax purposes. The second exception requires the recognition of gain if the total of the liabilities that are assumed or acquired by the transferee corporation from a transferor exceeds the total of the adjusted basis of the properties that are transferred by that transferor. The amount of gain recognized equals the excess of the amount of the transferor's liabilities that are assumed or acquired by the transferee corporation over the transferor's total adjusted basis for the transferred properties.

These rules are illustrated by the following:

**EXAMPLE 7-2.**   Tax A. Voider and two associates are creating a new corporation. Tax A. Voider plans to transfer equipment worth $500,000 and liabilities in the amount of $200,000 in exchange for one-third of the new corporation's stock that is worth $300,000. The adjusted basis of the transferred assets is $275,000. The realized gain is $225,000 [($300,000 + $200,000) − $275,000]. None of the gain is recognized since Tax A. Voider receives only stock in exchange for the property and the assumption of the liabilities is not the receipt of "boot."

A special exception exists to the rule which requires the recognition of gain when the liabilities transferred or assumed by the transferee corporation exceed the adjusted basis of the assets that are transferred. This exception is particularly important to cash method of accounting transferors who do not have any basis for their accounts receivable. For such a transferor, ordinarily none of the accounts receivable are included in the total assets transferred. On the other hand, all of the accounts payable and other current liabilities are included in the total liabilities transferred or assumed by the transferee corporation, even though none of these liabilities can be deducted until they are paid. For cash or hybrid method of accounting taxpayers the special exemption does not include in the liability total any liabilities that produce a tax deduction when they are paid. As a result, most accounts payable amounts are not counted for purposes of applying the gain recognition rules.

### Character of Recognized Gain

The gain recognized by a transferor is characterized as either a short-term or long-term capital gain if the transferred asset is a capital asset. If the property is not a capital asset, then one of the other types of gains described in Chapter 9 may apply. For example, if the transferred asset is a trade or business asset, the recognized gain will be characterized as a Section 1231 gain. In addition, the various recapture provisions (e.g., the depreciation recapture provisions of Sections 1245 and 1250) can apply to characterize part of the recognized gain as ordinary income.

A transfer of property into a corporation in exchange for stocks, securities, or other property that are worth more than the transferred property is worth can result in the excess amount being treated as a dividend paid to the transferors. Alternatively, the IRS may attempt to hold that such amounts are in fact compensation for services. In either case, the dividend or compensation amount is taxed currently to the transferor.

### Basis of the Stocks and Securities Received

Because the gain or loss on the transfer of assets to the corporation goes partially or totally unrecognized, the basis for the stocks and securities that are received by the transferor is not their fair market value. If a gain is deferred on the transfer, the basis for the stocks and securities received ordinarily is lower than their market value on the transfer date by the amount of the deferred gain. If a loss is deferred on the transfer, the basis for the stocks and securities received ordinarily is higher than their market value on the transfer date by the amount of the deferred loss. The boot property received takes a basis equal to its fair market value.

The total basis of the stocks and securities received is determined by using the following formula:

|  | Total basis of transferred property |
|---|---|
| Plus: | The amount of dividend income or gain recognized by the transferor on the transfer |
| Less: | The fair market value of the boot property (other than money) received by the transferor |
|  | The amount of money received by the transferor |
| Equals: | Total basis of nonrecognition property |

The amount of any liabilities assumed or acquired by the transferee corporation is treated as money for purposes of determining the adjusted basis of the stocks and securities that are received. Although they are not considered money for purposes of determining the recognized gain, the amount of liabilities assumed or acquired reduces the basis of the stocks and securities that are received. This money treatment for the liabilities assumed or acquired, however, does not apply to the liabilities of a cash- or hybrid-method-of-accounting transferor that are the subject of the special exception discussed earlier.

If a single class of stock is received by the transferor in the exchange, then the total basis of the nonrecognition property is allocated to it. If multiple classes of stock are received, or one or more classes of each stock and securities are received, then the total basis of the nonrecognition property is allocated to the various classes of stocks or securities based upon their relative fair market values.

### Holding Period for the Stocks and Securities

The holding period for stocks and securities received in a partially or completely tax-free transfer of property to a corporation involving a capital asset or a Section 1231 trade or business property (as defined in Chapter 9) includes the transferor's holding period for the property transferred. Stocks and securities received for other types of properties, or in a taxable transaction, have their holding periods begin on the date of the exchange. Since most asset transfers to a corporation involve multiple properties, the stock and securities received may have holding periods commencing on a variety of dates depending upon the nature of the properties transferred. The holding period for any boot property received begins on the transaction date.

### Recognition of Gain or Loss by the Transferee Corporation

No gain or loss is recognized by a corporation when it receives property or services in exchange for its stock. This nonrecognition rule applies whether the stock is treasury stock or stock that has not been previously issued. Likewise, no gain or loss is recognized when the transferee corporation issues its indebtedness in exchange for property and services.

A corporation excludes capital contributions from its gross income and includes them as part of its capital account. Voluntary, pro rata capital contributions made by a shareholder, for which no additional stock is issued, are treated as an additional price paid by the shareholder for the stock he already holds. The basis of the stock is increased by the amount of money or adjusted basis of the non-money property that is contributed. An involuntary contribution of property that satisfies an assessment made by a corporation is a transaction that is taxable to the shareholder. The shareholder recognizes a gain or loss if the contribution is made by using nonmoney property. The basis of the stock already held is increased by the amount of money or the fair market value of the nonmoney property contributed.

### Basis for Transferee
### Corporation's Properties

The transferee corporation's basis for contributed property equals the asset's basis in the transferor's hands, increased by the amount of gain recognized by the transferor on the transfer. Liabilities that are assumed or acquired by the transferee corporation do not reduce the transferee's basis for the property. The basis of services contributed by the transferor equals the value of the consideration that is transferred as compensation.

**EXAMPLE 7-3.** Tax A. Voider transfers properties to a new corporation in a partially tax-free transaction whereby he recognizes $20,000 of gain. The adjusted basis and fair market value of the transferred properties are $300,000 and $500,000, respectively. The new corporation also assumes $125,000 of Tax A. Voider's liabilities. The transferee corporation's basis for Tax A. Voider's assets is $320,000 ($300,000 + $20,000). This basis is different from Tax A. Voider's basis for his stock, which is $175,000 [$300,000 + $20,000 − $20,000 (cash received) − $125,000].

The lower adjusted basis accorded appreciated property received in a tax-free transaction results in the corporation losing some tax benefits. For example, assume one individual transfers inventory having an $10,000 fair market value and a $1,000 basis to a corporation. Another individual transfers $10,000 in cash. The cash is used to purchase inventory. Each individual receives one-half of the transferee corporation's stock. Who has contributed the most to the corporation? The answer is the second individual since the inventory purchased with his cash contribution produces $10,000 in tax deductions when it is sold. The inventory transferred by the first individual produces only $1,000 in tax deductions. Assuming both inventory items are sold for the same price, the first individual's inventory results in $9,000 of additional taxable income and $4,140 ($9,000 × 0.46) of additional taxes due. Because of the additional tax liability that results from the tax-free transfer, some consideration should be given to requiring the first individual to contribute additional cash for his 50% interest or making an adjustment to the number of shares that are issued to the two shareholders.

A transferee corporation can step-up the basis for the property it receives without making a cash outlay. The use of short-term notes as boot permits the transferee corporation to step-up the basis for the property while deferring the cash outlay for no more than 10 years.

EXAMPLE 7-4. Tax A. Voider transfers land that is a capital asset in her hands to a new corporation. The adjusted basis and fair market value of the land are $200,000 and $375,000, respectively. Tax A. Voider receives $200,000 of stock and $175,000 of short-term notes from the new corporation. The short-term notes require Tax A. Voider to recognize a $175,000 capital gain [($200,000 + $175,000) − $200,000]. The new corporation takes a $375,000 basis for the land. Tax A. Voider may face a problem because the receipt of the short-term notes does not provide any cash with which to pay the tax due on the capital gain.

### Holding Period for Transferee Corporation's Properties

The assets received by the transferee corporation in a tax-free exchange assume the transferor's holding period for all assets, regardless of their character. This rule applies whether or not a gain must be recognized with respect to the individual property that is transferred.

### Avoiding the Nonrecognition of Gain or Loss Rules

As mentioned earlier, a transaction that fails one or more of the six requirements for nonrecognition treatment is fully taxable to the transferor. The transferor recognizes his entire realized gain or loss and takes a basis for the stocks and securities equal to their fair market value. The transferee corporation takes the property's cost as its basis.

Parties creating a new corporation may desire to avoid tax free treatment in order to (1) increase the basis for the property to its fair market value; (2) recognize a loss on the transfer of a property which has declined in value; or (3) preserve capital gain treatment for appreciation that has taken place prior to the transfer.

In the first situation, the transferee corporation can claim an increased amount of depreciation, depletion, or amortization, or can use an increased cost of goods amount to offset its sales revenues if the transaction is taxable.

The nonrecognition rules extend to both gains and losses. Even if one of the six requirements is not met so that the transaction is taxable, the realized loss may not be recognized for tax purposes. The related party sales rules prohibit loss recognition on a transaction between an individual and a corporation that is more than 50% owned, directly or indirectly, by that individual. Further discussion on the related party sale rules are included in Chapter 9.

The type of gain that is recognized by the corporation when it later sells property received from a transferor depends solely on the property's use or character in the corporation's hands. Thus, a piece of land that was held as a capital asset by the transferor and is held currently as inventory by the transferee corporation produces ordinary income when sold by the corporation. In order to preserve the favorable capital gains treatment for the gains that accrued while the transferor held the property, a transaction that *avoids* the nonrecognition rules needs to be structured. This type of transaction results in the transferor's appreciation being taxed at a maximum 20% rate

(40% of the gain times a 50% rate) instead of being taxed at the maximum 46% corporate tax rate.

**EXAMPLE 7-5.**   Tax A. Voider has owned a parcel of land for a number of years. The land is worth $1,000,000 and has a basis of $100,000. The land is to be transferred to a new corporation where it will be subdivided and sold. If a tax-free transfer occurs, the land takes a $100,000 basis in the corporation's hands and the corporation's cost of goods sold is $100,000. A taxable transfer, on the other hand, results in a $900,000 long-term capital gain being recognized by Tax A. Voider and a $1,000,000 basis for the corporation. This reduces the corporation's ordinary income that results from the subdividing by $900,000 and converts it into a capital gain recognized by the transferor.

A number of ways exist for avoiding the nonrecognition rules. These include the following:

1.  Sale of the assets to the corporation.
2.  Failure to control the transferee corporation immediately following the exchange.
3.  Transfer of assets for stock or securities and cash, other property or short-term notes.
4.  Loan of funds to the corporation.
5.  Lease of property to the corporation.

### Organizational Expenditures

Organizational expenditures incurred by a corporation are capitalized and, with a special election, deducted over a period of 60 or more months, commencing with the month in which the corporation begins business. The election applies to all organizational expenditures that are incurred before the end of the taxable year in which the corporation begins business. If this election is not made, or the expenditures are incurred after the end of the corporation's first taxable year, then the organizational expenditures are capitalized and can not be deducted until the corporation is terminated. Examples of organizational expenditures eligible to be amortized include legal services incident to the organization of the corporation, fees paid to the state of incorporation, necessary costs of establishing an accounting system, and expenses of temporary directors meetings and organizational meetings of stockholders. Expenditures ineligible for this treatment include expenses incurred in selling stock (treated as a reduction in the capital received) and acquiring assets (treated as an increase in the basis of the assets).

## TRANSFERS TO PARTNERSHIPS

As is true throughout the tax laws for partnerships, the tax laws governing transfers to a partnership represent a mix of the aggregate and entity concepts. Under the entity concept, the partnership itself is treated as an entity separate from its owners so that there are questions about basis and holding periods of partnership assets. Under the aggregate concept, the partnership is in many ways treated only as the aggregate of the group of partners so that gain and loss are not generally recognized by the partners on the formation. The mix of these two sets of rules results in different treatments than for transfers to a corporation.

### Recognition of Gain or Loss by the Transferor

A transfer of property to a partnership in exchange for a partnership interest does not normally cause any gain or loss recognition for the transferor. The partnership is viewed as an aggregation of its partners and the transfer is considered to be only a change in the form in which the property is held. Note that the nonrecognition of gain or loss in a partnership formation is not dependent on requirements like those found in corporate formations. The nonrecognition rule applies for any contribution of property in exchange for a partnership interest, regardless of the size of the interest acquired.

There are three major exceptions to the nonrecognition rule. First, gain may be recognized if the partnership assumes the liabilities of the partner. Second, any realized gain is recognized if the partnership is one which would be treated as an investment company if it were incorporated. Third, a contribution of property to the partnership followed immediately by a distribution of cash or property by the partnership to the contributing partner may be treated as a sale between partners (and therefore taxable) or as a partial contribution of property to the partnership and a partial sale between the partnership and an individual who is not a partner (and therefore taxable). The first two of these exceptions are examined in the proceeding sections.

## Effect of Liabilities

The pervasive effect of liabilities in the partnership setting arises from the fact that general partners do not have limited liability. An increase in partnership liabilities is treated as a contribution of money by the partner and a decrease in liabilities is treated as a distribution of money by the partnership. Liabilities can have an additional impact as follows: if the partnership agrees to pay liabilities which had belonged to a partner as an individual, that partner is considered for all purposes as if he received a distribution of money from the partnership. Conversely, if a partner assumes a liability which formerly was owed by the partnership as a whole, the partner is treated for all purposes as if he made a contribution of money to the partnership. All of these deemed cash contributions and distributions are significant because gain must be recognized by a partner any time (whether in formation, during operation, or upon liquidation) that cash distributions (actual or deemed) are made in excess of his basis in the partnership interest.

Most contributions of property to a partnership are tax-free even if there are significant liabilities assumed by the partnership.

EXAMPLE 7-6.   Tax A. Voider contributes property with a basis of $10,000 and a fair market value of $20,000 in return for a 40% interest in the TAV partnership. TAV also assumes a $12,000 debt on the property. TAV has $1,000 of other liabilities at the time of the transaction. Tax A. Voider has a basis in his partnership interest of:

| | Carryover basis from property contributed | $10,000 |
|---|---|---|
| Plus: | Tax A. Voider's share of partnership liabilities | |
| | ($13,000 debts × 0.40) | 5,200 |
| Less: | Tax A. Voider's debt assumed by the partnership | (12,000) |
| Equals: | Tax A. Voider's basis in his TAV partnership interest | $ 3,200 |

Note that the liability on the contributed property in this example was greater than the adjusted basis of the property, but that fact alone did not result in recognition of gain by the contributing partner. Only in the rare case where the taxpayer's deemed distribution (from the assumption of his own liability by the partnership) exceeds his total contribution (both property and his share of partnership liabilities assumed) is income recognized on the contribution of property subject to a liability.

Clearly, this result differs significantly from the $2,000 gain which would be mandated if the same property were contributed to a corporation. The difference in treatment arises from the idea that the partner is liable for his share of all partnership liabilities.

As can be seen from Example 7-6, there is a relatively simple strategy which can be used to avoid the recognition of gain on the contribution of encumbered property. Remember that if the partnership incurs liabilities, each partner's basis is increased by his share of the liabilities. Remember also that a partner recognizes no gain until he receives a distribution in excess of his basis. Therefore, if the partnership has significant liabilities before the contribution of encumbered property (whether from partnership borrowings or from the contributions of other encumbered properties by other partners), the contributing partner is less likely to incur gain. However, a caveat is in order. The payment of partnership liabilities is considered a distribution of money to the partners. Tax A. Voider needs to be sure that the partnership liabilities are not paid off before he has a basis greater than his share of the debt repayment or he will be forced to recognize a gain.

**EXAMPLE 7-7.** Assume the facts remain the same as in Example 7-6. If the partnership immediately pays off $5,000 of its debt, Tax A. Voider's basis is reduced by his share of the liability reduction, or $2,000 ($5,000 × 0.40). His basis of $3,200 before the debt repayment is sufficiently large that he has a positive basis of $1,200 ($3,200 basis − $2,000 deemed distribution) after the debt repayment. If the partnership instead repays $10,000 in debts, Tax A. Voider's share of the repayment is $4,000 ($10,000 × 0.40) and he will recognize an $800 gain. The gain equals the amount by which his deemed distribution from the debt reduction exceeds his basis at the time of the debt repayment.

### Investment Diversification

Congress became aware that a taxpayer with a small portfolio of stocks and securities could diversify his holdings if he and other similarly situated taxpayers contributed the stocks and securities to a partnership. Each partner would then have an interest in a diversified investment portfolio. If there were no special exceptions to the partnership formation rules described above, the taxpayer would be able to accomplish this diversification without recognizing any gain since he would be exchanging property (stock and securities) for a partnership interest. Congress, accordingly, provided that a taxpayer would recognize gain (but not loss) on the transfer of property to a partnership "investment company." The tax laws define an investment company as one which immediately after the exchange holds more than 80% of the value of its assets (excluding cash and nonconvertible debt obligations) for investment, and the assets consist of readily marketable stocks, securities or similar assets. While this provision closes the door to a partnership whose sole purpose is the diversification of an investment portfolio, there clearly remains the possibility of achieving some diversification in a partnership which holds securities as well as some significant amount of other assets which are not readily marketable.

### Partnership Interest Received
### for Services

A partner must recognize income if he receives his partnership interest as compensation for his services. As in other situations in which a taxpayer receives property for his services, the taxpayer reports income equal to the value of the property received minus any amounts he paid for the property.

### Basis in Partnership Interest

Since a partner is considered to have exchanged one form of asset for another, it is not surprising that the partner's beginning basis in his partnership interest is derived in part as a carryover from his basis in the property he contributed. If the partner must recognize gain on the formation of the partnership because the partnership is an investment company, this gain also increases the initial basis. To the extent a partner includes in income the value of a partnership interest received for services, he will also increase his basis in his partnership interest.

As described in the previous example, a partner's basis in his partnership interest is greatly affected by liabilities owed by the partnership and by liabilities of the transferor partner which are assumed by the partnership. The formula for the partner's initial basis in the partnership interest can be summarized as follows:

|  | Basis of property contributed by transferor |
| --- | --- |
| Plus: | Gain recognized on the contribution |
|  | Income recognized from partnership interest received for services |
|  | Partner's share of all partnership liabilities |
| Minus: | Amount of partner's liabilities assumed by the partnership |
| Equals: | Initial basis in partnership interest |

An example of the computation of the initial basis in a partnership interest can be found in Example 7-16.

### Holding Period of Partnership Interest

Holding period rules for a partnership interest in large part parallel their counterparts in the corporate tax setting. If a partner acquires his partnership interest in exchange for a capital asset or Section 1231 trade or business property, his holding period for his partnership interest includes his holding period for the property he contributed. If he receives his partnership interest for other types of property or for services, his holding period for his partnership interest commences on the date he acquires his partnership interest.

Unlike the corporate formation rules, there are no provisions in the partnership tax law for determining the holding period for a partnership interest which is acquired in part for a capital asset or Section 1231 property and in part for other property. In fact, the only *safe* procedure for ensuring a long-term holding period treatment on the sale or exchange of such a partnership interest (acquired for both a capital asset and other property) is to hold the partnership interest for more than six months. If this is not possible, expert advice is essential.

### Tax Consequences to the Partnership

When a partnership is formed, the partnership itself recognizes no gain or loss on the transfer of partnership interests for property. When services are contributed to the partnership in return for a partnership interest, the partnership must account for the value of the services. There are two possible situations: (1) the services may be of a nature that would generate a deduction if performed by an outsider; or (2) the services may be of a nature that would be capitalized if performed by an outsider. An example of the former is services provided by a partner selling the partnership's product to ensure a demand for the product when the production process begins. The value of these services would be a deduction for the new partnership. An example of the latter type of situation are services provided by a partner as a contractor during the construction of the partnership's office building. These services must be included in the cost of the building and are depreciated over 18 or more years. (See Chapter 8 for a further discussion of the depreciation rules.)

When partners contribute property to a partnership, the partnership simply takes the transferor's adjusted basis for the property. This carryover basis is adjusted if the transferor has to recognize gain because the partnership is an investment company. The basis is not increased for any gain the transferor must recognize because of liabilities being transferred.

This carryover basis rule potentially causes two problems which must be considered. The first problem is that the partnership is likely to have a low basis (relative to fair market value) for investments which have appreciated in the partner's hands and for investments which are depreciable. This means that the partnership's deductions for depreciation may be much lower than they would have been if the same asset had been acquired by purchase.

The second problem is the determination of the proper allocation of any preacquisition gain or loss when the asset is finally sold by the partnership. Without any special allocations, the partners will simply share all gain or loss from the sale of the contributed asset as they share other gains and losses. It is possible, if the partners so desire, to allocate pre-contribution gain or loss to the contributing partner, while all post-contribution change in value is still shared among all partners.

Under the 1984 Tax Act the IRS must draft new rules indicating how income, gain, loss, and deductions with respect to contributed property is to be allocated between the partners so as to take into account (1) differences between the tax basis of the property at the time of the contribution and its fair market value and (2) contributions of accrued but unpaid items by a cash method of accounting partner. These new rules will make the allocation of built-in gain or loss to the contributing partner mandatory for contributions made after March 31, 1984.

EXAMPLE **7-8.** Tax A. Voider contributed land with a basis of $25,000 and a fair market value of $50,000 to the 2T Partnership for a 50% partnership interest. Todd contributed $50,000 cash for the other 50% interest. The 2T Partnership sells the land a year later for $60,000. If there is no special allocation agreement, Tax A. Voider and Todd will each report and pay taxes on one-half of the partnership's $35,000 gain ($60,000 sales price − $25,000 basis).

EXAMPLE **7-9.** Assume the facts remain the same as in the preceding example except that the partners agree that all pre-contribution gain will be allocated to Tax A. Voider. Any gain which accrues while the partnership holds the land will be divided equally between the partners. With this special allocation, a partnership sale of the land for $60,000 would result in Tax A. Voider reporting his pre-contribution gain of $25,000 ($50,000 fair market value at contribution minus the $25,000 basis) plus one-half of the $10,000 appreciation which has accrued since the contribution. Todd would then only be taxed on his share of the appreciation which has accrued during partnership operation ($5,000). Clearly the special allocation will be favored by Todd while Tax A. Voider is more likely to prefer that no special allocation be made.

The 1984 Tax Act provided special rules for determining the character of income or loss recognized when a partnership disposes of certain properties contributed after March 31, 1984. If a partnership disposes of property that was inventory in the hands of the contributing partner immediately before its contribution, then any gain on the recognition during the 5-year holding period following the contribution will be treated as ordinary income or loss. Gain or loss on the disposition of unrealized receivables contributed by a partner will be treated as ordinary income regardless of the date of disposition by the partnership. Any loss existing on the transfer of a capital asset to a partnership retains its capital loss characterization in the hands of the partnership for a period of 5 years after that date of contribution regardless of the asset's character in the hands of the partnership.

**EXAMPLE 7-10.**    Tax A. Voider contributed land with a basis of $100,000 and a fair market value of $60,000 to the TJ Partnership. Jack contributed $60,000 cash. Each individual receives an one-half interest in the partnership. The land was a capital asset in Tax A. Voider's hands. The land is held by the partnership as inventory. Sale of the land within 5 years of the date it was contributed to the partnership will not result in an ordinary loss to the partnership, but instead a capital loss. Once the 5-year period has passed, the land can be sold and an ordinary loss recognized. The amount of the capital loss recognized in the 5-year period can not exceed the built-in capital loss at the time of the contribution, or $40,000.

Like a corporation which receives property in a tax-free contribution, the partnership will have a holding period for each of its contributed assets which includes the holding period of the partner.

## Organizational Expenditures

Expenses incurred in the organization of a partnership can be treated as deferred expenses that are deductible when the partnership is liquidated. Alternatively, an election can be made to amortize the costs over a period of not less than 60 months commencing with the month in which the partnership begins business. The amortization election must be made in the partnership tax return covering the month in which the partnership begins business. The definition of organizational expenditures are the same for partnerships as for corporations. No deduction can be claimed for syndication fees associated with the sale of a partnership interest.

# 8

# ACQUISITION AND USE OF BUSINESS ASSETS

An important question facing any business is whether to acquire new properties or to make improvements to existing properties. Each investment decision involves a series of cash inflows and outflows throughout the asset's useful life. An important cash inflow derived from asset ownership occurs as a result of the deductions and tax credits available in the tax laws. These tax attributes are illustrated in Figure 8-1 for a $100,000 asset that is a new, personal property with a 10-year expected useful life. The acquisition is 100% debt financed and repayment occurs over the asset's useful life.

In the year of acquisition the asset is eligible for an investment tax credit equal to 10% of the asset's acquisition cost ($10,000). A deduction also can be claimed in Year 1 for part of the asset's acquisi-

**FIGURE 8-1** Tax benefits derived from asset ownership.

## FACTS

| | |
|---|---|
| Acquisition cost: | $100,000 |
| Debt financing: | 100% |
| Principal repayment: | $10,000 is repaid at the end of each year |
| Interest rate: | 12% |
| Investment tax credit: | $10,000 |
| Capital recovery deduction: | |

| Year | Capital Recovery Deduction |
|---|---|
| 1 | $14,250 |
| 2 | 20,900 |
| 3–5 | 19,950 |

| | |
|---|---|
| Sale price: | $25,000 |

## UNDISCOUNTED CASH FLOWS

| | Cash Outflows | | | Cash Inflows | | |
|---|---|---|---|---|---|---|
| Year | Principal Repayment | Interest Payment | Investment Tax Credit | Value of Deductions[a] | After-tax Sales Proceeds | Net Cash Outflow (Inflow) |
| | (1) | (2) | (3) | (4) | (5) | (6) = (1) + (2) − (3) − (4) − (5) |
| 1 | $ 10,000 | $12,000 | $10,000 | $12,075 | | 75 |
| 2 | 10,000 | 10,800 | | 14,582 | | (6,218) |
| 3 | 10,000 | 9,600 | | 13,593 | | (6,007) |
| 4 | 10,000 | 8,400 | | 13,041 | | (5,359) |
| 5 | 10,000 | 7,200 | | 12,489 | | (4,711) |
| 6 | 10,000 | 6,000 | | 2,760 | | (13,240) |
| 7 | 10,000 | 4,800 | | 2,208 | | (12,592) |
| 8 | 10,000 | 3,600 | | 1,656 | | (11,944) |
| 9 | 10,000 | 2,400 | | 1,104 | | (11,296) |
| 10 | 10,000 | 1,200 | | 552 | $13,500[b] | 2,852 |
| Total | $100,000 | $66,000 | $10,000 | $74,060 | $13,500 | ($68,440) |

Present value of cash flow (discounted at 10% rate)          $39,638

[a] Value of deductions = 0.46 (Depreciation + Interest payment)

[b] After-tax sales proceeds = Sales price − Income tax due on recognized gain

$13,500 = $25,000 − (0.46 × $25,000)

tion cost under the Accelerated Cost Recovery System. These tax benefits reduce the net cash outflow in Year 1 to $75. Even though the property has a 10-year useful life, the taxing authorities permit its acquisition cost to be recovered over a 5-year period. In Year 10 the property is sold for $25,000, and because the property has been fully depreciated, the entire amount realized is recognized as a gain (ordinary income). Had the property been disposed of before the end of Year 5, part or all of the investment tax credit would have to be repaid. This example is used again at various times throughout the remainder of this chapter to illustrate the application of the tax laws to the asset acquisition decision.

This chapter examines the impact that the tax laws have on the asset acquisition or improvement decision by reviewing the determination of the asset's basis; the alternatives for recovery of the capital investment through depreciation, amortization, or depletion; and the available tax credits which can reduce the needed initial cash outlay.

## BASIS RULES

In order to determine the annual capital recovery deductions, it is necessary to determine the property's initial basis and its adjusted basis. The property's basis begins as its original carrying value on the tax books of the corporation. An asset's adjusted basis is determined as follows:

|  | Initial basis |
|---|---|
| Plus: | Capital improvements |
| Less: | Capital recoveries (depreciation, amortization, tax-free dividends, deductible casualty losses) |
| Equals: | Adjusted basis |

The rules for determining a property's basis for two situations are described in the proceeding sections.

### Purchased Property

The basis of purchased property is its cost. An asset's acquisition cost includes the amount of money given up, the fair market value of any nonmoney property given up, and the amount of any debt obligations that are incurred or assumed by the purchaser. Any additional costs incurred in placing the property in service also must be capitalized. Examples of such outlays include legal fees, transfer costs, and special foundations. Interest charges incurred on debt financing during the time period from when the asset is acquired to when it is placed in service can be deducted. A special election to capitalize interest and taxes related to the purchase and installation of personal property is available. Capitalizing these charges makes them eligible for the investment tax credit and allows the taxpayer to recover the costs through depreciation or amortization.

### Conversion of Personal Assets
### Into Income-Producing Property

The basis of "converted properties" on the conversion date is used to determine the realized gain. The lower of the property's basis or fair market value on the conversion date is used to determine the realized loss. The "loss" basis is used to compute the depreciation and capital recovery amounts.

EXAMPLE 8-1.   Tax A. Voider purchased a house to be used as a personal residence for $60,000. She converted it into a rental property when its fair market value was $100,000. Tax A. Voider computes her depreciation based on the property's $60,000 basis. Had the property declined in value to $40,000 prior to conversion, the depreciation deduction would be based on the $40,000 market value on the conversion date. Use of the lower market value prevents the taxpayer from claiming a depreciation deduction for the $20,000 decline in value, which represents a nondeductible personal loss.

## DEPRECIATION

### General

The tax laws permit as a depreciation deduction "a reasonable allowance for the exhaustion, wear, and tear (including a reasonable allowance for obsolescence)—(1) of property used in the trade or business, or (2) of property held for the production of income." No depreciation deduction is available for nonbusiness assets, such as a personal residence. Assets having both a business and a personal use are treated as two properties with only the business portion being depreciable.

Two sets of capital recovery rules are found in the tax laws. For assets acquired before 1981, a set of depreciation rules similar to those used in financial accounting are employed. The Accelerated Cost Recovery System (ACRS) was enacted in 1981, to stimulate capital investment by increasing the capital recovery tax incentives. These rules are mandated, with a few limited exceptions, for assets acquired after 1980. The ACRS rules simplified the cost recovery process by eliminating questions of useful life, salvage value, and depreciation method for most properties. Now, nearly all depreciable personal and real properties are categorized into a series of "recovery classes." Each recovery class has a period of time over which the asset's cost is recovered and a series of recovery percentages that indicate how fast or slow the asset's cost is deducted. Even though the new system was enacted, properties acquired before 1981 continue to be depreciated under the old system. Only rules for current acquisitions are discussed below.

### Property Eligible for Depreciation

Both tangible and intangible property can be depreciated. Tangible properties can be depreciated only if they are subject to wear and tear, exhaustion, or obsolescence. Thus land is not depreciable. Land improvements, however, can be depreciated. Certain natural resources that are subject to physical exhaustion, such as a mineral deposit, can be depleted under the tax laws. Intangible property that has a limited useful life, which can be determined with reasonable accuracy, can be amortized. Examples of intangibles with a limited life are patents or copyrights. An intangible asset that has an indefinite useful life (goodwill, for example) is not eligible for depreciation or amortization.

Where a single price is paid for a group of assets, part of the acquisition cost must be allocated to each of the individual assets. A number of methods can be used for such an allocation. The first method allocates the acquisition cost to the individual assets (including goodwill, if any) based upon their relative market values. An alternative allocation method is to assign to each individual asset the amount determined by the purchaser and seller as part of the sales negotiations. These negotiations can produce larger cost allocations to the inventory and short-lived depreciable properties than would a fair market value allocation and, therefore, permit a quicker recovery of the purchase price. A third allocation method assigns each tangible property a basis amount equal to its fair market value. Any portion of the acquisition cost not allocated to tangible property is allocated to goodwill. To the extent that the goodwill can be attributed to an asset having a limited useful life—such as customer lists, customer routes, or subscription lists—the cost of these assets can be amortized. Goodwill that can not be attributed to a specific property can not be amortized but results in a capital gain or loss being recognized if it is sold or exchanged.

### Post-1981 Capital Recovery Rules

The post–1981 rules represent a marked departure from the depreciation concept used in financial accounting. Use of recovery classes with standardized capital recovery percentages for each year in the capital recovery period obviates the need to determine an asset's useful life. Further, there is no need to determine an asset's salvage value.

#### *Property Eligible for ACRS Treatment*

The ACRS rules are mandatory for real or personal property placed in service by the taxpayer in taxable years beginning after December 31, 1980. Special "anti-churning" rules prevent the sale or exchange of property in use in 1980 to a related party in order to bring it under the ACRS rules. Transactions covered by these rules include: sales or exchanges between family members; sales or exchanges between a corporation and a controlling shareholder; and tax-free formations, liquidations or reorganizations of a corporation or a partnership. The acquiring party in these types of transactions is restricted to the same recovery method that was used by the selling or transferor party. Also excluded from the ACRS rules are properties that the taxpayer elects to depreciate under the units of production method, income forecast method, or any other specialized method not expressed in a term of years. Pre–1981 properties that are "substantially improved" so their use is changed, or useful life is lengthened, can elect to come under the ACRS rules.

### Recovery Classes

The basic foundation of the ACRS rules is a series of recovery classes. The properties included in the recovery classes are illustrated in Figure 8-2. Certain special use properties are excluded from this listing. Most personal property is included in the 5-year recovery class. Real property, on the other hand, usually has an 18-year recovery period.

**FIGURE 8-2**   Property included in recovery classes.

| | |
|---|---|
| *3-Year Class:* | Automobiles, light-duty trucks, machinery and equipment used in researh and experimentation activities, and special tools used in manufacturing. |
| *5-Year Class:* | Machinery, equipment, furniture, and any tangible personal property not included in the 3-, 10-, or 15-year property classification. |
| *10-Year Class:* | Railroad tank cars, residential mobile homes, prefabricated homes, coal-fired boilers and burners, real property used in theme and amusement parks, and limited types of public utility properties. |
| *15-Year Public Utility Property Class:* | Public utility property not included in the 3- or 10-year class including electric utility production plants and water utility property. |
| *15-Year Low-Income Housing Property:* | Includes federally-financed low-income housing projects and certain rehabilitation expenditures. |
| *18-Year Real Property:*[a] | Real property not included in the 10-year class, building components, elevators and escalators. |

[a] A 15-year recovery period applies to real property placed in service prior to March 16, 1984. Special transitional rules can delay the application of the 18-year recovery period for certain properties placed in service by January 1, 1987.

*Recovery Percentages*

The recovery percentages of personal and real property (other than low-income housing) are illustrated in Figures 8-3 and 8-4, respectively. The recovery percentages shown are the same for both new and used property. The recovery percentages for personal property shown in Figure 8-3 are determined by using the 150% declining-balance method and then switching to the straight-line method at the most advantageous time. One-half year's depreciation is claimed in the year of acquisition. The recovery percentages for real property shown in Figure 8-4 are determined by using the 175% declining-balance method and then switching to the straight-line method at the most advantageous time. Although not reproduced here, the capital recovery percentages for low-income housing permit an even more rapid recovery of an investor's capital investment. These recovery percentages are determined by using a 15-year recovery period and the 200% declining-balance method and then switching to the straight-line method.

The net effect of the ACRS rules has been twofold. First, the re-

**FIGURE 8-3**  Recovery percentages for personal property.

| If the Recovery Year Is | The Applicable Percentage for the Class of Property Is | | | |
|---|---|---|---|---|
| | 3-Year | 5-Year | 10-Year | 15-Year Public Utility Property |
| 1 | 25 | 15 | 8 | 5 |
| 2 | 38 | 22 | 14 | 10 |
| 3 | 37 | 21 | 12 | 9 |
| 4 | | 21 | 10 | 8 |
| 5 | | 21 | 10 | 7 |
| 6 | | | 10 | 7 |
| 7 | | | 9 | 6 |
| 8 | | | 9 | 6 |
| 9 | | | 9 | 6 |
| 10 | | | 9 | 6 |
| 11 | | | | 6 |
| 12 | | | | 6 |
| 13 | | | | 6 |
| 14 | | | | 6 |
| 15 | | | | 6 |

**FIGURE 8-4**  Recovery percentages for 18-year recovery period real property (other than low-income housing).

| If the recovery year is | The applicable percentage is (use the column for the month in the first year the property is placed in service) | | | | | | | | | | | |
|---|---|---|---|---|---|---|---|---|---|---|---|---|
| | 1 | 2 | 3 | 4 | 5 | 6 | 7 | 8 | 9 | 10 | 11 | 12 |
| 1 | 9 | 9 | 8 | 7 | 6 | 5 | 4 | 4 | 3 | 2 | 1 | 0.4 |
| 2 | 9 | 9 | 9 | 9 | 9 | 9 | 9 | 9 | 9 | 10 | 10 | 10.0 |
| 3 | 8 | 8 | 8 | 8 | 8 | 8 | 8 | 8 | 9 | 9 | 9 | 9.0 |
| 4 | 7 | 7 | 7 | 7 | 7 | 8 | 8 | 8 | 8 | 8 | 8 | 8.0 |
| 5 | 7 | 7 | 7 | 7 | 7 | 7 | 7 | 7 | 7 | 7 | 7 | 7.0 |
| 6 | 6 | 6 | 6 | 6 | 6 | 6 | 6 | 6 | 6 | 6 | 6 | 6.0 |
| 7 | 5 | 5 | 5 | 5 | 6 | 6 | 6 | 6 | 6 | 6 | 6 | 6.0 |
| 8 | 5 | 5 | 5 | 5 | 5 | 5 | 5 | 5 | 5 | 5 | 5 | 5.0 |
| 9 | 5 | 5 | 5 | 5 | 5 | 5 | 5 | 5 | 5 | 5 | 5 | 5.0 |
| 10 | 5 | 5 | 5 | 5 | 5 | 5 | 5 | 5 | 5 | 5 | 5 | 5.0 |
| 11 | 5 | 5 | 5 | 5 | 5 | 5 | 5 | 5 | 5 | 5 | 5 | 5.0 |
| 12 | 5 | 5 | 5 | 5 | 5 | 5 | 5 | 5 | 5 | 5 | 5 | 5.0 |
| 13 | 4 | 4 | 4 | 5 | 4 | 4 | 5 | 4 | 4 | 4 | 5 | 5.0 |
| 14 | 4 | 4 | 4 | 4 | 4 | 4 | 4 | 4 | 4 | 4 | 4 | 4.0 |
| 15 | 4 | 4 | 4 | 4 | 4 | 4 | 4 | 4 | 4 | 4 | 4 | 4.0 |
| 16 | 4 | 4 | 4 | 4 | 4 | 4 | 4 | 4 | 4 | 4 | 4 | 4.0 |
| 17 | 4 | 4 | 4 | 4 | 4 | 4 | 4 | 4 | 4 | 4 | 4 | 4.0 |
| 18 | 4 | 3 | 4 | 4 | 4 | 4 | 4 | 4 | 4 | 4 | 4 | 4.0 |
| 19 | | 1 | 1 | 1 | 2 | 2 | 2 | 3 | 3 | 3 | 3 | 3.6 |

covery period for real and personal property has been substantially shortened from its actual economic life or its life under the pre–1981 rules. Second, the recovery rate for new personal property and certain real property has been lowered, thus reducing the acceleration of the deductions that was formerly available.

### Capital Recovery Allowances

The capital recovery allowance for a taxable year is determined by multiplying the property's unadjusted basis times the appropriate recovery percentage for the recovery year. The recovery percentage shown in the table is applied to all personal property for the first year of ownership without regard to whether it was acquired at the beginning or the end of the taxable year. If personal property is disposed of before the end of its final recovery year, no capital recovery allowance can be claimed for the year of disposition. Different rules are applied to real property. The appropriate real property recovery percentage depends upon the month in which the property was placed into service. If real property is disposed of before the end of its final recovery year, the capital recovery allowance is prorated according to the portion of the year the property was in service.

The property's unadjusted basis is not reduced by any salvage value amount. The unadjusted basis must be reduced if an election is made to expense a portion of an asset's cost in the year of acquisition, or an investment tax credit or special rehabilitation credit is claimed for an asset acquisition. These adjustments are described below.

The ACRS rules are illustrated by the following example:

**EXAMPLE 8-2.**    TAV Corporation purchases a new asset for $100,000 in March, 19X1. A comparison is presented below of the capital recovery allowance that can be claimed if the property is a 3-year or 5-year personal property or an 18-year real property. (Note: No adjustment is made here to the personal property calculations for any investment tax credit that can be claimed.)

|  | Capital Recovery Allowances for: | | |
| --- | --- | --- | --- |
|  | 3-Year Personal Property | 5-Year Personal Property | 18-Year Real Property |
| 19X1 | $ 25,000 | $ 15,000 | $  8,000 |
| 19X2 | 38,000 | 22,000 | 9,000 |
| 19X3 | 37,000 | 21,000 | 8,000 |
| 19X4 |  | 21,000 | 7,000 |
| 19X5 |  | 21,000 | 7,000 |
| 19X6 |  |  | 6,000 |
| 19X7–19Y2 |  |  | 5,000 (each year) |
| 19Y3–19Y8 |  |  | 4,000 (each year) |
| 19Y9 |  |  | 1,000 |
| Total | $100,000 | $100,000 | $100,000 |
| Present value (discounted at 10%) of capital recovery allowances | $ 81,855 | $ 74,971 | $ 51,237 |

The substantial reduction in the capital recovery benefits that are available as the recovery period is lengthened from 3 to 18 years is illustrated by the 37% decline in the present value of the capital recovery allowances.

### Straight-Line ACRS Election

Not all taxpayers may want to use the accelerated ACRS rules. Four common reasons for not using the accelerated ACRS rules are:

1.  The taxpayer is in a loss situation and can not obtain a tax benefit from additional capital recovery allowances.
2.  The taxpayer anticipates being in a higher marginal tax bracket in future years and hopes to achieve additional tax savings from deferring the deduction to these years.
3.  The taxpayer wants to avoid recognizing ordinary income under the depreciation recapture rules when 15-year or 18-year real property is sold or exchanged at a gain.
4.  The taxpayer wants to avoid recognizing a tax preference item, with respect to 15-year or 18-year real property and leased personal property, which could result in a corporate minimum tax or alternative minimum tax liability.

If a straight-line ACRS election is made, it is effective for all personal property included in a specific recovery class that is placed in service during that taxable year. The election does not effect property in other recovery classes acquired in the same year nor any property acquired in subsequent taxable years. A straight-line ACRS election for 15-year or 18-year real property is made on an asset-by-asset basis.

The straight-line election lets you use any one of the following periods:

| ACRS Class for Property | Allowable Straight-Line Recovery Periods |
| --- | --- |
| 3-year | 3,  5, or 12 years |
| 5-year | 5, 12, or 25 years |
| 10-year | 10, 25, or 35 years |
| 15-year public utility | 15, 35, or 45 years |
| 15-year real | 15, 35, or 45 years |
| 18-year real and low-income housing | 18, 35, or 45 years |

The straight-line election for personal property requires that a half-year of depreciation be claimed in the year of acquisition. This restriction requires the recovery period to be extended by one-half year. The straight-line ACRS election for real property is based on the actual number of months that the property is in service.

The impact of the straight-line ACRS election can be seen below.

**EXAMPLE 8-3.**   Assume Tax A. Voider purchased 5-year class property for $100,000. The capital recovery allowances that can be claimed under the accelerated ACRS rules and the straight-line ACRS election for the $100,000 of 5-year, recovery period property that was acquired are as follows (ignore any investment tax credit effects):

| Year(s) | Accelerated ACRS | Straight-Line ACRS 5-year period | 12-year period | 25-year period |
|---|---|---|---|---|
| 1 | $ 15,000 | $ 10,000 | $ 4,167 | $ 1,111 |
| 2 | 22,000 | 20,000 | 8,333 | 2,222 |
| 3–5 (each) | 21,000 | 20,000 | 8,333 | 2,222 |
| 6 | | 10,000 | 8,333 | 2,222 |
| 7–12 (each) | | | 8,333 | 2,222 |
| 13 | | | 4,166 | 2,222 |
| 14–25 (each) | | | | 2,222 |
| 26 | | | | 1,121 |
| Undiscounted total | $100,000 | $100,000 | $100,000 | $100,000 |
| Present value (discounted at 10%) of capital recovery allowances | $ 74,971 | $ 64,940 | $ 54,200 | $ 19,254 |

The discounted cash flows illustrate that the value of the deduction is severely reduced if the 12- or 25-year straight-line election is made. It is doubtful that many taxpayers will make such an election for personal property because of the availability of a 15-year carryover for NOLs.

### Special Restrictions

The 1984 Tax Act imposed special restrictions on claiming the investment tax credit and the ACRS capital recovery allowances on luxury automobiles, property used only partially for business purposes, and on property leased to the government and other tax exempt entities. The ACRS portion of these rules are outlined below.

1.  *Luxury Automobiles.*  The ACRS capital recovery deduction (excluding the special expensing deduction available in the year of acquisition) for passenger automobiles used predominantly (more than 50%) for business is limited to $4,000 in the year the property is placed in service and $6,000 in subsequent years for properties placed in service after June 18, 1984. As a practical matter, any passenger automobile costing $16,000 or more will be subject to these restrictions ($4,000 = $16,000 × 0.25 the first year ACRS percentage for three-year property). The ceiling amounts are reduced if the property is used less than 100% of the time for business purposes (e.g., the ceiling is $3,200 for the year the property is placed in service if the property is used only 80% of the time for business purposes). These dollar amounts are to be adjusted for inflation starting in 1985. Any portion of the adjusted basis that has not been recovered by the end of the recovery period because of the ceiling can be recovered in later years (but not in excess of the annual limitations).

The ceiling does not apply to certain special-use vehicles such as ambulances, vans, and so on or to lessors of vehicles.

**EXAMPLE 8-4.**  Tax A. Voider purchases a $35,000 foreign-made automobile. The automobile is to be used 60% of the time for business. The total capital recovery allowances over the life of the vehicle are limited to $21,000 ($35,000 × 0.60) assuming no change in the percentage of time devoted to business usage. The first year capital recovery allowance is limited to $2,400 ($4,000 × 0.60), the subsequent year capital recovery allowances are limited to $3,600 ($6,000 × 0.60). The ceiling on capital recovery deductions has extended the useful life of the automobile for tax depreciation purposes out to 7 years ($2,400 + (5 × $3,600) + $600 = $21,000 recovery over 7 years).

2.  *Dual Purpose Assets.*  The special restrictions on the dual purpose asset applies to passenger automobiles, aircraft, entertainment, recreation, or amusement facilities, and computer and periph-

eral equipment (other than those items used exclusively at a regular business establishment). Only properties placed in service after June 18, 1984 and not meeting the requirements outlined below are subject to these restrictions. To be eligible to use the accelerated ACRS rules, the property must be predominantly used in a qualified business use; that is, its business use percentage must be more than 50%. Excluded from the business use is leasing the property to a 5% or more owner of the business or a related person. Taxpayers must maintain adequate records to support the satisfaction of the 50% minimum.

If the property fails the 50% test, the straight-line ACRS rules must be used over the following recovery periods: 3-year property, 5 years; 5-year property, 12 years; and 18-year realty and low-income housing, 40 years. Depreciation recapture will occur any time that the business use percentage for an asset for a single year drops below the 50% threshold. Thus, if an asset was predominantly used for business in the first two years of its 5-year recovery period, and fell below the 50% minimum in the third year, the excess of the actual depreciation deductions claimed in years 1 and 2 over the amount that would have been claimed using the straight-line ACRS rules and the extended recovery period would be included in the third year's gross income.

Employees are not allowed to claim the ACRS deductions on the dual purpose asset unless it is used for the convenience of the employer and is required as a condition of his employment. Otherwise, the straight-line ACRS rules will apply with the extended recovery period.

## SPECIAL RULES FOR EXPENSING THE COST OF DEPRECIABLE PROPERTY

An election can be made to expense a limited amount of qualifying property in the year it is placed in service. The dollar limitation is $5,000 for 1985 through 1987, $7,500 for 1988 and 1989, and $10,000 for 1990 and later years. If this election is made, no investment tax credit can be claimed with respect to the portion of the acquisition cost that has been expensed. The portion of the acquisition cost that is *not* expensed is depreciated under the ACRS rules and is eligbible for the investment tax credit. Any taxpayer can make this election except trusts, estates, and certain noncorporate lessors who are ineligible to claim the investment credit with respect to property. The dollar limitation is applied separately to a partnership or S corporation and again to its partners or shareholders. Thus, a partnership is limited to a $5,000 deduction in 1985, and each partner is also limited to a total of $5,000 in deductions from property acquisitions made as an individual, in partnerships, and in S corporations in which he has an interest.

**EXAMPLE 8-5.** TAV Corporation acquires the $100,000 of tangible personal property illustrated in Figure 8-1 from an unrelated party in 1985. An election can be made to expense $5,000 of this acquisition cost in 1985. The $95,000 balance of the acquisition cost comes under the ACRS rules and is eligible for the investment tax credit.

Qualifying property is tangible personal property that is eligible for the investment tax credit (also known as Section 38 property) acquired by purchase from an unrelated person for use in a trade or business. Property acquired from a family member, a shareholder that controls the corporation's stock, or another member of a controlled group can not come under this election. Also excluded is depreciable property that is used in an activity not characterized as a trade or business. Property acquired in a like-kind exchange is eligible for the election only to the extent that the basis of the property acquired exceeds the basis of the property given up.

The election to expense a portion of an asset's cost may or may not be advisable. For many taxpayers, the loss of the investment tax credit for the expensed portion of the acquisition cost is a detriment which cannot be overcome by the acceleration of the capital recovery deduction.

## DEPLETION

Taxpayers owning an economic interest in natural resources (i.e., a mineral deposit or standing timber) can claim a deduction for either cost or percentage depletion. This deduction represents the utilization of a portion of a wasting asset as the mineral deposit is extracted or the standing timber is cut, and is the means by which the owner of the deposit or timber recovers his capital investment. This portion of the chapter examines the determination of the depletion deduction.

### Who Can Claim a Depletion Deduction?

Depletion is only available to a taxpayer who has an economic interest in a mineral deposit or standing timber which results in income being received from the extraction of the mineral or the cutting of the timber. The income can be derived by the taxpayer's own extraction or production activities or from a lease which permits a lessee to engage in the production activities for a cash or in-kind payment to the lessor. The lessee of property can also claim a depletion deduction for his capital investment in the leasehold (e.g., drilling and development costs). No depletion can be claimed if a taxpayer receives compensation from the owner of the natural resources for his production or extraction activities, since he does not have an economic interest in the property.

### What Costs Are Depletable?

The owner of an economic interest must classify all expenses as capital costs or deductible expenditures. Expenditures made to acquire the natural resource or the lease must be capitalized. These outlays must be allocated between the cost of the mineral deposit or timber and the cost of the surface land. The surface land costs are not depletable. Tangible equipment costs that are incurred (e.g., oil derricks, pipelines, etc.) must be capitalized and are recovered through depreciation deductions. In drilling oil and gas wells, taxpayers are permitted to capitalize or deduct their intangible drilling costs. Intangible drilling costs (IDC) include all expenditures made for the drilling and preparation of an oil and gas well including, for example: wages, fuel, repairs, hauling, and supplies used in clearing the ground, in drilling the well, and in constructing the derricks, and other physical structures used in the drilling of the wells and in the preparation of the wells for production. If IDC is capitalized by an owner or lessee, it is recoverable as any other asset. If the election is made to expense these costs, the taxpayer deducts them in the year they are incurred. For most taxpayers, the deduction for IDC is one of the important benefits of engaging in an oil and gas drilling activity.

### Cost Depletion

Cost depletion represents the recovery of the taxpayer's depletable costs over the property's productive life. A property's productive life is defined in units of the natural resource that remain at the beginning of a year. Thus, an oil or gas property would have its capacity measured in barrels of oil or cubic feet of gas that are estimated to remain at the beginning of the year as a result of a geological survey. The cost depletion amount is determined as follows:

$$\begin{matrix} \text{Cost} \\ \text{depletion} \\ \text{amount} \end{matrix} = \begin{matrix} \text{Unrecovered} \\ \text{depletable} \\ \text{costs} \end{matrix} \times \frac{\text{Units sold during the taxable year}}{\begin{matrix}\text{Units remaining to be produced at} \\ \text{the beginning of the year}\end{matrix}}$$

The property's unrecovered depletable costs equals the property's original depletable amount minus any cost or percentage depletion claimed in earlier taxable years. A taxpayer's cost depletion is limited to his unrecovered depletable basis.

**EXAMPLE 8-6.**    Tax A. Voider has an economic interest in a coal deposit. Its adjusted basis at the beginning of 19X6 is $500,000. The estimated coal reserves at the beginning of 19X6 are 2,000,000 tons. No change in these estimates occurred during 19X6. 19X6 production was 300,000 tons. Only 270,000 tons were sold. Tax A. Voider's cost depletion amount is:

$$\$67,500 = \$500,000 \times \frac{270,000 \text{ tons}}{2,000,000 \text{ tons}}$$

### Percentage Depletion

Percentage depletion represents a recovery of the taxpayer's depletable costs as the property produces income. Over the productive life of the property the percentage depletion claimed may exceed the taxpayer's investment. The gross income derived from the property can be reduced by a percentage or cost depletion deduction.

A lessee can also claim a percentage depletion deduction with respect to the production. The lessee's percentage depletion is based upon the gross income derived from the lease minus the amount of the royalty paid to the lessor. This prevents the depletion from being claimed by both the lessee and lessor on the same income.

Percentage depletion rates range between 5 and 22%. This rate is multiplied by the taxpayer's income from the property. The percentage depletion deduction for a taxable year is limited to 50% of the taxable income (excluding the depletion deduction) derived from the property. Subject to this limit, a taxpayer can claim the larger of the cost or percentage depletion amounts. Unlike cost depletion, percentage depletion can be claimed even though the taxpayer's investment in the property has been fully recovered. The taxpayer's unrecovered depletable basis is reduced by the amount of the actual depletion claimed.

**Example 8-7.**   Assume the facts remain the same as in Example 8-6. The mineral is eligible for percentage depletion based upon 10% of gross income. The average price paid Tax A. Voider for his coal was $5 per ton. Gross income for 19X6 is $1,350,000. Net income is $300,000. The 19X6 percentage depletion is $135,000 (0.10 × $1,350,000). The net income limitation of $150,000 (0.50 × $300,000) does not limit the depletion that can be claimed. The unrecovered basis for the property at the beginning of 19X7 is $365,000 ($500,000 − $135,000).

Special rules apply to oil and gas properties. Percentage depletion has been restricted to production by independent producers and royalty owners having average daily production of less than 1,000 barrels or 6 million cubic feet of natural gas. The percentage depletion rate is 15%. Only cost depletion is available on oil and gas properties owned by parties ineligible for percentage depletion and on quantities of oil and gas in excess of the maximums. A special limitation for oil and gas depletion is 65% of the taxpayer's taxable income. This limit is in addition to the 50% limit applied to the property's taxable income.

Natural resource production can create special tax preference items. Percentage depletion claimed once a property's adjusted basis has been reduced to zero is a tax preference item for both the corporate minimum tax and alternative minimum tax. In addition, the amount by which the "excess" intangible drilling costs deducted on an oil and gas property exceed the property's net income for a taxable year represents a tax preference item for noncorporate taxpayers. Excess intangible drilling cost are those deductions that are claimed in excess of the amount that would have been deductible had straight-line amortization over a 10-year period been used to recover the costs.

## LEASEHOLD IMPROVEMENTS

Taxpayers who lease property may need to make improvements to the property to make it suit their needs. Special capital recovery rules apply to leasehold improvements. Leasehold improvements made after 1980 are recovery property and come under the ACRS rules. If the recovery period is shorter than the remaining lease term, the ACRS rules are used. If the recovery period is longer than the remaining lease term, then straight-line amortization is used over the remaining lease term. In making these calculations, a taxpayer can elect to use the optional straight-line recovery method.

**EXAMPLE 8-8.** TAV Corporation has a 20-year lease to occupy one floor of an office building. The lease does not include any option to renew. TAV adds a number of movable partitions (personal property) to make the leased space suit its needs. A capital recovery allowance can be claimed for the movable partitions under the ACRS rules over a 5-year recovery period.

Special rules apply to leases that have renewal periods. When the term remaining on the lease at the time of the completion of the leasehold improvements (excluding any renewal period which may be elected by the lessee) is less than 60% of the recovery period, both the remaining term of the original lease plus the renewal period must be counted in determining whether the improvement can come under the ACRS rules. The renewal period is ignored if the taxpayer can establish that it is more probable that the lease will not be renewed.

## INVESTMENT TAX CREDIT AND OTHER SPECIAL BENEFITS

The investment tax credit generally equals 10% of an asset's acquisition cost. This credit reduces the taxpayer's tax liability in the year the property is placed in service. In Figure 8-1 the investment tax credit helped reduce to $75 the net cash outflow needed in Year 1 to acquire the $100,000 asset. If property is disposed of prior to the end of its recovery period, part or all of the investment tax credit previously claimed is "recaptured" and increases the taxpayer's tax liability for the year of disposition. Similar types of credits can be claimed for the acquisition of special energy conservation properties and the rehabilitation of buildings that are in excess of 30 years of age or that are certified historical structures. An examination of each of these sets of rules is as follows:

### Investment Tax Credit

#### *Eligible Property*

The investment tax credit can be claimed for new and used "Section 38" properties. These include the following:

1. Tangible personal property that is subject to an allowance for depreciation.
2. Tangible real property (other than buildings and structural components) that is used as an integral part of manufacturing or production, or for furnishing transportation or certain public utility services.

3. Elevators and escalators.

4. Single purpose agricultural and horticultural structures.

5. Certain rehabilitation expenditures incurred in connection with a building that is 30 or more years old.

6. Properties acquired in connection with the planting, growing, cutting, or commercial production of timber products.

7. Livestock (other than horses).

8. Movie and television films.

9. Storage facilities (other than a building or its components) used for the distribution of petroleum products.

10. Coin-operated vending machines and coin-operated washing machines and dryers.

Buildings and structural components do not qualify as Section 38 property, so structures such as apartment buildings, factory and office buildings, warehouses, barns, garages, and stores do not qualify for the investment tax credit. A facility is not a "building" if (1) it is essentially an item of machinery or equipment, or (2) it houses property used as an integral part of a manufacturing or production activity *and* the use of this structure is so closely related to the use of the property that the structure can be expected to be replaced when the property it initially houses is replaced. Special facilities within a building such as refrigerated freezer rooms, special doors leading to truck terminal docks, and special foundations and pads for machinery and equipment all qualify as Section 38 property. A number of accounting, engineering and consulting firms offer specialized services to indicate which properties in a new facility are eligible for the investment tax credit. If these services are used during the designing of the facility, changes may be possible which can increase the proportion of the acquisition cost related to Section 38 property.

The investment tax credit can be claimed by individuals and certain closely held corporations only to the extent that they are "at risk" in the qualifying property. A property cannot be qualifying property if the taxpayer finances the acquisition by borrowing funds for which he is not personally liable. If a taxpayer purchased a $1,000,000 asset, otherwise qualifying as Section 38 property, by investing $100,000 of his own funds and borrowing the remaining $900,000 of financing through nonrecourse financing that is provided by the asset's manufacturer, only $100,000 of the acquisition cost is eligible for the investment tax credit. Two key exceptions to these rules apply. First, if the taxpayer is at risk in an amount equal to 20% of the property's basis, he is considered to be at risk for all amounts borrowed from banks and unrelated creditors. Second, the rules do not apply to real estate and a limited group of other activities. Most often these rules will be applied to restrict leveraged lease arrangements.

### Ineligible Property

The investment tax credit cannot be claimed for the following properties among others:

1. Property having a useful life of less than three years.
2. Buildings and building components (other than those listed above).
3. Property used predominantly outside the United States (a limited number of exceptions to this rule exist).
4. Property used to provide nontransient lodging (other than coin-operated vending machines and coin-operated washing machines and dryers);
5. Property used by tax-exempt organizations.
6. Property expensed in the year of acquisition.
7. Self-contained air conditioning and heating units.

Used property placed in service during a taxable year that is eligible for the investment tax credit is limited to $125,000 annually. If used property in excess of this limitation is acquired, a taxpayer can select which properties are eligible for the credit. A single $125,000 limitation applies to a controlled group. Partnerships and S corporations must apply this limitation at the entity level and again at the partner and shareholder level.

The acquisition of a passenger automobile that is used predominantly for business purposes is subject to a ceiling on the amount of investment tax credit that can be claimed (in addition to the ACRS deduction ceiling described earlier). The investment tax credit is limited to $1,000. If the taxpayer uses the special two percentage point reduction in the investment tax credit election (described below), then the credit limitation is reduced to $667. If the portion of the automobile being used for business purposes is less than 100%, then the credit limitations are reduced in the same manner. A reduction in the portion of the automobile used for business purposes from the original estimate results in a portion of the investment tax credit being recaptured.

A special investment tax credit rule applies for that group of dual-purpose assets that are subject to the special rules for assets not predominantly used for business purposes. The investment tax credit is denied when the business-use percentage is 50% or less. Thus, if the taxpayer purchases a personal computer for business and personal use, and cannot document the more than 50% business use that is needed, then he is denied any investment tax credit for the asset acquisition. If the asset is initially used predominantly for business purposes, and then subsequently fails the 50% test, the investment tax credit that was previously claimed must be recaptured.

### Credit Rate

The investment tax credit for Section 38 property placed in service after 1981 is based upon the recovery class for ACRS purposes. A 6% investment tax credit can be claimed for 3-year recovery property. A 10% investment tax credit can be claimed for 5-, 10-, and 15-year recovery properties.

EXAMPLE 8-9. TAV Corporation acquires and places in service the $100,000 of tangible personal property illustrated in Figure 8-1 on December 31, 1984. Since the property is 5-year recovery property, TAV Corporation can claim a $10,000 investment tax credit ($100,000 × 0.10) on the acquisition. Had the property instead been 3-year recovery property, TAV Corporation's credit is only $6,000 ($100,000 × 0.06). An election to expense $5,000 of the 5-year class property's acquisition cost would reduce the Section 38 property amount to $95,000, and the investment credit amount to $9,500 ($95,000 × 0.10).

## Special Energy Credit

A special tax credit is available for certain energy conserving properties that are purchased in an attempt to reduce the United States' dependence on oil and natural gas. This tax credit is available through 1985, in addition to the regular 10% investment tax credit. The special credit percentages are as follows:

| Type of Property | Energy Credit Percentage |
| --- | --- |
| Solar, wind, or geothermal property | 15% |
| Ocean thermal property | 15% |
| Hydroelectric generating property | 11% |
| Intercity buses | 10% |
| Biomass property | 10% |

These credits are available to new properties placed in service before 1986 that have a useful life of at least three years. The special credit is reduced by one-half if the property is financed by industrial development bonds.

EXAMPLE 8-10.    Assume the property acquired by TAV Corporation in the preceding example was a 5-year recovery class item that was used to provide solar heating to one of its factory buildings. A regular investment tax credit of $10,000 can be claimed in 1984 plus a special energy credit of $15,000 ($100,000 × 0.15).

## Limitation on Credit

The investment tax credit and special energy tax credit amounts are part of the group of "business" credits that are in total limited by the amount of the taxpayer's tax liability. The credit limitation for these credits equals 100% of the tax liability up to $25,000 plus 85% of the tax liability that exceeds $25,000. Controlled groups of corporations are treated as a single taxpayer and must apportion the $25,000 eligible for a 100% offset. In the case of a partnership or an S corporation that passes-through investment tax credit benefits, the business credit limitation is determined at the partner or shareholder level. This pass-through permits partnerships and S corporations with losses to benefit from the investment tax credit.

Any business credits that exceed the limitation are carried back to the three preceding taxable years and forward to the fifteen succeeding taxable years. These excess credits are used in the following sequence: credit carryovers, current-year credits, and credit carrybacks. Such a sequencing permits any credit carryovers in existence at the beginning of a taxable year to be used before any current year credits are used. Losses of unused credits are thus minimized.

**Example 8-11.** TAV Corporation reports tax liabilities of $20,000 and $100,000 in 19X3 and 19X4, respectively. New Section 38 properties acquired in 19X3 and 19X4 are $500,000 and $700,000, respectively. None of this property is 3-year recovery property. No excess credits earned in 19X3 or 19X4 can be carried back to 19X2 or earlier years. No other current year business tax credits are available. TAV Corporation's tentative investment tax credit (before the limitation) is $50,000 and $70,000 in 19X3 and 19X4, respectively. The business tax credit limitations for 19X3 and 19X4 are $20,000 and $88,750 [$25,000 + .85 ($100,000 − $25,000)]. An excess credit amount of $30,000 ($50,000 − $20,000) is created in 19X3. This excess amount can be carried over to 19X4 and is used before any of 19X4's $70,000 current credit amount. Only $58,750 of the current credit amount ($88,750 − $30,000) can be used. The $11,250 ($70,000 − $58,750) unused credit amount from 19X4 can be carried over to 19X5 and subsequent years.

One-half of the amount of any business tax credits that remain unused at the end of the 15-year carryforward period can be claimed as a deduction in the taxpayer's next taxable year.

### Special Credit Reduction Election

One-half of any investment tax credit claimed on Section 38 property reduces the property's basis. This basis adjustment, of course, reduces the available capital recovery deductions. Similarly, one-half of any investment tax credits that are recaptured increases the basis of the property (as determined immediately preceding the recapture event). A special election is available which eliminates the need for the basis reduction and permits the ACRS capital recovery allowances to be claimed for the entire acquisition cost. This election requires the investment tax credit to be reduced by two percentage points. A comparison of the investment tax credit (ITC) rates and the portion of the property's acquisition cost eligible for "depreciation" under ACRS is summarized as follows:

|  | 3-Year Property | | 5-Year Property | |
|---|---|---|---|---|
|  | ITC | ACRS | ITC | ACRS |
| Basic rule: | 6% | 97% | 10% | 95% |
| Special election: | 4% | 100% | 8% | 100% |

A comparison of the benefits of this election can be found in Figure 8-5 for the acquisition of the $5,000 of Section 38 property. This comparison illustrates that for a corporate taxpayer in the 46% marginal tax bracket and having a 10% discount rate, the advantage of the additional investment tax credit for both the 3-year and 5-year property outweighs the advantage of the larger capital recovery deductions in later years. However, the amount of this difference is small (not in excess of 2% of the total discounted tax benefits).

A comparison of the benefits of expensing the cost of a $5,000 asset acquisition versus capitalizing the cost, claiming a full or reduced investment tax credit, and using the ACRS rules to depreciate the property is also illustrated in Figure 8-5. For our corporate taxpayer, little difference is again seen between the three alternatives

**FIGURE 8-5** Comparison of discounted tax benefits for alternative capital recovery treatments.

| Facts: | Acquisition cost: | $5,000 |
|---|---|---|
|  | Marginal tax rate: | 46% |
|  | Discount rate: | 10% (all payments received at the end of the year) |

|  | Recovery Class | |
|---|---|---|
|  | 3-year | 5-year |
| General rate (6 or 10% investment tax credit, accelerated ACRS on reduced basis) | $2,101 | $2,092 |
| Special ITC adjustment (4 or 8% investment tax credit, accelerated ACRS on 100% of basis) | 2,066 | 2,088 |
| Special expensing election | 2,091 | 2,091 |

for either 3-year or 5-year recovery property. These results could be different, for example, if the taxpayer were in the 15 or 18% marginal tax bracket in the year the property was acquired, and he expects to be in the 46% tax bracket in the other years. Here the capitalization alternative might provide a significantly better discounted value.

## SPECIAL RULES FOR REAL ESTATE

A number of special rules apply to real estate investments. These rules provide a special credit for the rehabilitation of buildings 30 or more years old or certified historic structures. There is also a restriction on the deductibility of interest and taxes incurred during the construction of real property.

### Rehabilitation Credit

The special tax credit available for rehabilitation expenditures incurred in connection with buildings at least 30 years old provides an incentive to rehabilitate these structures instead of replacing them with a new building. The rates for this credit are as follows:

| Rehabilitation Expenditures Incurred With Respect to a: | Credit Rate |
| --- | --- |
| Nonresidential building: | |
| 30 to 39 years old | 15% |
| 40+ years old | 20 |
| Residential and nonresidential | |
| certified historic structure | 25 |

The rehabilitation credit is available for any building and its structural components that (1) has been substantially rehabilitated, (2) was placed in service before the beginning of the rehabilitation, (3) retains at least 75% of the external walls, and (4) satisfies the minimum "age" requirement by the time the rehabilitation work began and the building was placed in service. The rehabilitation credit is not available for any portion of the asset's original acquisition cost or any costs incurred to enlarge the building. A substantially rehabilitated building is one where the expenditures made during the eligible period exceed the greater of the adjusted basis of the building as of the first day of the eligible period or $5,000.

The credit for a certified historic structure is similar to the basic rehabilitation credit but has additional requirements. A certified historic structure is a building located in a registered historic district. The rehabilitation must be certified by the Secretary of the Interior as consistent with the historic character of the property, or the district in which the property is located, in order to be eligible for the credit.

Claiming this credit restricts the availability of certain other tax benefits. Rehabilitation expenditures that are also Section 38 property are ineligible for the investment tax credit and the special energy credit. The basis of the 30-year to 40-year buildings must be reduced by the full amount of the rehabilitation credit claimed. The basis of a certified historic structure is reduced by one-half of the rehabilitation credit claimed. Rehabilitation expenditures are eligible only for the straight-line ACRS writeoffs. The remaining costs of the rehabilitated building or certified historic structure can be depreciated by using the accelerated ACRS rules.

**EXAMPLE 8-12.** TAV Corporation purchases a 40-year old building for $175,000. The costs attributable to the land are $75,000. Rehabilitation expenditures of $200,000 are incurred. A $40,000 tax credit can be claimed for the rehabilitation expenditures. The $100,000 acquisition cost attributable to the building can be recovered by using the accelerated 18-year real property rules. Rehabilitation expenditures in the amount of $160,000 ($200,000 − $40,000) can be recovered over a minimum of 18 years by using the straight-line ACRS rules. Many states and localities also provide special tax and nontax incentives to rehabilitate older buildings. TAV Corporation may also be able to obtain special tax credits or capital recovery allowances for state income tax purposes, special property tax exemptions, or special low-interest-rate financing.

The benefits in the above example are not only available to an owner-user of a building. A lessee can claim the credit for qualified expenditures made as a leasehold improvement provided the remaining term of the lease is at least 18 years. Similarly, a lessor can claim the credit for outlays made on rental property.

### Capitalization of Interest and Taxes

Interest and taxes incurred during the construction period for real property were at one time deductible by all taxpayers. This deduction permitted a substantial tax benefit by eliminating the need for the taxpayer to have to capitalize these costs and then depreciate them over the building's useful life. Taxpayers who were unable to take advantage of the interest and tax deductions during the construction period were still able to capitalize the charges as part of the asset's cost.

These interest and tax amounts now must be capitalized and amortized over a 10-year period. Alternatively, an election can be made to capitalize the charges and recover them under the ACRS rules. Amortization commences with the later of (1) the year following the year in which the expense is paid or accrued, or (2) the year in which the property is ready to be placed in service or is ready to be held for sale. The capitalization requirement does not apply to (1) low-income housing, (2) residential rental property acquired or constructed by a regular corporation, or (3) real property not held in a trade or business or as part of a profit-making activity. The residential rental property exception to the capitalization requirement only applies through 1984.

## SPECIAL RULES FOR LESSORS

Leasing activities are most commonly found in two forms—operating leases and financing leases. Operating leases typically are entered into for a term substantially shorter than the property's useful life. The lessee's periodic payments are treated as ordinary income by the lessor. The lessee deducts the amount of the lease payments as an ordinary and necessary business expense.

A financing lease involves a lease term (or lease term plus renewal period) that is substantially equivalent to the property's useful life. The lessor purchases the property from the manufacturer, or has it constructed to the user's specifications, by making a small equity investment and borrowing the remainder of the purchase price from a bank or other financial institution. The lessee then makes periodic lease payments over the term of the lease which covers the cost of the property plus the cost of the financing arrangement. The lessor is treated as the owner of the property. As such, he is able to take advantage of all of the tax benefits arising from the ownership of the property (e.g., investment tax credit and depreciation). The lessee deducts the amount of the lease payments as an ordinary and necessary business expense. Many lease arrangements contain a provision whereby the lessee can purchase the property for a specified amount. One common form that this provision takes is for the lessee to acquire the property for $1, or other nominal amount, at the expiration of the lease term.

The investment tax credit rules permit the lessor to either claim the investment tax credit associated with the purchase of new ACRS properties or to elect to pass-through the credit to the lessee. The pass-through of the investment tax credit treats the lessee as the purchaser of the property. The choice between the two alternatives usually depends upon which party can obtain the greater tax savings. Ordinarily, the decision as to which party claims the credit is reflected in an increase or decrease to the amount of the required lease payments. (If the lessee claims the investment tax credit, the lease payment should be adjusted upward. If the lessor claims the credit, the lease payment should be adjusted downward.) Noncorporate lessors may be prohibited from claiming the investment tax credit. They may claim the credit only if they manufactured or produced the property as part of their business, the life of the lease (including renewals) is less than one-half of the property's useful life, and the lessor's business expenses during the first year of the lease exceed 15% of the rental income. Normally these restrictions prevent the noncorporate lessor from obtaining any investment tax credit benefits.

The financing lease offers a number of advantages to the lessee, including the following:

1.  The ability to acquire the use of equipment or buildings with little or no initial commitment of funds.
2.  The ability to acquire tax benefits that otherwise might not be available. The lessor, as the owner of the property, can take advantage of the interest deductions, ACRS deductions, and investment tax credits. These tax benefits are passed-through to the lessee in the form of reduced lease payments. A loss company, or a marginally profitable company, may not be able to take full advantage of these benefits of asset ownership. The financing lease can provide a mechanism whereby these benefits can be obtained in an indirect manner.
3.  The ability to acquire title to an asset at a later date by exercising a purchase option.

One disadvantage that can occur with a leveraged lease is that the lease arrangement may be treated as a conditional sale for tax purposes. The taxing authorities then treat the lessor as having sold the property to the lessee. The lessee is required to capitalize the "purchase" price. He can not deduct the periodic rental payments made to the lessor. The ACRS and investment tax credit benefits are only available to the lessee. The tax savings resulting from these benefits may be diminished, because one of the primary reasons for entering into such an arrangement is the reduced lease cost available when the lessor can take advantage of tax benefits that are not otherwise available to the lessee if an outright purchase were made.

The IRS has published guidelines for taxpayers constructing direct leasing transactions involving noncorporate lessors. These guidelines permit the taxpayer to apply for an advance ruling in order to determine whether the transaction will be treated as a "lease arrangement" or a "conditional sale." These guidelines set forth: minimum investment requirements; a minimum residual value at the end of the initial lease term; a minimum amount for purchase options; a profit requirement (exclusive of tax benefits); and a safe-haven rent payment schedule for uneven rents. Congress has also enacted special rules for financing leases entered into by corporate lessors. These rules apply only to certain categories of qualifying property, and if met permit the transaction to be treated as a lease arrangement instead of a conditional sale.

A number of special finance lease provisions are found in the tax laws. The 1984 Tax Act enacted a number of restrictions on the tax benefits which are available on leasing property to, or for the use of, a tax-exempt entity. These rules in general restrict the availability of the ACRS allowances and the investment tax credit benefits. Special finance lease rules are found in the Internal Revenue Code which permit the parties to the lease to elect to have the transaction treated as a lease. Originally these provisions were to go into effect at the beginning of 1984. The 1984 Tax Act deferred these safe harbor rules until 1988.

## SALE-LEASEBACK TRANSACTIONS

A sale-leaseback transaction is a means by which a corporation can raise capital. The transaction is divided into two parts. First, the sale of a property takes place at the market value. This is followed by the seller entering into a lease agreement with the buyer. Normally the terms of both transactions are negotiated at the same time.

**EXAMPLE 8-13.**    TAV Corporation has a 10-story office building. The building has been owned for a number of years and is now worth about four times its original acquisition cost. TAV Corporation can realize a substantial immediate cash inflow by selling the building to an insurance company or other group of investors and then leasing part or all of the building back under a long-term lease. The building will no longer appear on TAV's balance sheet, but recognition of the lease commitment in the financial statements will likely be required. By making the sale, TAV will forgo any subsequent price appreciation that would be realized on holding the asset.

Normally the tax laws give separate recognition to the two parts of a sale-leaseback transaction involving independent parties. The seller will recognize gain or loss on the sale of the property. The lessor will acquire the property along with all of the tax benefits of asset ownership (investment and special tax credits, depreciation, etc.). The lessee will deduct the rental payments as they are paid or incurred. The IRS will carefully scrutinize sale-leaseback transactions involving related parties (e.g., family members) to see if they constitute a sham or tax avoidance device. The extra scrutiny is required because of the ability of these transactions to permit high-tax-bracket taxpayers to shelter income through the availability of interest and depreciation deductions, or to allow for the division of the income earned from the property among a number of family members.

EXAMPLE **8-14.** Tax A. Voider sells an office building used in her dental practice to the TAV Trust. The sales proceeds are to be paid over a 20-year period. Tax A. Voider will lease the building from the trust for a 20-year period. The beneficiaries of the trust are Tax A. Voider's three minor children. This type of sale-leaseback transaction will permit Tax A. Voider's children to receive some income from the dental practice. Means by which Tax A. Voider can help to ensure that the transaction is accepted by the IRS, and the courts, include: having the trust holds title to the property; ensuring that the trust has a substantial equity interest in the property; developing a valid business purpose for the transaction; and appointing an independent trustee to have control over the trust.

# 9

# Disposition of Business and Investment Assets

Companies may need to dispose of some of their business or investment assets. Some of these dispositions are voluntary; for example, the trade-in of a company automobile or the conversion of short-term investments into cash. Other dispositions may be involuntary; for example, a casualty, theft, or condemnation involving a business property.

This chapter examines the general rules for determining the amount of realized and recognized gain or loss, the character of the recognized gain or loss, the transactions that permit nonrecognition of gain or loss, the need for recapturing previously claimed investment tax credits, and the tax planning techniques available for dispositions of investment properties.

**195**

## AMOUNT OF REALIZED AND
## RECOGNIZED GAIN OR LOSS

The taxpayer's *realized* gain or loss on any sale is determined as follows:

|        | Amount realized: |
|--------|------------------|
|        | Cash |
|        | Fair market value of noncash property |
|        | Debt obligations of the seller assumed or acquired by the purchaser |
| Minus: | Adjusted basis |
| Equals: | Realized gain or loss |

It should be noted that this computation is based upon the taxpayer's total investment in the property rather than merely his equity interest. The amount of any debt obligations assumed with the original purchase by the taxpayer becomes part of his basis in the property. No subsequent adjustment is made if part or all of the debt is repaid. At the time of sale, the amount of any unpaid debt obligation assumed by the buyer is treated as part of the amount realized.

**EXAMPLE 9-1.**   Tax A. Voider purchases land for $400,000 by paying $75,000 down and taking out a $325,000 mortgage. The land is held for 6 years during which time interest and $65,000 of mortgage principal is repaid. The land is sold for $200,000 and the $260,000 unpaid mortgage being assumed by the buyer. Tax A. Voider realizes a $60,000 gain [($200,000 + $260,000) − $400,000] on the sale.

The entire amount of the realized gain or loss is recognized (reported as part of his taxable income) unless authority can be found in the tax laws to defer or exempt the gain from taxation. Some of the transactions receiving special treatment are like-kind exchanges, involuntary conversions, and wash sales.

## LIKE-KIND EXCHANGES

A like-kind exchange can reduce the amount of gain recognized when a property is sold or exchanged. Such an exchange permits the taxpayer's capital investment to remain intact. Through the use of the carryover basis rules, a gain is deferred only until the property received in the like-kind exchange is subsequently disposed of in a taxable transaction. This gain could be deferred indefinitely if the taxpayer's future property disposition is also tax-free (e.g., a second like-kind exchange). The like-kind exchange rules also prevent a taxpayer from recognizing a realized loss. Taxpayers can obtain a tax benefit from recognizing the loss only if they can manage to avoid the like-kind exchange rules.

### Eligible Property

The nonrecognition rules apply when property (held either for productive use in a trade or business or for investment) is exchanged solely for property of a like-kind (to be held either for productive use in a trade or business or for investment). These rules allow an exchange of property used in the conduct of a trade or business for an investment property or vice versa. The only restriction imposed on the term "like-kind" is that personal property must be exchanged for personal property and real property must be exchanged for real property. An exchange of real property (land) for personal property (an airplane) would not qualify as an exchange of like-kind property even if both were to be used in the conduct of a trade or business. No restrictions are imposed on exchanging new and used properties, or improved and unimproved properties. Thus, a like-kind exchange could involve the swapping of unimproved land for an apartment building where both are to be held for investment purposes.

The like-kind exchange rules do not apply to inventory, property held primarily for sale, stocks, bonds, securities, notes, or other evidences of indebtedness or interest, even though such property is held for investment purposes or is used in the conduct of a trade or business. Even though an exchange of stocks or bonds cannot be tax-free under the like-kind exchange rules, in some circumstances such a transaction may qualify as a tax-free reorganization and permit the gain to receive a tax exemption.

### Recognition of Gain or Loss

The like-kind exchange rules may apply to one or both of the parties to the transaction. If both parties are exchanging solely like-kind properties, then the nonrecognition rules will apply to both parties to the transaction. The nonrecognition rules will only apply to the exchanging party when property used in a trade or business is traded-in, together with cash, for other property of a like-kind that is held by a dealer and which will be used in a trade or business. The dealer can not receive a tax exemption because the inventory he surrenders can not be like-kind property.

**EXAMPLE 9-2.**   Tax A. Voider operates a contracting business. He trades-in earth moving equipment having an adjusted basis of $25,000 and $15,000 of cash for new earth moving equipment having a list price of $50,000. Tax A. Voider treats the transaction as a like-kind exchange and will recognize no gain or loss. The dealer will be taxed on his profit from the transaction.

If the taxpayer receives money or property (other than the like-kind property) as part of the exchange, then he must recognize gain to the extent of the lesser of (1) his realized gain or (2) the sum of the money and the fair market value of the other property received. No loss can be recognized. The non-like-kind property is commonly referred to as "boot." The giving of cash boot does not result in the recognition of gain. Giving noncash boot leads the exchanging shareholder to recognize gain or loss as if he had sold the boot property for cash immediately before the like-kind exchange. These rules are illustrated by the following example:

**EXAMPLE 9-3.**   Tax A. Voider trades-in an old truck for a new truck. The new truck has a fair market value of $10,000. The amount of gain or loss that is recognized for a series of situations is illustrated below.

| Situation No. | Adjusted Basis of Truck Given up | Type of Boot Given up or Received | FMV of Boot Given up | Adjusted Basis of Boot Given up | FMV of Boot Received | Realized Gain (Loss) | Recognized Gain (Loss) |
|---|---|---|---|---|---|---|---|
| 1 | $ 7,000 | Cash | $2,000 | $2,000 | –0– | $1,000 | –0– |
| 2 | 9,000 | Cash | 2,000 | 2,000 | –0– | (1,000) | –0– |
| 3 | 7,000 | Stock | 2,000 | 1,000 | –0– | 2,000 | $1,000 |
| 4 | 7,000 | Cash | | | $2,000 | 5,000 | 2,000 |
| 5 | 11,000 | Cash | | | 2,000 | 1,000 | 1,000 |
| 6 | 13,000 | Cash | | | 2,000 | (1,000) | –0– |

No gain or loss is recognized in Situation Nos. 1–3 as a result of receiving boot property. The gain recognized in Situation No. 3 is the result of transferring appreciated stock as boot. The gains recognized in Situation Nos. 4 and 5 follow the general gain recognition rule for receiving boot property. No loss can be recognized in Situation No. 6 even though boot is received. The recognized gain can be reported by using the installment method of accounting if the boot is to be paid in a period later than the one in which the exchange occurred, or it is to be paid in a series of installments.

### Basis of Property Received

Two different basis rules apply to the property received in a like-kind exchange. First, boot property receives a basis equal to its fair market value. Second, like-kind property receives a basis that carries over from the basis of the property that is surrendered. The like-kind rule is as follows:

|  | Adjusted basis of like-kind property given up |
|---|---|
| Plus: | Amount of money given up |
|  | Adjusted basis of noncash boot property given up |
|  | Gain recognized |
| Minus: | Amount of money received |
|  | Fair market value of noncash boot property received |
|  | Loss recognized |
| Equals: | Basis of like-kind property received |

The short-cut method illustrated below can also be used to determine the basis of like-kind property.

|  | Fair market value of like-kind property received |
|---|---|
| Plus: | Amount of the deferred loss |
| Minus: | Amount of the deferred gain |
| Equals: | Basis of the like-kind property |

The loss that must be deferred becomes available either in the form of a larger depreciation deduction or by reducing (increasing) the gain (loss) recognized upon a subsequent disposition. Taxpayers can obtain an immediate tax benefit from the deferred loss only by avoiding the like-kind exchange rules. The deferred loss that results from the trade-in in Situation No. 6 of Example 9-3 could have been recognized by selling the old truck to a third party and then making a cash purchase of the new truck.

A deferred gain reduces the basis of the like-kind property acquired and results in a larger gain (smaller loss) when the property is subsequently disposed of in a taxable transaction. This gain can receive a permanent tax exemption if the property is held until death. The decedent's heirs will take a property basis equal to its fair market value on the date of death, or the alternate valuation date, without being taxed on any of the deferred gain or appreciation. Deferral of the gain, however, does reduce the capital recovery allowances on the property. Consideration should be given to selling the old property, recognizing a current capital gain, and purchasing new property for cash. This would permit the capital recovery allowance to be based on the acquisition cost of the new property instead of the lower, carryover basis that would result from a like-kind exchange. Remember that the depreciation recapture rules or the Section 1239 related-party sale rules described later may require gain on a sale to be recognized as ordinary income. Recognizing a dollar of ordinary income today—in order to step-up the basis on property to obtain additional capital recovery deductions in later years—is not usually an advisable action.

**EXAMPLE 9-4.** Reference is made to the facts in Example 9-3. The basis for the like-kind property received in each of the six situations is determined as follows:

| | | Plus: | | | | Minus: | | |
|---|---|---|---|---|---|---|---|---|
| Situ-ation No. | Adjusted Basis of Truck Given Up | Money Given Up | Adjusted Basis of Boot Given Up | Gain Recog-nized | Money Received | FMV of Boot Received | Loss Recog-nized | Basis of Truck Re-ceived |
| 1 | $ 7,000 | $2,000 | | | | | | $ 9,000 |
| 2 | 9,000 | 2,000 | | | | | | 11,000 |
| 3 | 7,000 | | $1,000 | $1,000 | | | | 9,000 |
| 4 | 7,000 | | | 2,000 | $2,000 | | | 7,000 |
| 5 | 11,000 | | | 1,000 | 2,000 | | | 10,000 |
| 6 | 13,000 | | | | 2,000 | | | 11,000 |

### Assumption of Liabilities

An assumption of a liability by the transferee or the transfer of a property subject to a liability is treated as if the transferor received money. An exchange of two properties and their related liabilities is treated as an exchange of the properties plus an exchange of the "net" amount of the two liabilities. The smaller liability reduces the amount of the larger liability, and the "excess" liability given up is treated as money received. Cash that is paid by the party giving up the "excess" liability reduces the amount of the money that the party receives upon his release from the "excess" liability. An example will clarify this rule.

**EXAMPLE 9-5.** Tax A. Voider owns an apartment building which has an adjusted basis of $500,000 and which is subject to a mortgage of $150,000. She transfers the apartment building and mortgage to A, receiving in exchange $50,000 in cash, and an apartment building having a fair market value of $600,000. Tax A. Voider realizes a $300,000 gain on the exchange, of which $200,000 is recognized.

|  |  | Basic Facts | An Alternate Situation |
|---|---|---|---|
| Amount realized by Tax A. Voider: |  |  |  |
|  | Cash | $ 50,000 | $        0 |
|  | Apartment building | 600,000 | 800,000 |
|  | Liability assumed by A | 150,000 | 0 |
|  | Total amount realized | $800,000 | $800,000 |
| Less: | Adjusted basis of building | (500,000) | (500,000) |
| Equals: | Realized gain | $300,000 | $300,000 |
|  |  |  |  |
|  | Boot received | $200,000 | 0 |
|  | Recognized gain | 200,000 | 0 |

Tax A. Voider's basis for her "new" building is $500,000 [$500,000 + $200,000 − $50,000 − $150,000].

It is unlikely that the direct exchange that was illustrated could have taken place without some form of advance planning. Quite often the seller (Tax A. Voider) will have negotiated the transaction with the purchaser (A) and then realize that its tax cost is too great. The seller then seeks alternative ways to reduce the capital impairment which takes place when the taxes due on the transaction must be paid. One way to structure the exchange would be to use a three-party like-kind exchange. Tax A. Voider initially locates the suitable like-kind property to be received and has A purchase the property from a third party (B). A then exchanges his newly-acquired property for Tax A. Voider's property. Tax A. Voider's gain can then be partially or totally deferred. A will likely have no gain on the transaction since only a very short period of time will lapse between his acquisition of the replacement property and the exchange. If this procedure was being used in the previous example, Tax A. Voider's tax result could have been improved had he selected a replacement property having a $800,000 market value and then had A take out a $150,000 mortgage to cover the increased cost for the property (Alternate Situation). The two mortgages being exchanged would have offset one another, and Tax A. Voider would have received no boot. The selection of the more expensive building would have also eliminated the need to use $50,000 of cash. Tax A. Voider then could have deferred his entire $300,000 realized gain.

Some times an exchange may be delayed because the selling party is unable to locate a suitable replacement property. Rather than delaying the exchange, Tax A. Voider may agree to transfer the property in exchange for a commitment from A that a suitable like-kind property having a value equal to that of the property given up will be found within a specified time period. Once the appropriate replacement property is located, it can be purchased by A and transferred to Tax A. Voider to complete the exchange. When the replacement property's value is less than the value of the property given up, the purchasing party must pay cash to close the transaction. The cash represents boot and is taxable to the selling party. The 1984 Tax Act imposed new restrictions on these nonsimultaneous like-kind exchanges. The property to be received in the exchange must be identified within 45 days of the date on which the transferor surrenders his like-kind property. The like-kind property so identified must be received by the earlier of 180 days after the date on which the transferor surrenders his like-kind property or the due date (determined without regard to any extension) for the transferor's tax return for the taxable year in which he surrenders his like-kind property. If either of these two requirements is not met, then all property that is received by the transferor will not qualify for like-kind exchange treatment. Thus, the entire realized gain on the transaction will have to be recognized.

Taxpayers should always obtain competent tax advice before structuring a three-party like-kind exchange or a nonsimultaneous like-kind exchange to ensure that the transaction will, in fact, be tax-free.

## INVOLUNTARY CONVERSIONS

The destruction of a property in an involuntary conversion and the receipt of insurance proceeds to cover the loss represents a disposition of the property and can result in the recognition of gain or loss. An exception to this rule permits the taxpayer's realized gain to go unrecognized when the property is either directly converted into similar property, or is converted into money which is used to purchase similar property. The requirements for using this exception are outlined below.

### Definition of Eligible Occurrences

An involuntary conversion may occur as the result of the partial or total destruction of property, the theft of property, the requisition or condemnation of property, or the threat or imminence of requisition or condemnation of property. Special rules expand this definition for farmers and ranchers to include some additional occurrences such as the destruction, sale, or exchange of livestock as a result of disease.

### Indirect Conversions

Most involuntary conversions represent an indirect conversion of one property into the replacement property. The taxpayer receives the proceeds from the conversion and invests part or all of the payment in a replacement property. If the replacement property is "similar or related in service or use to the converted property," and its cost equals or exceeds the proceeds from the conversion, then an election can be made to avoid recognizing the realized gain. Gain must be recognized only to the extent that the proceeds are not reinvested. The recognized gain equals the lesser of the taxpayer's realized gain or the sum of (1) the money not reinvested, plus (2) the cost of the property acquired that is *not* similar or related in service or use to the converted property. This latter amount represents the taxpayer's boot. Losses realized on an involuntary conversion must be recognized. The replacement period for an involuntary conversion is generally within two years after the close of the first taxable year in which any part of the conversion gain is realized. If the conversion is a condemnation of real property, the two-year period is extended to three.

The basis for the replacement property depends upon whether a gain or loss was realized, and whether part or all of the gain is deferred. If a loss is recognized, the basis equals the replacement property's cost. If a gain is realized, the basis equals the replacement property's cost minus the amount of the deferred gain. Thus, if all of the gain is recognized, the basis equals the replacement property's cost.

Example **9-6.** Tax A. Voider owned an apartment building having an adjusted basis of $75,000 that was condemned. His condemnation award was $85,000. A replacement property was acquired within one year for $90,000. Tax A. Voider realizes a $10,000 gain ($85,000 − $75,000), none of which must be recognized if the appropriate election is made. The replacement property's basis is $80,000 ($90,000 − $10,000). If the replacement property cost $75,000 or less, the entire realized gain must be recognized, and the replacement property's basis equals its cost. If the converted property instead had a $95,000 adjusted basis, Tax A. Voider would realize a $10,000 loss ($85,000 − $95,000), all of which must be recognized. The replacement property's basis equals its cost, or $90,000.

A taxpayer might choose not to defer the gain on an involuntary conversion, particularly if he has a large amount of capital losses or ordinary losses against which the gain can be offset. Such an action would permit the basis of the replacement property to be stepped-up to its replacement cost at little cost to the taxpayer.

### Replacement Property

The qualifications for replacement property are more restrictive than for like-kind exchanges. Two different tests are applied to determine if the replacement property is "similar or related in service or use to the converted property."

1. *Functional-Use Test.* This test applies to owner-users of property and requires that the replacement property serve the same functional use as the converted property. The proceeds derived from the conversion of a manufacturing plant must be used to acquire a manufacturing plant having a similar functional use.

2. *Owner-Investor Test.* This test is applied to owner-investors such as a lessor and only requires that the replacement property be of the "same general class" as the converted property. Using this test, funds received from the conversion of an office building that was rented out by the taxpayer could be invested into residential apartment buildings to be rented out.

The funds received from the involuntary conversion do not have to be used to acquire new property. These funds can be spent to upgrade existing property that meets the appropriate "functional-use" test or "owner-investor" test. The replacement property may also be a controlling interest in the stock of a corporation that owns the necessary replacement property. "Control" is defined as ownership of at least 80% of the voting power and at least 80% of all other classes of stock of the acquired corporation.

## SALE OR EXCHANGE OF A RESIDENCE

The sale or exchange of the taxpayer's principal residence can produce a substantial profit for an individual. Many times because of inflation, or the differential cost of housing in different locations, the entire sales proceeds must be expended to acquire a replacement residence. Taxation of the profit would deprive the taxpayer of the ability to acquire a similar replacement residence without borrowing additional funds. In order to reduce or eliminate such a burden, the gain realized when a principal residence is sold can be deferred provided the funds are reinvested in an equally expensive or more expensive residence. This gain can be repeatedly deferred throughout the taxpayer's lifetime by reinvesting the proceeds of each home sale. At some point in time, a taxpayer may decide that he does not need a larger, more expensive residence. If the taxpayer is at least 55 years of age, he can permanently exclude from taxation up to $125,000 of his realized gain even if he makes no reinvestment at all.

### Reinvestment Requirements

Under the usual rules, the gain realized on the sale of a principal residence is eligible for a tax deferral if (1) the taxpayer replaces it with a new principal residence within a period beginning 24-months before the sale date and ending 24-months after the sale date, and (2) the cost of the replacement residence equals or exceeds the adjusted sales price of the old residence. Even if the reinvestment is not enough to defer all of the gain, the realized gain is recognized only to the extent that the replacement cost of the new residence is less than the "adjusted sales price" of the old residence. Deferral of the realized gain is mandatory if the previously described conditions are met. Losses realized on the sale of a personal residence are never deductible.

Acquisition of a replacement residence can involve purchasing an existing residence or constructing a new residence. Reinvestment occurs only to the extent that the funds are spent for the construction of a new residence, or the acquisition and reconstruction of an existing residence, within the 48-month replacement period. The stock of a cooperative housing corporation also qualifies as a replacement residence. Replacement is not considered to have occurred when the funds are used to acquire a facility that is not used as the taxpayer's principal residence—such as a vacation home or condominium or the rental portion of a duplex.

The adjusted sales price of the old residence equals its selling price less the total of any selling expenses and fixing-up expenses. Fixing-up expenses are outlays made for work performed on the old residence in order to help sell it. These outlays do not reduce the realized gain but do reduce the reinvestment that is required if the work is performed within 90 days of the sales contract date on the old residence, and are paid within 30 days of the date of the sale of the old residence.

The new personal residence's basis equals its cost minus the amount of the realized gain that did not have to be recognized. If the old residence was sold at a loss, the basis of the new residence equals its cost.

**EXAMPLE 9-7.** Tax A. Voider decides to sell her personal residence for $300,000 plus the purchaser's assumption of the $100,000 outstanding mortgage balance. A sales commission of $24,000 was paid. The residence cost $125,000 ten years ago. Capital improvements in the amount of $25,000 have since been made. Fixing-up expenses in the amount of $12,000 have been incurred and paid within 90 days of the sales contract date and 30 days of the sales date. Computation of the realized gain and adjusted sales price occurs as follows:

| Cash | $300,000 | | |
|---|---|---|---|
| Plus: Assumption of mortgage | 100,000 | | |
| Proceeds from sale | $400,000 | | |
| Less: Selling expenses | (24,000) | | |
| Equals: Amount realized | $376,000 | → Amount realized | $376,000 |
| Less: Adjusted basis | (150,000) | Less: Fixing-up expenses | (12,000) |
| Equals: Realized gain | $226,000 | Equals: Adjusted sales price | $364,000 |

No gain is recognized if the cost of the replacement residence equals or exceeds $364,000.

Taxpayers who sell a personal residence and take back either a first or second mortgage from the purchaser need to be careful about the interest rate that is charged. Sometimes pressure is placed on the purchaser to accept a higher sales price and a lower rate of interest to increase the portion of the transaction reported as a capital gain and reduce the portion of the transaction reported as ordinary income (interest). Although the original issue discount rules do not apply to the sale of a personal residence, a set of imputed interest rules for deferred payment sales do apply. These rules apply to transactions taking place before July 1, 1985 and require the seller to charge 9% interest, or be required to impute interest at a 10% rate. Look for additional changes to these rules during 1985.

In some cases an employee's home may be purchased by his employer. The employee's gain or loss is reported according to the rules outlined earlier. The employer must treat any gains and losses derived from acquiring an employee's home under a relocation plan as resulting from the ownership of a capital asset. This can be a significant disadvantage if the residence is subsequently sold at a loss. An advantage may be obtained by having the employer contract with a relocation company to sell the house and pay a fee for the service. This fee would be deductible by the employer as a trade or business expense.

### Lifetime Exclusion

Once in his lifetime a taxpayer can elect to exclude from gross income up to $125,000 of gain realized on the sale or exchange (including involuntary conversion) of a principal residence. This exclusion is available if the taxpayer is at least 55 years old before the sale or exchange occurs *and* the property has been owned or used by the taxpayer as his principal residence for at least three years out of the five-year period preceding the sale. Unlike the earlier tax deferral for reinvesting in a new residence, this provision permanently excludes the gain from taxation.

This election can be used in addition to the tax deferral provided for reinvestment in a new principal residence. In fact, this exclusion combined with the normal tax deferral on reinvestment means that much or all of the lifetime gain on home ownership escapes taxation completely. The over-55 exclusion acts to reduce the taxpayer's adjusted sales price for the old residence. The "reduced" adjusted sales price must be compared with the cost of the replacement residence to determine the amount of the realized gain that must be recognized.

**EXAMPLE 9-8.**   Assume the facts remain the same as in the preceding example except that Tax A. Voider is 60 years of age, has continuously used the property that was sold as her personal residence, and acquires a condominium that cost $200,000 as a replacement residence. No previous election to exclude a gain from the sale of a principal residence has been made. The realized gain and adjusted sales price are reduced by the $125,000 excluded gain, and become $101,000, and $239,000, respectively. The recognized gain is $39,000—the smaller of the realized gain ($101,000) or the boot ($239,000 − $200,000). The basis for the replacement residence is $138,000 [$200,000 − ($101,000 − $39,000)].

## WASH SALES

The wash sale rules prevent a taxpayer from recognizing a loss for tax purposes while maintaining essentially the same economic position in a stock or security. A wash sale involves (1) the sale or exchange of stock or securities at a loss and (2) substantially identical securities being purchased within a period beginning 30 days before the date of the sale or exchange and ending 30 days after such date (a 61-day period).

When a quantity of securities is reacquired that is less than the quantity sold, the loss is disallowed only for the portion of the securities sold or exchanged that are identical in quantity to those reacquired. The difference between the selling price of the "old" securities and the purchase price of the replacement securities is added to the basis of the "old" securities to determine the basis for the replacement securities.

The wash sale rules can restrict a taxpayer's year-end tax planning, if he wants to maintain the same economic position in the stock to obtain future price appreciation.

**EXAMPLE 9-9.** Tax A. Voider owns 1,000 shares of Amalgamated Conglomerate common stock that were acquired 4 years ago at $100 per share. Tax A. Voider sells the Amalgamated Conglomerate stock for $60 per share on December 27, 19X5 and realizes a $40,000 long-term capital loss [1,000 × ($60 − $100)]. In order to recognize the loss and maintain a 1,000 share economic position, the replacement Amalgamated Conglomerate shares must be acquired before November 27, 19X5 or after January 26, 19X6. If 1,000 shares are acquired for $62,000 during the prohibited 61-day period, the $40,000 loss is disallowed and Tax A. Voider's basis for the "new" shares becomes $102,000 [$100,000 + ($62,000 − $60,000)]. The holding period for the stock sold is added to the holding period of the new shares if the loss is disallowed.

## RELATED-PARTY SALES

These rules prevent a taxpayer from recognizing a loss for tax purposes by selling property to a related person, whether or not the loss has economic substance. The related-party sale rules apply when the property is sold or exchanged at a loss and the selling and purchasing parties are related. These rules do not apply to losses incurred on the complete liquidation of a corporation, or to losses coming under the wash sale rules.

A related party includes (but is not limited to) the following:

1.   Members of a family—including brothers, sisters, spouse, ancestors, and lineal descendants.

2. An individual and a corporation more than 50% owned by or for that individual.

3. A corporation and a partnership where the same person(s) owns more than 50% of each entity.

4. Two corporations that are members of the same controlled group.

5. An S corporation and a C corporation if the same persons own more than 50% of the stock of each corporation.

In order to determine whether two parties are in fact related, special attribution rules are used which can cause an individual to be treated as the owner of stock actually owned by other family members or by partnerships, S corporations, regular corporations, trusts, or estates in which he has an ownership or beneficial interest.

The purchaser's basis for the property is its acquisition cost. When the purchaser subsequently sells or exchanges the property on which the loss was disallowed, the second owner's gain is recognized only to the extent that it exceeds the amount of the first owner's disallowed loss. If the disallowed loss exceeds the realized gain, the excess loss is never recognized. A previously disallowed loss cannot be recognized if the second sale or exchange occurs at a loss.

**EXAMPLE 9-10.** Tax A. Voider owns 60% of the TAV Corporation stock. During 19X2 she sells TAV some XYZ Corporation stock for $120,000. The stock has a basis of $200,000. TAV holds this stock for 5 years and sells it for $260,000. The $80,000 ($120,000 − $200,000) loss realized by Tax A. Voider on the 19X2 sale cannot be recognized. The stock has a $120,000 basis in TAV's hands. The second sale results in TAV realizing a $140,000 ($260,000 − $120,000) gain, only $60,000 of which must be recognized.

## CHARACTER OF RECOGNIZED GAIN OR LOSS

The final step in the determination of the tax consequences of a sale or exchange is to ascertain the character of the gain or loss. The character of the gain or loss is determined by the nature and use of the asset that is sold or exchanged. In some cases, Congress has extended preferential tax treatment to some transactions. Some of the most important provisions for determining the character of gain or loss are described in the pages that follow.

## Section 1231

Section 1231 provides the taxpayer with the best of both worlds—the possibility of reporting a long-term capital gain when a qualifying property is sold at a gain and an ordinary loss when a qualifying property is sold at a loss. The price extracted for such preferential tax treatment is the awesome complexity of the provisions. Nevertheless, it is well worth the time required to understand these provisions.

### Section 1231 Property

Section 1231 rules apply to (1) sales or exchanges of property used in the taxpayer's trade or business, and (2) involuntary conversions of (a) property used in the taxpayer's trade or business *and* (b) capital assets held for more than six months that are used in the taxpayer's trade or business or held for a profit-making transaction. "Property used in the trade or business" includes depreciable property that is used in the trade or business *and* which has been held for more than 6 months and real property used in the trade or business that has been held more than 1 year. (The 6-month holding period applies to depreciable property acquired after June 22, 1984. For all other properties a 12-month holding period is required.) Excluded from this definition are:

1. Inventory items.
2. Property held primarily for sale to customers in the ordinary course of the business (i.e. lots held by a real estate developer).
3. Copyrights, literary, musical, or artistic compositions, and similar items that were prepared or produced by or for the taxpayer or such property when it has a carryover basis from a party who prepared the property or for whom the property was

prepared (e.g., a painting held by the artist or a painting acquired as a gift from the artist).

4.  U.S. government publications acquired at a reduced cost or for free.

5.  Any property held 6 months or less.

Exclusion of these properties from the Section 1231 definition means that any profit or loss recognized on their disposition is ordinary gain or loss.

The Section 1231 property definition also includes the following: timber that is held for more than 6 months and that is cut by the taxpayer; timber, coal, or domestic iron ore that is held for more than 6 months, and which is sold under a royalty contract whereby the taxpayer retains an economic interest in the property; cattle and horses held by the taxpayer for more than 24 months and used for draft, breeding, dairy, or sporting purposes; other livestock held for more than 6 months and used for draft, breeding, dairy, or sporting purposes; and unharvested crops on land used in the conduct of a trade or business which are held for more than 6 months and that are sold, exchanged, or involuntarily converted at the same time as the land and to the same person. Section 1231 treatment for these properties converts what would otherwise be ordinary income into long-term capital gain.

### Treatment of Section 1231 Gains and Losses

The Section 1231 taxation rules have become simpler in 1984. The 1984 Tax Act eliminated most of the complexity by having the personal casualty and theft losses treated under the capital asset rules (see Chapter 2). The determination of the taxation of Section 1231 gain or losses takes three steps:

1.  All gains and losses from "Section 1231 property" and eligible capital asset transactions are separated into "business casualty and theft transactions" and "other transactions."

2.  All gains and losses from "casualty and theft" transactions are combined into a "net" gain or loss position.

(a)  If a net loss results, all casualty and theft gains and losses are treated as ordinary gains and losses. (Consequently, all casualty and theft transactions will fall outside Section 1231.)

(b)  If a net gain results, the net gain is included with the gains and losses from the "other" Section 1231 transactions.

3.  All gains and losses from the "other" Section 1231 transactions and the net "casualty and theft" gain (if any) are combined into a single "net" gain or loss position.

(a)  If a net loss results, all gains and losses are treated as ordinary gains and losses.

(b)  If a net gain results, the net gain is included with the total of the taxpayer's long-term capital gains and losses to determine "net long-term capital gain or loss." Further combining of the net long- and short-term capital gains and losses follow the rules outlined in Chapter 2.

The application of the Section 1231 gain or loss rules are illustrated by the following examples:

**EXAMPLE 9-11.**  TAV Corporation's 19X4 property transactions result in the following:

| | |
|---|---:|
| Net long-term capital gain | $ 5,000 |
| Net short-term capital loss | (2,000) |
| Section 1231 "other" transactions: | |
| Gains | 12,000 |
| Losses | (7,000) |
| Section 1231 business "casualty and theft" occurrences: | |
| Gains | 8,000 |
| Losses | (6,000) |
| Ordinary gain on property held less than 12 months | 600 |

The first step combines the "casualty and theft" gains and losses into a net $2,000 gain which is then combined with the other Section 1231 transaction gains and losses to produce a net $7,000 gain ($2,000 + $12,000 − $7,000). This net gain is combined with the long-term and short-term capital gains and losses to produce a $10,000 long-term capital gain ($7,000 + $5,000 − $2,000).

In the past a taxpayer could engage in tax planning by separating the recognition of Section 1231 gains and losses into two different taxable years so as to preserve the advantages of both the long-term capital gain and the ordinary loss treatment. The ability to separate Section 1231 gains and losses into two different taxable years so as to take advantage of the capital gain and ordinary loss treatments has been ended for 1985 and later years. Section 1231 losses for the 5 most recent preceding taxable years (beginning after December 31, 1981) must be recaptured as ordinary income when Section 1231 gains are recognized. The amount of ordinary income recognized in a given taxable year is the lesser of the excess of the Section 1231 gains over Section 1231 losses for the taxable year or the amount of the net Section 1231 losses from the preceding 5 taxable years that have not yet been recaptured.

## Section 1245

The Section 1245 depreciation recapture rules prevent taxpayers from claiming depreciation deductions against ordinary income during a property's life and subsequently selling the property and obtaining long-term capital gain treatment. The Section 1245 rules override Section 1231 and require previously claimed depreciation deductions to be recaptured as ordinary income when the property is sold, exchanged, or otherwise disposed of.

### Section 1245 Property

The Section 1245 property definitions have changed over time. Prior to 1981, Section 1245 property included tangible and intangible property if it was, or had been, subject to depreciation. Limited forms of real property and other property (e.g., livestock and professional sports player contracts) were also included in the definition.

Under the ACRS rules (generally applied to all property placed in service after 1980), all recovery property is Section 1245 property *except* for the following:

1.  15-year or 18-year real property and low-income housing which is residential rental property.
2.  15-year or 18-year real property and low-income housing which is used predominantly outside the United States.
3.  15-year or 18-year real property and low-income housing for which an election to use the straight-line recovery method is in effect.
4.  15-year or 18-year real property which qualifies as low-income housing under the rules for certain federally-funded housing projects or is eligible for 60-month amortization of rehabilitation expenditures.

### Ordinary Income Amount

The ordinary income amount equals the lesser of the realized gain or the post–1961 depreciation that has been claimed. The Section 1245 rules do not apply to property sold at a loss. Losses come under the Section 1231 rules.

Because Section 1245 provides for 100% recapture of previously claimed depreciation deductions, the likelihood of Section 1245 property being sold and producing a Section 1231 gain is limited to two circumstances—property that was sold for an amount in excess of its purchase price; or property that was placed in service prior to 1962.

For Section 1245 purposes, the depreciation amount includes not only the capital recovery (or depreciation) allowances claimed by the taxpayer, but also the amount of the basis reduction required because an investment tax credit was claimed and the amount of the purchase price that was expensed in the year of acquisition. The depreciation amount is reduced by one-half of the amount of any investment tax credits that are recaptured. A sale or exchange of property, for which part of the acquisition cost was expensed in the year of acquisition, results in the lesser of the amount so expensed or the sales price being recaptured under Section 1245.

The application of the Section 1245 rules is illustrated by the following example:

**EXAMPLE 9-12.** TAV Corporation acquired a 5-year recovery class property. The property is sold 2½ years after its acquisition. The asset acquisition permitted a $1,000 investment tax credit to be claimed. The sale transaction causes $600 of this credit to be recaptured. The Section 1245 consequences of the sale are illustrated in the following three different situations:

| | Situation Number | | |
| --- | --- | --- | --- |
| | 1 | 2 | 3 |
| Acquisition cost (1) | $10,000 | $10,000 | $10,000 |
| Capital recovery allowance claimed (2) | 3,515[a] | 3,515 | 3,515 |
| Investment tax credit adjustment: | | | |
| At acquisition (3) | 500[b] | 500 | 500 |
| At sale (4) | 300[c] | 300 | 300 |
| Section 1245 recapture potential | | | |
| (5) = (2) + (3) − (4) | 3,715 | 3,715 | 3,715 |
| Adjusted basis | | | |
| (6) = (1) − (2) − (3) + (4) | 6,285 | 6,285 | 6,285 |
| Sale price (7) | 7,500 | 3,000 | 12,000 |
| Recognized gain (loss) | | | |
| (8) = (7) − (6) | 1,215 | (3,285) | 5,715 |
| Character of gain (loss): | | | |
| Section 1245 gain | 1,215 | 0 | 3,715 |
| Section 1231 gain (loss) | 0 | (3,285) | 2,000 |

[a] [($10,000 − (0.50 × 0.10 × $10,000)) × (0.15 + 0.22) = $3,515]
[b] 0.50 × $1,000 = $500
[c] 0.50 × $600 = $300

The entire gain in Situation No. 1 is Section 1245 gain since the recognized gain is less than the Section 1245 recapture potential. Section 1245 does not apply to Situation No. 2 since the property is sold at a loss. Sections 1245 and 1231 apply to Situation No. 3 since it is sold for an amount in excess of its acquisition cost. The price appreciation up to the acquisition cost is recaptured as Section 1245 ordinary income, the remaining price appreciation is eligible for long-term capital gain treatment under Section 1231.

## Section 1250

The intent behind the Section 1250 rules parallels that of the Section 1245 rules. Taxpayers cannot depreciate real estate and offset ordinary income and then recognize a long-term capital gain when the real estate is sold. The Section 1250 rules have changed several times, and have resulted in differing definitions for Section 1250 property and differing amounts of depreciation being recaptured as ordinary income.

### Section 1250 Property

Prior to 1981, Section 1250 property included any real property (other than the limited forms of real property included in the Section 1245 property definition) that had been subject to an allowance for depreciation. This definition still remains applicable for property placed into service prior to 1981 (pre-ACRS properties) and for property for which an election out of the ACRS rules is made.

Under the ACRS rules, real property comes under either the Section 1245 or 1250 recapture rules. All real property comes under the Section 1245 definition other than the four exceptions outlined previously in this chapter. First, residential rental property remains Section 1250 property. Second, real property for which a straight-line ACRS election is made is excluded from both Sections 1245 and 1250 so all of the recognized gain receives Section 1231 treatment.

### Ordinary Income Amount

The Section 1250 recapture rules do not call for 100% recapture of all previously claimed depreciation deductions as do the Section 1245 rules. The Section 1250 rules recapture only "additional depreciation"—the excess of actual depreciation claimed for the taxable year over the amount of depreciation that would have been claimed had the straight-line method of depreciation been used. The straight-line calculation is performed using the property's useful life (if non–ACRS property) or the 15-year or 18-year recovery period (if ACRS property).

The portion of the additional depreciation that is recaptured depends on the nature and use of the property. The recapture percentages that apply to the "additional depreciation" claimed after 1975 are as follows:

| Type of Property | Recapture Percentage for Additional Depreciation Claimed for Property Acquired in | |
| --- | --- | --- |
| | 1975–1980 | 1981–Present |
| Commercial real estate | 100% recapture | Section 1245 property[a] |
| Residential rental | 100% recapture | 100% recapture |
| Low income housing and rehabilitation expenditures | 100% recapture minus 1% for each month the property is held in excess of 100 months[b] | 100% recapture minus 1% for each month the property is held in excess of 100 months[b] |

[a] Unless used predominantly outside the United States or a straight-line ACRS (or depreciation) election is made.
[b] No recapture occurs if the property is held for at least 16 years and 8 months.

If the property was held less than 6 months, 100% of all depreciation claimed is recaptured. The Section 1250 rules do not apply to losses.

The application of the Section 1245 and 1250 rules to realty are illustrated by the following example:

EXAMPLE **9-13.** Tax A. Voider purchases some real estate for $1,250,000 on January 1, 19X2. An allocation of $250,000 of the purchase price is made to the land. The land and building are sold on January 1, 19X5 for $1,200,000, of which $900,000 is allocated to the building. The calculation of the depreciation recapture amount under the Section 1245 and 1250 rules is made below using three different assumptions, regarding the character of the property and the type of capital recovery method that is used.

| | Situation Number | | |
| | 1 | 2 | 3 |
|---|---|---|---|
| Type of Property | Commercial Real Estate | Residential Rental Property | Commercial Real Estate |
| Cost (1) | $1,000,000 | $1,000,000 | $1,000,000 |
| ACRS capital recovery method[a] | Accelerated | Accelerated | Straight-line |
| ACRS capital recovery allowance in: | | | |
| 19X2 | $ 120,000 | $ 120,000 | $ 66,667 |
| 19X3 | 100,000 | 100,000 | 66,667 |
| 19X4 | 90,000 | 90,000 | 66,666 |
| Total (2) | $ 310,000 | $ 310,000 | $ 200,000 |
| Hypothetical straight-line capital recovery allowance[a] | $ 200,000 | $ 200,000 | $ 200,000 |
| Excess depreciation | $ 110,000 | $ 110,000 | 0 |
| Amount realized | $ 900,000 | $ 900,000 | $ 900,000 |
| Less: Adjusted basis (3) = (1) − (2) | (690,000) | $ (690,000) | $ (800,000) |
| Realized and recognized gain | $ 210,000 | $ 210,000 | $ 100,000 |
| | | | |
| Character of gain: | | | |
| Sec. 1245 | $ 210,000 | | |
| Sec. 1250 | | $ 110,000 | |
| Sec. 1231 | | $ 100,000 | $ 100,000 |

[a] 15-year recovery period

In Situation No. 1, the Section 1245 rules cause all of the recognized gain to be ordinary income. In Situation No. 2, the residential rental character of the property reduces the recapture amount to the excess depreciation, or $110,000. The remainder of the gain is taxed as a long-term capital gain under Section 1231. Situation No. 3 is the critical one from a decision-making standpoint. An election to use the straight-line ACRS rules reduces the capital recovery allowances by $110,000 during 19X2–19X4. A positive benefit accrues in that $100,000 of the gain that was taxed as ordinary income in Situation No. 1 is taxed now as a long-term capital gain under Section 1231. Whether the benefit of this tax savings offsets the cost of forgoing the additional depreciation deductions in years 19X2–19X4 must be determined based upon the taxpayer's facts and circumstances. The $50,000 gain recognized on the sale of the land is Section 1231 gain. It should be noted that the result in Situation No. 3 would be the same if the realty were instead residential rental property.

Special rules apply to a corporate taxpayer selling or exchanging a Section 1250 property. The amount of ordinary income recognized on the sale of Section 1250 property is increased by 20% (15% for 1984 and before) of the amount of additional ordinary income that would have been recognized had the property instead been subject to recapture under Section 1245. Thus, in Situation No. 3 in the preceding example, a corporate taxpayer would recognize $20,000 of ordinary income (0.20 × $100,000) and $80,000 of Section 1231 gain on the disposition.

### Section 1239

As a result of the Section 1239 rules, the gain recognized on a related-party sale (that would otherwise be a capital gain) converts into ordinary income if the property is of a depreciable nature in the purchaser's hands. Related parties for purpose of this rule include a corporation and an 80% shareholder, a partnership and an 80% partner, and any taxpayer and a trust in which the taxpayer (or his spouse) has a beneficial interest. Thus, the entire gain recognized by Tax A. Voider on the sale of the residential rental property in Situation No. 2 in Example 9-13 would be ordinary income if the purchaser were a related party (e.g., a corporation wholly owned by Tax A. Voider).

### Abandonment

The depreciation provisions are designed to account for normal obsolescence. Abnormal obsolescence may render a property useless before the end of its useful life. In such a case, a taxpayer can claim a loss for the property's unrecovered basis. Such a loss is an ordinary loss. These rules apply to both tangible or intangible property, and must be accompanied by an actual physical abandonment of the property. Abandonment can be advantageous since the loss does not arise from a sale or exchange, and therefore is outside the purview of Section 1231.

## RECAPTURE OF INVESTMENT TAX CREDITS

A sale or exchange of Section 38 property before the end of its recovery period results in the recapture of part or all of any previously claimed investment tax credits. The portion of the credit that is recaptured is based on the following table:

| Recovery Property Ceases to Be Section 38 Property After: | Recapture Percentage for: | |
| | 3-Year Property | 5-, 10-, and 15-Year Property |
| --- | --- | --- |
| Less than 1 year in service | 100% | 100% |
| At least 1 year (but less than 2 years) in service | 66% | 80% |
| At least 2 years (but less than 3 years) in service | 33% | 60% |
| At least 3 years (but less than 4 years) in service | 0 | 40% |
| At least 4 years (but less than 5 years) in service | 0 | 20% |
| At least 5 years in service | 0 | 0 |

EXAMPLE 9-14.　On March 1, 19X7, TAV Corporation sells Section 38 property that it had acquired for $100,000 on January 1, 19X5. An investment tax credit of $10,000 (0.10 × $100,000) was originally claimed. The asset has been held for 2 years and 2 months. The credit that is recaptured is $6,000 ($10,000 × 0.60). Even though this amount must be repaid by increasing TAV's 19X7 tax liability, no interest and penalties are charged by the government for failing to have the property in service for the entire 5-year recovery period. One-half of the $6,000 recapture amount increases the property's adjusted basis and reduces the Section 1245 recapture potential.

Dispositions other than an outright sale of the property can result in a recapture of previously claimed investment tax credits. Transactions resulting in a recapture include the following:

1. Like-kind exchanges (including trade-ins).
2. Involuntary conversions.
3. Liquidations.
4. Gifts.
5. Property ceasing to be Section 38 property (e.g., property converted to personal use).

Events that do not result in recapture include the following:

1. Formation of a corporation or partnership that is treated as a "mere change in the form of conducting a trade or business."
2. Making of an S corporation election.
3. Certain tax-free reorganizations.
4. Transfers occurring as a result of death.

## SALE OF A BUSINESS

Sometimes a taxpayer will dispose of his entire business. Three primary alternatives are available: (1) sell the individual assets; (2) sell his ownership interest (e.g., corporate stock or a partnership interest); or (3) exchange the assets or ownership interest in a tax-free transaction. If the first alternative is selected, the transaction is treated as the disposition of the individual assets of the business. Sales of investment assets, Section 1231 properties, and goodwill at a gain will produce capital gains. Sales of accounts receivable, inventory, Section 1245 property and Section 1250 property at a gain will produce ordinary income. Recapture of previously claimed investment tax credits will also be required. If the business is conducted by using the corporate form, a sale of the assets followed by a liquidation all taking place within a 12-month period will permit part or all of the gain realized on the asset sale to go unrecognized.

The sale of a corporation's stock generally results in a capital gain or loss being recognized. The Section 1244 rules permit an ordinary loss to be recognized when the corporation is a small business corporation. A stock sale has the advantage of transferring the depreciation and investment tax credit recapture potential to the purchasing party. The sale of a partnership interest is a taxable transaction that generally results in a capital gain or loss being recognized. Ordinary income may have to be recognized if the partnership has "hot assets"—substantially appreciated inventories, Section 1245 and 1250 properties, and unrealized receivables.

The stock or assets of a corporation can be exchanged in a tax-free reorganization. Gain is recognized by the corporation or its shareholders only to the extent that boot is received. Losses are not recognized. The reorganization rules permit a corporation, or the shareholders to exchange a stock interest in one corporation for the stock of another corporation, without incurring any tax liability. The partnership rules provide that both the liquidation of an existing partnership and the formation of a new partnership are generally tax-free events. (See Chapters 7 and 12.)

## TAX PLANNING FOR CAPITAL GAINS AND LOSSES

Some asset dispositions made by a business are eligible for preferential treatment as capital gains or losses. Ordinarily capital gain or loss treatment results from a taxpayer having disposed of a capital asset *and* having had a substantial investment purpose for acquiring or holding the asset. Ordinary gain or loss treatment can result when the asset either does not qualify as a capital asset or the asset is held for a business purpose.

### Timing of Capital Asset Transactions

Some tax planning considerations can reduce the tax cost of realizing a capital gain or increase the tax benefits of realizing a capital loss. A number of these opportunities are presented below. (For a review of the capital gain and loss rules, see Chapter 2.)

### Planning with Capital Gains

1. *Spread Out the Capital Gains Over More Than 1 Year.* By spreading out the capital asset sales so that they occur in two taxable years, a taxpayer can spread out the recognition of the capital gains. This may reduce the marginal tax rate that applies to the income. If only a single asset is sold, the gain can be spread over two or more taxable years by having the proceeds paid in a series of installments. Even if a "bunching" problem cannot be avoided, income averaging can be used to reduce the tax liability.

2. *Defer the Reporting of the Gain Into a Later Taxable Year.* Because of the time value of money, a taxpayer may benefit from deferring a capital gain to a later year even if his marginal rate is the same in each year. The advantage of the tax deferral becomes even greater if the marginal tax rate can be expected to be lower in the later year. A taxpayer can defer the reporting of a current transaction by receiving the payment in a later taxable year. Such a transaction is treated as an installment sale, and the gain is reported in the year the sales proceeds are collected.

3. *Elect Not to Report a Transaction Under the Installment Method.* A taxpayer may desire to report a gain in the currrent year in order to avoid losing a loss or credit carryover, or to obtain a greater tax benefit from a loss realized earlier in the year. The advantage of such an election is illustrated by the following example:

EXAMPLE **9-15.** Tax A. Voider uses the cash method of accounting. She purchases 1,000 shares of ABC Corporation stock at $10 per share on December 28, 19X4. The trade is made and confirmed on that date. The shares are paid for on January 4, 19X5 (the fifth working day after the sale, the settlement date). The shares are sold on December 31, 19X5 for $25 per share. The trade is made and confirmed on that date. The cash is made available to Tax A. Voider on January 7, 19X6 (the settlement date). The sale of a security by a cash method of accounting taxpayer normally is not reported until the cash is received. For transactions occurring on a securities exchange this is normally the settlement date. (The trade dates are used to determine the security's holding period.)

Two alternatives are available for reporting the transaction. Because the transaction is considered an installment sale, the taxpayer can report the transaction in the year of collection or settlement. Alternatively, the taxpayer can elect not to report the transaction using the installment method, and recognize the gain in the year the trade is executed. Thus, the taxpayer might consider recognizing the $15,000 gain [1,000 × ($25 − $10)] in 19X5 if she wanted to use a capital loss carryover. Reporting the $15,000 gain in 19X6 would, of course, defer the payment of the taxes for 1 year. The election not to use the installment method is made when the tax return is filed, which can be as much as 8½ months after year-end.

4.  *Use Specific Identification of the Properties Sold to Control the Amount and Character of the Gain or Loss Recognized.*   Normally, stocks and securities are considered to be sold on a first-in, first-out basis. By using specific identification of the stocks and securities that are sold, a taxpayer may be able to increase or decrease the amount of gain or loss that is recognized, or control whether such gain or loss is short-term or long-term.

### Planning with Capital Losses

The following tips can increase the value of a capital loss or decrease the possibility that a carryover will be lost:

1.  *Recognize Unrealized Capital Losses Before They Become Long-Term.* A short-term capital loss is deductible on a dollar-for-dollar basis. Two dollars of long-term capital loss are required to produce one dollar of deduction. Sale or exchange of capital assets in order to recognize a short-term loss (rather than a long-term loss) should be considered. Cut your economic loss and get larger tax benefits.
2.  *Avoid Capital Loss Carryovers When the Taxpayer Is Elderly.*   A tax advisor should be careful to recognize any unrealized

capital losses prior to death. Any losses which have accrued prior to death but which were not recognized by the decedent cannot be used by the estate or any beneficiaries as a deduction or to offset capital gains. If a capital loss carryover should develop, planning should be undertaken to generate a sufficient amount of capital gains to use the carryover as quickly as possible. Because the carryover cannot be used by the estate or a beneficiary, the possibility of losing the carryover is high with an elderly taxpayer.

3. *Recognize Losses by Making Year-End Sales.* Cash method of accounting taxpayers normally report a transaction when the cash is received or made available. An exception to this general rule permits securities that are sold at a loss at the year-end to be reported on the transaction date (instead of the settlement date). This permits tax planning to take place up until the year-end.

4. *Use the Wash Sale Rules to Avoid Recognizing a Loss.* A taxpayer may discover after year-end that it would be more advantageous if he had not recognized a loss on the sale or exchange of a stock or security. This loss can be deferred if within 30 days of the sale date the taxpayer acquires a similar quantity of the same stock or security. The loss can then be recognized at some later date with only an additional transaction cost being incurred.

### Planning Year-End Transactions

Year-end transactions can enhance the value of a loss or reduce the cost of having previously recognized a gain. Similarly, deferring a transaction from one year to the next can prevent the loss of preferential tax benefits. Taxpayers should review their year's transactions at least one month before their year-end to allow time to make any necessary transactions. Some year-end planning techniques for individual taxpayers are illustrated as follows:

1. *If the Taxpayer's Transactions Have Resulted in a Net Gain to Date, Consider Recognizing Offsetting Paper Losses Before Year-end.* A taxpayer having a net short-term gain position might consider realizing either short-term or long-term losses to offset the gain. Long-term losses are particularly advantageous here since they fully offset short-term gains without any need for a 2-for-1 reduction

as would be the case if they were offset against ordinary income. Additional short-term losses might also be recognized to offset ordinary income.

2.  *If the Taxpayer's Transactions Have Resulted in a Net Short-Term Loss to Date, Avoid Recognizing a Long-Term Capital Gain Before Year-End.*  The preferential treatment available for a long-term capital gain would be lost if it were recognized before year-end, since it must first offset the short-term capital loss. Short-term capital gains might be recognized before year-end to "lock-in" the profit and use up any losses that are in excess of the $3,000 annual limitation on deducting capital losses.

3.  *If the Taxpayer's Transactions Have Resulted in a Net Long-Term Loss To Date, Consider Recognizing Short-Term Gains to Offset the Losses.*  Short-term gains offset the long-term loss and prevent the taxpayer from having to use two dollars of loss to create one dollar of deduction. If no short-term gains can be recognized, consider recognizing short-term losses which are deducted up to the $3,000 limitation. The long-term losses could then be carried over until next year when short-term gains can be realized.

4.  *If the Taxpayer's Transactions Have Resulted in a Net Long-Term Gain to Date, Consider Not Recognizing Any Capital Losses.*  Only 40% of long-term capital gains are taxed. Since this is the best possible way to recognize gain, capital losses could be saved to offset short-term capital gains or ordinary income in other years. Alternatively, consider recognizing long-term losses to offset the gains and then recognize additional short-term capital losses up to the $3,000 deduction limitation. The long-term losses defer the tax due on the long-term gains. The short-term losses permit the taxpayer to offset other ordinary income.

Other tax strategies are possible. Many of these strategies involve making short sales, writing or buying puts or calls, or entering into straddles. These transactions are beyond the scope of this text but may be advantageous for a taxpayer. Consult your tax advisor for more information.

# ————— 10

# EMPLOYEE COMPENSATION

In Chapter 4, the advantage of withdrawing funds from a corporation by making salary payments was illustrated. A substantial tax savings was achieved because the double taxation associated with dividend payments was avoided. This type of tax savings is the mere "tip of the iceberg" of a very specialized form of tax planning that is known as compensation planning. Various strategies can be adopted which can make the compensation tax free, defer the taxation for one or more years, or permit taxation at preferential capital gains rates.

No single compensation plan can be developed that is suitable for all individuals since compensation planning generally must be tailored for each individual. For a longtime, compensation planning was thought to be a tax-sheltering technique available only to highly compensated individuals. This is no longer true. Recent changes in tax laws permit larger numbers of individuals to take advantage of the compensation planning techniques explained here. These devices are available whether the individual works part-time or full-time, is paid by the hour or by salary, or is an employee or self-employed. However, the greatest benefits of compensation planning still accrue to highly compensated individuals who have the flexibility to receive part of their compensation in a noncash form and can participate in the employer's growth.

This chapter is divided into four parts: current and deferred compensation; fringe benefits; equity-oriented plans; and retirement plans. A number of alternative types of compensation forms are examined in each category.

Each compensation alternative can be categorized according to (1) the deductibility of the payment by the employer; and (2) the taxability of the payment to the employee. One possible breakdown of the compensation alternatives is found in the following matrix:

|  | Taxability of Compensation to Employee | | | | |
|  | Taxed in a Future Period As: | | Taxed in Current Period As: | |
|  | Not Taxed | Long-term Capital Gain | Ordinary Income | Long-term Capital Gain | Ordinary Income |
|---|---|---|---|---|---|
| Deductible currently | 1 | 2 | 3 | N.A. | 4 |
| Deductible in a future period | 5 | N.A. | 6 | 7 | 8 |
| Never deductible | 9 | 10 | 11 | 12 | 13 |

N.A. = Not available.

The numbers indicate a possible ranking (with 1 being the preferred choice) for the compensation alternatives in each category. Using this table, one can see that a higher ranking would be given to (1) a fringe benefit payment not taxed to the employee but deductible currently by the employer (a ranking of 1) over (2) a salary payment currently taxed to the employee and deductible currently by the employer (a ranking of 4). A breakdown of selected compensation alternatives into the categories included in the above matrix is presented in Figure 10-1.

A number of tax factors other than the taxability/deductibility of the compensation alternative must be considered in determining its suitability as part of a compensation package for an individual employee. Some of these factors include the following:

1. Current marginal tax rate of the employee and the employer.
2. Future marginal tax rate of the employee and the employer.
3. Amount of the employee's tax preference items.
4. After-tax rate of return for employer and employee pension plan contributions.
5. Size of the taxpayer's estate and the marginal estate tax rate (if the compensation is to be received by the taxpayer's estate).
6. Marginal tax rate applicable to beneficiary (if the compensation is to be received after the employee's death).

Each variable must be considered in the selection of the "appropriate" compensation package. As the tax and nontax variables change, the compensation plan must be reexamined and, if necessary, changed in order to better suit the employer and employee's needs.

## ILLUSTRATIVE EXAMPLE OF COMPENSATION PLANNING

One way to illustrate the advantages of compensation planning is to determine the tax savings that are available to our friend Tax A. Voider, the chief executive officer of TAV Corporation, when he receives a portion of his compensation in the form of nontaxable fringe benefits. The plan on page 234, represents one alternative to the corporation paying Tax A. Voider his entire compensation package of $150,000 in cash. In order to keep our plan quite simple, it does not include any compensation forms that are keyed to the performance of TAV Corporation (e.g., stock options).

**FIGURE 10.1** Classification of selected payments made by a corporation.

| Treatment to Employer | Deductible | Deductible | Deductible | Deductible |
|---|---|---|---|---|
| Treatment to Employer | Not Taxed | Taxed as Ordinary Income Currently | Taxed as Ordinary Income in Future Period | Taxed as LTCG in Future Period |
| | 1. Group-term life insurance (in excess of $50,000 of insurance)<br>2. Retired lives reserve insurance<br>3. Employee death benefits<br>4. Accident and health insurance<br>5. Medical reimbursement plans<br>6. Medical examinations<br>7. Insurance on wrongful acts<br>8. Workers' compensation<br>9. Disability insurance<br>10. Meals and lodging for the convenience of the employer<br>11. Group legal services<br>12. Educational assistance<br>13. Free parking<br>14. Van pooling arrangements for commuting<br>15. Day-care centers<br>16. Normal discounts on employee purchase<br>17. Travel and entertainment<br>18. Entertainment facilities<br>19. Office accommodations<br>20. Moving expense reimbursement (up to amount of deductible expenses)<br>21. Occupational dues and publications<br>22. Attendance at seminars<br>23. Shareholder-directed contributions | 1. Salary<br>2. Bonuses<br>3. Funded-deferred compensation arrangements<br>4. Restricted stock or property where special election is made<br>5. Restricted stock or property where no substantial risks of forfeiture exists<br>6. Group-term life insurance (in excess of $50,000 of insurance)<br>7. Permanent life insurance<br>8. Key-person life insurance—employee is beneficiary<br>9. Discriminatory medical reimbursement plan<br>10. Split-dollar life insurance<br>11. Above normal employee discounts<br>12. Commuting cost paid by employer<br>13. Personal use of company automobile<br>14. Moving expense reimbursement (in excess of deductible expenses)<br>15. Investment and financial counseling services<br>16. Nonqualified stock options (current compensation portion)<br>17. Unrestricted stock plans<br>18. Vacation pay<br>19. Imputed interest on interest-free or low-interest loans | 1. Qualified pension, profit-sharing and stock bonus plan<br>2. Annuity plans<br>3. Bond purchase plans<br>4. Salary reduction plans<br>5. Employee stock ownership plans<br>6. Individual Retirement Arrangements<br>7. Simplified Employee Pension Plan<br>8. Social Security payments | 1. Qualified pension, profit-sharing and stock bonus plan (attributable to pre-1974 service)<br>2. Restricted stock or property where a substantial risk of forfeiture exists and the special election is made (price appreciation) |

232

| Deferred Deduction | Nondeductible | Nondeductible | Nondeductible |
|---|---|---|---|
| Taxed as Ordinary Income in Future Period | Taxed as Ordinary income | Taxed as LTCG | Not taxed |
| 1. Unfunded deferred compensation arrangements<br>2. Restricted stock where a substantial risk of forfeiture exists<br>3. Phantom stock plans<br>4. Stock appreciation rights | 1. Incentive stock options (when sold before satisfying holding period requirement)<br>2. Dividend<br>3. Stock redemption treated as dividend<br>4. Unreasonable compensation paid to shareholder<br>5. Travel and entertainment expenses when related to personal business or extravagance | 1. Incentive stock options (price appreciation)<br>2. Nonqualified stock options (price appreciation)<br>3. Stock redemption treated as exchange transaction<br>4. Distribution in liquidation of corporation | 1. Key-person life insurance when company is beneficiary<br>2. Return of capital portion of distribution<br>3. Stock dividend<br>4. Redemption of debt |

| Type of Compensation | Amount | Taxable to Tax A. Voider | Tax-free to Tax A. Voider | Deductible by Corporation |
|---|---|---|---|---|
| Salary | $ 75,450 | $75,450 | | $75,450 |
| Salary reduction plan | 14,090 | | $14,090 | 14,090 |
| Fees for serving as a director of TAV Corporation | 3,000 | 3,000 | | 3,000 |
| Qualified pension plan | 15,000 | | 15,000 | 15,000 |
| Premium on $250,000 group-term life insurance | 1,710 | 1,368 | 342 | 1,710 |
| Premium on accident/health insurance for entire family | 3,000 | | 3,000 | 3,000 |
| Premium on medical and dental reimbursement plan for entire family | 2,000 | | 2,000 | 2,000 |
| Medical check-up | 250 | | 250 | 250 |
| Premium on disability income insurance | 2,000 | | 2,000 | 2,000 |
| Company car (50% business use) | 6,000 | 3,000 | 3,000 | 6,000 |
| Professional memberships (luncheon clubs and country club) | 4,000 | | 4,000 | 4,000 |
| Group legal plan | 1,500 | | 1,500 | 1,500 |
| Executive financial counseling | 1,000 | 1,000 | | 1,000 |
| Liability insurance (while serving as an officer/director) | 2,000 | | 2,000 | 2,000 |
| Professional education (seminars, etc.) | 5,000 | | 5,000 | 5,000 |
| Travel and entertainment (taxable portion attributable to Tax A. Voider's spouse accompanying him on some trips) | 10,000 | 2,500 | 7,500 | 10,000 |
| Charitable contributions made by corporation to Tax A. Voider's charities | 3,000 | | 3,000 | 3,000 |
| Parking (in special space in employee lot) | 1,000 | | 1,000 | 1,000 |
| Total | $150,000 | $85,868 | $63,682 | $150,000 |

The advantage of this type of plan is that over 40 percent of the compensation is tax-free. If Tax A. Voider were in the 50% marginal tax bracket, the tax savings from these items would approach $25,000. (The tax savings would not be the full 50% of the tax-free compensation because some of the expenditures would be deductible if made by Tax A. Voider individually.)

## IMPORTANCE OF EMPLOYEE
## STATUS TO THE INDIVIDUAL

Whether an individual is self-employed (an independent contractor) or an employee (under the tax laws) is important for two reasons. First, it determines the amount of employment taxes owed. Second, it determines the individual's eligibility to receive certain fringe benefits tax free. An employer-employee relationship is present when the person for whom the services are performed has the right to control and direct the individual who performs the services; not only as to the result to be accomplished, but also as to the means by which that result is accomplished.

A shareholder can also be an employee of the corporation. For most tax law purposes, a sole proprietor or partner is not considered an employee. For many owners of closely held businesses, the ability to retain employee status is an important advantage of incorporating the business.

When an individual is an employee, the employer assumes four federal tax responsibilities which are as follows:

1.  To withhold the employee's share of the social security taxes.
2.  To withhold federal income taxes.
3.  To pay the employer's share of the social security taxes.
4.  To pay federal unemployment taxes.

For 1985, the social security taxes are levied on the employer at a 7.05% rate on the first $39,600 of wages. The employee also pays social security taxes on the first $39,600 of wages, but at a 7.05% rate (for 1985). The federal unemployment taxes are 3.5% of wages up to $7,000. A credit of 2.7% is available for state unemployment taxes paid that can reduce the actual federal rate down to 0.8%.

On the other hand, self-employed individuals are not responsible for social security taxes. Instead, they must pay a self-employment tax. For 1985 this tax is 11.8% of the individual's self-employment income. The amount of self-employment income that is taxed cannot exceed $39,600 minus the amount of the individual's wages that have been subjected to social security taxation.

Most fringe benefits are only tax-exempt when paid to an employee. Employees are eligible for qualified pension, profit sharing, or stock bonus plans. Self-employed individuals are not eligible to contribute to such plans, but instead contribute to H.R. 10 (Keogh) plans. Some fringe benefits provisions do consider self-employed individuals to be "employees." Examples of such provisions include those providing a tax exemption for benefits paid under an employee education assistance plan or a dependent care assistance program. More details on the specific compensation forms are presented next.

## CURRENT AND DEFERRED CASH COMPENSATION

The variety of current and deferred cash-compensation plans is limitless. Our discussion here is divided into three parts—current compensation, short-run deferred compensation, and long-run deferred compensation.

### Current Cash Compensation

The payment of current cash compensation is largely motivated by the employee's current consumption needs. Quite often some portion of the employee's cash compensation represents a bonus based upon his performance or the firm's performance. The payment of bonuses provides the employer with the flexibility to make discretionary payments when times are good and to withhold the payments when times are bad.

The base wages (and any bonuses that are paid) are taxable to the employee when received. These amounts are deductible by the employer when accrued or paid depending upon the employer's method of accounting. An employer that uses the accrual method of accounting should accrue the bonuses prior to year-end in order to accelerate the deductibility of the expense.

### Deferred Cash Compensation

Deferred compensation is any plan under which the payment for services is received in a year later than the year in which the services were rendered. One type of deferred compensation plan is a "pure" cash arrangement whereby the payment of a cash amount is deferred for one or more years.[1] Some of the plans are short-term and provide for a portion of the compensation to be paid each year over a relatively short period (e.g., 5 years). The plan might also call for partial or complete forfeiture of the deferred compensation if the individual terminates his employment. Other arrangements are longer-term and may result in monies being paid when the employee reaches retirement age. For example, one football star signed a contract for the 1983 season that called for deferred compensation payments to begin in the year 2018.

The tax consequences of the plan depend upon whether it is a funded or unfunded plan. An unfunded plan is one where the employer does not unconditionally fund the liability until it comes due. Thus, the employee takes the position of a general creditor. An employee who uses the cash method of accounting does not report the income from an unfunded plan until the amount is actually or constructively received. The compensation payment cannot be deducted by the employer until the employee is taxed on the income.

A funded plan ordinarily involves the employer establishing a trust to receive the payment on behalf of the employee, or the employer providing the employee with a negotiable promissory note. The employee is taxed on the deferred compensation amount at the time his right to payment becomes nonforfeitable. Funded plans are attractive when some doubt exists as to the employer's ability to pay the deferred compensation liability. Two alternative forms of the funded plan that permit the employee to obtain a tax deferral involve (1) having the payments made to an escrow agent who invests the funds and does not make the money available to the employee until a specified date, or (2) having the payments made to the trust be forfeitable if a certain occurrence takes place. Both arrangements provide for funding of the liability, yet do not result in constructive receipt and current taxation of the income by the employee.

**EXAMPLE 10-1.**    Tax A. Voider earns $250,000 annually from the Big Wheel Corporation. $150,000 of this amount is paid in current cash compensation. The remainder is to be paid at the time of Tax A. Voider's death, or in 10 annual installments payable after Tax A. Voider's retirement. Tax A. Voider is currently taxed on $150,000 of the compensation. The remainder of the income is not taxed until it is paid to Tax A. Voider or his estate, since it is an unfunded deferred compensation arrangement.

**EXAMPLE 10-2.**    Assume the facts remain the same as in the preceding example except that Big Wheel annually transfers $100,000 to a trust to hold and invest the funds for the executive's benefit. The executive's right to these monies (plus interest) is nonforfeitable. Tax A. Voider is taxed on the entire $250,000, since the deferred compensation liability has been funded and it is not forfeitable. A tax deferral could have been obtained had the funds instead been transferred to an escrow agent who invested them on behalf of the employer and these amounts were not made available to Tax A. Voider until the designated dates.

## RESTRICTED PROPERTY RULES

### General Rule

The restricted property rules apply when a taxpayer (ordinarily, an individual) performs services (either as an employee or an independent contractor) and receives in exchange real or personal property at no cost or a reduced cost. Ordinarily, the excess of the property's fair market value over the amount (if any) paid for the property is taxable when the property is received. The income recognition is deferred if the property rights are not transferrable or are subject to a substantial risk of forfeiture. This tax deferral lasts until the first taxable year in which the property rights are transferable or are not subject to a substantial risk of forfeiture. The property is valued without regard to any of the restrictions, except those restrictions whose terms will never lapse.

**EXAMPLE 10-3.** Tax A. Voider is an employee of Oilco. Under the terms of her employment agreement she can purchase 1,000 shares of Oilco stock on the last day of each year during the period 19X0–19X4. The purchase price of each share is $10. On December 31, 19X0 Oilco stock is selling for $100 per share. If Tax A. Voider purchases the shares on that date for the $10 price, she realizes $90,000 of compensation [($100 − $10) × 1,000]. This income is taxable in 19X0. The basis for the shares equals the sum of Tax A. Voider's cost ($10,000), plus the amount of income that is recognized ($90,000), or $100,000. Her holding period commences on the purchase date.

**EXAMPLE 10-4.** Assume the facts remain the same as in the preceding example except that the stock may not be transferred for a period of 5 years from the date of the stock purchase, or December 31, 19X5. The stock's fair market value on December 31, 19X5 is $160 per share. Tax A. Voider does not recognize any income in 19X0. Instead, she must recognize $150,000 [($160 − $10) × 1,000] in 19X5. The basis for the shares in 19X5 equals the sum of the amount expended for the shares ($10,000), plus the income that is recognized ($150,000), or $160,000. The holding period commences at the earlier of the date that the property becomes transferable, or the date it is not subject to a substantial risk of forfeiture.

One special type of restricted property plan that has become extremely popular with the high technology firms involves the use of a second class of stock that is known as junior stock. Junior stock is issued to an employee at a price that is below the price of the company's common stock. This stock cannot be sold and can only be transferred back to the employer corporation. Employees may exchange their junior stock for common stock when certain performance goals have been achieved. The receipt of junior stock is tax-free since there is a substantial risk of forfeiture.

### Substantial Risk of Forfeiture

A substantial risk of forfeiture is present when the property rights that are transferred are directly or indirectly conditioned upon the future performance of substantial services or the occurrence of some other condition. Examples of substantial risks of forfeiture include the requirement that an employee: (1) sell stock back to the corporation (at his original acquisition cost) should he terminate his employment before a predetermined date; (2) return the stock to the corporation if the employer's earnings do not exceed a predetermined level; or (3) return stock to a former employer should he violate a noncompetition covenant. The risk that the value of property will decline during a certain period of time does not constitute a substantial risk of forfeiture.

### Transferability of Property

An individual's property rights are transferable when any interest in the property can be transferred to any other person *and* the transferee's rights to the property are not subject to a substantial risk of forfeiture.

### Special Election

A special election is available which permits the taxpayer to report income from the receipt of restricted property in the taxable year in which the property is received. The income reported equals the excess of the property's fair market value at the time of the receipt over the amount (if any) paid for the property. Valuation of the property again takes place without regard to any of the restrictions, except those restrictions whose terms will never lapse.

This election permits the ordinary income to be determined as of the date of the transfer (instead of the date that the property rights become transferable, or are first not subject to a substantial risk of forfeiture). Any subsequent appreciation receives capital gain treatment. If no election is made, the appreciation represents a mix of ordinary income and capital gain as illustrated in the Example 10-5. The election is irrevocable (except with IRS consent) and must be made no later than 30 days after the transfer date.

The restricted property's basis equals the sum of the amount paid for the property, plus any income reported as a result of the special election. The holding period for the property commences on the date the property transfer occurs. If the election is made and the property forfeited, the amount of loss that can be claimed equals the excess of the amount paid for the property over the amount realized on the forfeiture. No deduction can be claimed for income recognized as a result of making the special election. Ordinarily, the loss represents a capital loss.

EXAMPLE 10-5.   Assume the facts remain the same as in Example 10-4 except that the 1,000 shares of Oilco stock are sold for $200 per share in 19X7. A comparison of the results with and without the special election is presented as follows:

|  | No Election | Special Election |
|---|---|---|
| Income recognized in 19X0 | None | $ 90,000 (ordinary income) |
| Income recognized in 19X5 | $150,000 (ordinary income) | None |
| Income recognized in 19X7 | 40,000 (long-term capital gain) | 100,000 (long-term capital gain) |
| Total income recognized | $190,000 | $190,000 |

If no special election is made, the $150,000 of ordinary income calculated in Example 10-4 must be recognized when the substantial risk of forfeiture is eliminated. Only the excess of the $200 selling price over the property's $160 basis ($150 + $10) receives capital gain treatment. The special election accelerates the recognition of the ordinary income by 5 years. Here the price appreciation is sufficient to offer an offsetting advantage of $60,000 of additional long-term capital gain. Such an advantage may not always be there. For example, if the stock price did not increase from 19X0 to 19X7, both alternatives would require the recognition of $90,000 [ ($100 − $10) × 1,000] of ordinary income. The special election would put the taxpayer at a disadvantage since it would accelerate the income recognition process by 5 years.

### Employer Deduction

The employer claims a deduction equal to the ordinary income recognized by the taxpayer. This deduction is available in the employer's taxable year in which or with which ends the taxable year in which the taxpayer recognizes the income. When the taxpayer providing the services is an employee, no deduction can be claimed unless federal income taxes are withheld from the compensation amount.

## FRINGE BENEFITS

Numerous exclusions for fringe benefits are available to employees as you can see in Figure 10-1. Fringe benefits may fit into one of three categories. Some benefits are completely tax-free. Others are tax-free up to a dollar limit. Still other fringe benefits do not qualify for any exclusion. In general, the tax-favored status for a fringe benefit results from a policy decision about the desirability of this form of social welfare being provided by employers.

### Life Insurance

Premiums paid on a group-term life insurance policy provided by an employer are not taxable to an employee if the face amount of the policy is $50,000 or less. If the face amount of the policy exceeds $50,000, the employee is taxed on the premiums "paid" on the portion of the policy in excess of $50,000. Special tables provided by the IRS indicate the monthly premiums for $1,000 of insurance coverage that are considered to be "paid" by the employer and are taxable to the employee. Even if the premium on the group policy is taxable to the employee, the resulting cost is often less than the expenditure that would be required for the employee to purchase an individual policy. The $50,000 exclusion is not available if the plan discriminates in favor of a "key" employee (e.g., an officer of the corporation or one of the corporation's 10 largest shareholders).

Premiums paid by an employer on an individual-term or individual-permanent life insurance policies are taxable to the employee when the benefits are payable to a beneficiary designated by the employee. The premiums are deductible by the employer. If the employer takes out such a policy on an employee and the employer is the beneficiary (key-man life insurance policy), the premium is not taxable to the employee since he derives no direct benefit from the policy. However, the employer can not deduct these premiums. The proceeds from key-man insurance are tax-free to the employer and may provide an indirect benefit to an employee such as funding the firm's acquisition of the employee's stock from his estate.

Split-dollar life insurance policies involve an employer and an employee combining to pay the premium on an individual  life insurance policy. The employer advances and pays the portion of the policy's annual premium equal to the current year's increase in the policy's cash surrender value. The employee pays the remainder of the premium. The employee is not taxed on the advances made by the employer unless they are paid for insurance coverage (instead of being applied towards the cash surrender value). The employer can deduct only the portion of the employee's premium that represents compensation.

### Employee Death Benefits

Employee death benefits represent another exclusion. Employee death benefits are payments made by an employer to the surviving family of an employee solely because of the employee's death. If the payments were, in any way, owed to the employee (e.g., uncollected salary, vested interests under a nonqualified pension plan, etc.) the death benefit exclusion is generally not available. The maximum exclusion is $5,000.

### Medical-Related Benefits

Accident and health insurance premiums paid by the employer are not included in the employee's income. The payments are deductible by the employer. Self-employed individuals are not employees for purposes of these rules. Benefits under these insurance plans are usually excluded from the employee's income as long as they are payments for medical expenses incurred or are for the permanent loss of, or the loss of the use of, a member or function of the employee, spouse, or dependent's body. Also excluded are amounts received under workmen's compensation for work-related injuries or sickness. Payments under a self-insured plan are included in the employee's gross income only if the plan discriminates in favor of "highly compensated" employees.

### Reduced-Cost Services

A third type of fringe benefit exclusion relates to providing employees with reduced cost services—similar to those that they would otherwise have to purchase out of after-tax dollars. The employer can retain a law firm to provide legal services to employees, the employee's spouse, the employee's dependents, or the employee's estate. The employees are not taxed on the cost of the services nor on the benefit they receive. The group legal services plan must not be discriminatory; that is, it must not discriminate in favor of officers, shareholders, or highly compensated individuals. For this exclusion, partners and proprietors are treated as employees.

The value of child care services provided for, or paid for, by the employer in order to enable an employee to work can be excluded from the employee's income. This exclusion is available only if it is provided by the employer as part of a nondiscriminatory plan. If married, each employee's exclusion is limited to the lesser of the earned income for the employee or the employee's spouse. For this exclusion, partners and proprietors are treated as employees.

The value of qualified transportation services provided by an employer can be excluded by an employee. In order to qualify, transportation must meet rather stringent standards. While few companies will find this a significant employee benefit, it does have potential for firms located in relatively small towns or towns that have inadequate public transportation. The value of a parking lot furnished by the employer is not taxed to an employee.

Educational assistance payments made by an employer are excluded from the employee's income and deducted by the employer if they are made under a qualifying plan. A qualifying plan must be in writing and not discriminate in favor of officers, owners, or highly compensated employees. Reimbursements for books, tuition, fees, and supplies can be excluded from income under these plans. (The related employee expense is, of course, nondeductible.) For this exclusion, partners and proprietors are treated as employees. The exclusion is available even when the educational expense would not otherwise qualify for a deduction.

One of the often overlooked fringe benefits available for employees is meals and lodging which are furnished for the benefit of the employer. For the value of meals provided to an employee to be excluded, they must be provided on the business premises of the employer and must be provided for the convenience of the employer. For example, free meals provided to doctors and nurses in a hospital cafeteria so that they will be on call in case of an emergency qualify for the exclusion. For the value of lodging to be excluded from the employee's income, the lodging must be on the employer's business premises; it must be provided for the convenience of the employer; and the employee must be required to accept the lodging as a condition of employment. While the traditional example of "excluded lodging" is the value of an apartment complex manager's apartment, the law is broad enough to cover lodging as diverse as a construction camp located in a foreign country or the White House.

### Miscellaneous Fringe Benefits

A number of miscellaneous forms of fringe benefits are less often encountered. Because of their limited use, only a brief discussion as to their taxability will be presented.

Many employers provide company-owned cars for use in business travel. If the employee also uses the automobile for personal activities (e.g., vacations, weekend use, or commuting), then a portion of the value of the automobile must be reported as compensation. Alternatively, the employee can reimburse the employer for the expenses related to the personal use of the automobile. One often-used method for determining the reimbursement amount is to establish a per mile charge that is paid by the employee for personal use of the automobile.

Some firms provide their employees with country club and social club memberships to be used for business entertainment. Provided that the country club is primarily used for business purposes, the portion of the dues related to business usage of the membership are deductible by the employer and not taxed to the employee. Similarly, dues paid to professional organizations and for attendance at meetings and seminars are not taxable to the employee.

### New Fringe Benefit Rules

The 1984 Tax Act changed the taxability of fringe benefits by creating a series of four new tax-exempt fringe benefit categories. These categories place into the Tax Code for the most part the tax exemption that most of these fringe benefits formerly had under the accepted IRS practices. The four categories are:

1. *No Additional Cost Services.* These include any service provided by an employer for use by an employee if the service is offered for sale to customers in the conduct of its trade or business and the employer incurs no additional cost in providing the service to the employee (e.g., airline travel for employees provided on a space-available basis).

2. *Qualified Employee Discount.* These include discounts on property (other than real property or property held for investment purposes) or services that are offered for sale to customers in the employer's trade or business in which the employee is performing the services. The discount offered must not exceed the employer's gross profit percentage for the property items or 20% of the selling price for service items.

3. *Working Condition Fringes.* These are any property or services provided to an employee of the employer to the extent that, if the employee paid for such property or service, the payment would be deductible. This type of fringe benefit also includes parking provided to an employee on or near the business premises of the employer and the value of any on-premises athletic facilities provided by the employer even though such amounts would not normally be deductible.

4. *De Minimis Fringe Benefits.* A "de minimis" fringe benefit means any property or service which is so small so as to make ac-

counting for it unreasonable or administratively impracticable. Employer-provided eating facilities provided for employees is a de minimis fringe if the facility is located on or near the business premises of the employer and the revenue derived from the facility equals or exceeds the facility's operating costs.

Application of the above rules is not intended to replace statutory exemptions already in the Tax Code for fringe benefits. The no-additional cost services, qualified employee discounts, and subsidized dining facility exclusions must be available to all employees with no discrimination in favor of an officer, owner, or highly-compensated employee of the firm. The rules are effective January 1, 1985. Because of the complexity of the area and the money involved, one may expect to see extensive interpretations of these exclusions for particular benefits to be forthcoming from the IRS.

## QUALIFIED PENSION, PROFIT SHARING, AND STOCK BONUS PLANS

Qualified pension, profit sharing, and stock bonus plans are special compensation plans that receive preferential treatment under the tax laws. This portion of the chapter examines the advantages and disadvantages of these plans, the types of plans, the requirements for a qualified plan, the taxation of the benefits to the employee, and the deduction available to the employer.

### Advantages/Disadvantages of a Qualified Plan

The primary benefits of a qualified plan are as follows:

1. Employer contributions to the plan are tax-free to the employee until he receives the benefits.
2. Employer contributions to the plan are deductible when paid.
3. The income of the plan accumulates tax-free.

4.  In the event of the employee's death, part or all of the distribution to a beneficiary may be excluded from the estate tax.

5.  Lump-sum distributions from the plan are eligible for special 10-year income averaging and/or capital gains treatment.

These benefits can be contrasted to benefits from a similar plan that does not meet the special tax law requirements (a nonqualified plan). Under a nonqualified plan, employer contributions are taxed to the employee, as soon as they are not subject to a substantial risk of forfeiture. The employer can deduct the contributions only when they are taxable to the employee. The income of the plan is taxed when it is earned. Distributions from the plan are taxed when received (either as an annuity or a lump-sum) without any special averaging provision (other than the regular 4-year income averaging benefits).

Major disadvantages of the qualified plans are as follows:

1.  The plan must satisfy a rather rigid set of rules regarding vesting, participation, and discrimination in order to qualify for the special tax benefits.

2.  The administration and compliance costs may be higher for a qualified plan than for a nonqualified plan.

### Types of Plans

The qualified pension, profit sharing, and stock bonus plan rules provide for a number of different compensation arrangements. The more common of these plans are described below.

1.  *Pension Plan.*  A pension plan provides benefits for employees or their beneficiaries after retirement. The benefits paid do not depend on the amount of the employer corporation's profits. There are two types of pension plans. A *defined contribution plan* requires that each employee have a separate account into which a share of the employer's contributions is paid and a share of the plan's annual income is credited. The employer's contributions are made based on a predetermined formula (e.g., a given amount per hour worked).

The retirement benefits to be received by an employee are based upon the amount in the individual's account at retirement. A *defined benefit plan* provides retirement benefits to an individual employee according to a specified formula (e.g., retirement benefits under the plan are pegged at 2% times the number of years of service times the employee's average compensation for his last three years of employment).

2.   *Profit-Sharing Plan.*   A profit-sharing plan is a defined contribution plan established by an employer to permit his employees or their beneficiaries to participate in profits. The plan provides a specified formula for allocating the contributions to the plan among the participants and for distributing the funds accumulated under the plan after a fixed number of years, the attainment of a stated age, or upon the occurrence of an event (e.g., retirement or disability).

3.   *Stock Bonus Plan.*   A stock bonus plan is a defined contribution plan established by an employer to provide benefits similar to a profit-sharing plan, except that the employer contributions do not depend upon profits and the benefits are paid in stock of the employer corporation.

4.   *Cash or Deferred Pay Plans.*   Some profit-sharing and stock bonus plans permit the employee to receive cash now or to have the employer make a cash contribution of a portion of his salary to an employee trust. The amount of salary contributed to the trust is treated as a salary reduction and is not taxed to the employee until it is distributed. Some plans provide for the employer to partially or fully match the employee's contribution to the plan.

Qualified plans can contain a number of special arrangements such as employee stock ownership plans (ESOPs); tax-sheltered annuities; special savings plans; and payments for sickness, accident, hospitalization and medical expenses of retired employees. These plans are beyond the scope of our coverage here.

### Requirements

The qualified pension, profit-sharing and stock bonus plan requirements are quite complex, and competent tax advice should be sought before a business establishes a plan. The principal requirements are outlined as follows:

1. If the plan payments are made to a trust, the trust must meet the tax law requirements for an employee trust.

2. The plan must be permanent and for the exclusive benefit of the employees or their beneficiaries.

3. Contributions to the plan must not discriminate in favor of the shareholders, officers, or highly compensated individuals. These contributions may be made by the employer, the employee, or both.

4. Benefits provided by the plan must not discriminate in favor of shareholders, officers, or highly compensated individuals.

5. The plan must cover at least (1) 70% of all employees or (2) 80% of all eligible employees, provided at least 70% of all employees are eligible to participate in the plan.

6. The plan must meet minimum vesting standards. This means that the employee's rights under the plan must be nonforfeitable according to one of three alternative vesting schedules—the 10-year rule, the 5–15 year rule or the rule of 45.

7. For defined contribution plans, the annual addition to the employee's account must not exceed the lesser of $30,000 or 25% of the employee's compensation. For defined benefit plans, the benefit that is payable to an employee must not exceed the lesser of $90,000 or 100% of the employee's compensation for the three years in which he earned the largest amount of compensation. (These amounts will be adjusted for changes in the cost of living starting in 1988.)

8. For both defined benefit and defined contribution plans, certain minimum funding standards must be satisfied.

9. Special rules apply to "top heavy" plans. Top heavy plans are those defined benefit or defined contribution plans where the benefits or contributions provided by the plan to key employees exceed 60% of the aggregate benefits or contributions provided by the plan.

10. The plan must comply with all of the reporting and disclosure requirements provided for qualified plans.

## Taxability of the Benefits to the
## Employees or Their Beneficiaries

Benefits paid by the employee trust to an employee or his beneficiary are taxable as ordinary income. When the payments are received other than in a lump-sum, the annuity rules described in Chapter 3 apply. Because the employer makes contributions to the plan that are tax-exempt to the employee, normally the employee does not have any investment in the plan. Thus, all distributions are fully taxable as ordinary income. An employee has an investment in the plan only to the extent that he has made contributions to the plan. To the extent that such an investment does exist, it is recovered by using the general annuity formula or the special three-year cost recovery rule outlined in Chapter 3.

Employees or their beneficiaries can also receive lump-sum distributions from a qualified plan. Three tax treatments are possible for these distributions. First, the portion of the distribution that is attributable to pre–1974 service is eligible for capital gain treatment. The remainder of the distribution is treated as ordinary income and is eligible for a special 10-year income averaging benefit. Alternatively, an election can be made to forgo the capital gain treatment and apply the 10-year averaging rules to the portion of the distribution attributable to pre–1974 service. If a lump-sum distribution includes appreciated stock or securities of the employer corporation, the appreciation is received tax free. The appreciation will be taxed at capital gains rates when the stock or securities are sold. Lump-sum distributions also can be received tax free if they are contributed ("rolled over") into an IRA within 60 days of their receipt.

## Deduction for the Employer
## Corporation

Contributions made by the employer corporation are deductible. The deduction for a pension plan is limited to the greater of: (1) the amount needed to satisfy the minimum funding requirements for the plan, or (2) (a) the normal cost of the plan plus an amount equal to one-tenth of the past service credits or (b) the amount needed to fund the unfunded current and past service credits of all employees at a level amount over the remaining future service time of each employee. Amounts paid in excess of this limitation are carried over and deducted in future years.

Employer contributions to a stock bonus and/or a profit-sharing plan are limited to 15% of the compensation paid or accrued during the taxable year to all employees under the stock bonus or profit-sharing plan. If contributions fall below the 15% ceiling, the unused limitation amount can be carried forward and used in future years to permit additional contributions to be deducted. If contributions are in excess of the 15% ceiling, the excess contributions can be used against the excess limitation from an earlier year or carried over to a later year.

Contributions made to a stock bonus and/or a profit-sharing plan *and* a pension plan are limited to the greater of 25% of the compensation paid or accrued during the taxable year to all employees covered by the plans, or the amount of the minimum funding requirement. Excess contributions can be carried over and deducted in later years. Contributions made to a qualified plan can be made after the end of the employer-corporation's taxable year, provided they are made by the due date for the tax return (including any extensions).

## H.R. 10 (KEOGH) PLANS

H.R. 10 (Keogh) plans are the self-employed individual's equivalent to a qualified pension plan. For many years there was a substantial disparity in the benefits provided to shareholder-employees under the qualified plan rules and the benefits provided to a self-employed individual under the H.R. 10 plan rules. The difference was so substantial that it provided a major incentive for incorporating a business. Tax law changes enacted in 1982 removed nearly all of the major differences between these two types of retirement plans for tax years beginning in 1984.

The H.R. 10 plans offer the same three major advantages as the qualified plan: (1) a current deduction for contributions made to the plan; (2) a tax exemption for income earned by the plan; and (3) a tax deferral for plan contributions and earnings until received by a beneficiary.

### Types of Plans

The contributions to H.R. 10 plans are generally made to a separate trust or custodial account with a bank or financial advisor serving as the custodian or trustee. Alternatively, the funds can be invested in annuity contracts, special investment certificates, or special U.S. bonds. Contributions made to H.R. 10 plans must vest immediately for the employee's benefit.

An H.R. 10 plan can be either a pension plan or a profit-sharing plan. The pension plan can be either a defined contribution or a defined benefit type of plan. The profit-sharing plan form has its contributions and benefits dependent upon the unincorporated entity's profits. Benefits can not be withdrawn from the plan until age 59½ (except in the case of a disability). Withdrawals must start at the later of age 70½ or the time of retirement.

### Eligibility

H.R. 10 plans are available for self-employed individuals. Not all partners are eligible to contribute to an H.R. 10 plan. A partner who is not active in the partnership and derives only a return on his partnership interest can not contribute to an H.R. 10 plan based upon his allocable share of the partnership's earnings.

H.R. 10 plans come under the same coverage requirements outlined earlier for qualified plans. As a result, the 70 and 80% minimums must be satisfied for all employees of a partnership or proprietorship in order to permit the partner or proprietor to participate in a qualified type of plan.

### Contributions to H.R. 10 Plans

Contribution limits for H.R. 10 plans are the same as for qualified pension plans. For a defined contribution plan, contributions can not exceed the lesser of $30,000 or 25% of the self-employed individual's earned income. For a defined benefit plan, the benefit provided must not exceed the lesser of $90,000 or 100% of the self-employed individual's compensation for his three years in which he earned the largest amount of compensation. Like a qualified plan, these amounts will be adjusted for changes in the cost of living starting in 1988.

Contributions to H.R. 10 plans are deductible in determining A.G.I. The ceiling on the deduction is $30,000 or 25% of the individual's earned income. These contributions can be made after the end of the taxable year.

### Distributions from H.R. 10 Plans

Distributions from an H.R. 10 plan are taxed according to the annuity or lump-sum distribution rules that were described for a qualified plan. Like a qualified plan, these distributions may be eligible for capital gain treatment if attributable to pre-1974 service or may be taxed using the special 10-year averaging provisions. An individual may recover (as a return of capital) part of his contribution to an H.R. 10 plan, if he has made voluntary contributions which were not deductible.

## INDIVIDUAL RETIREMENT ACCOUNTS (IRAs)

An IRA has become a very popular vehicle for providing for retirement. Nearly all individuals can contribute to an IRA provided they earn income during the taxable year and make their contributions before they reach age 70½.

An IRA is a personalized pension arrangement that receives the same tax-favored treatment available as with a qualified pension plan or an H.R. 10 plan. IRA contributions are deductible when made. Interest income is earned and accumulates tax-free. Distributions of both the original contributions to the IRA and the interest income are taxable when received.

### Types of IRAs

Many IRAs are set up as domestic trusts through brokerage firms, banks, savings and loan associations, or credit unions. The trust must satisfy certain requirements regarding its creation and operation. The trust assets can be invested in stocks, bonds, certificates of deposit, or other types of income-producing assets. Other forms of IRAs can involve annuity or endowment contracts purchased from an insurance company or certain special issue federal bonds. The rates of return and risks associated with an IRA vary with the type of investment made. As an alternative to the creation of an IRA, some employers will create a "simplified employee pension" (see the following discussion) or permit the employee to make voluntary contributions to a qualified pension plan. Contributions to both of these types of plans are also deductible.

### Deductibility of Contributions

An individual can annually deduct (as a FOR A.G.I. deduction) contributions to an IRA equal to the lesser of $2,000 or 100% of the individual's taxable compensation. Compensation includes all "earned income" minus any FOR A.G.I. deductions that are related to the compensation. For an employee "earned income" includes wages, salaries, bonuses, and taxable fringe benefits. For a self-employed individual this includes professional fees and other forms of self-employment income (after reduction for any expenses) that are derived from performing personal services. Items excluded from "earned income" include nontaxable fringe benefits, interest, dividends, rentals, pensions, annuities, and amounts attributable to a capital investment in an unincorporated entity (e.g., the income earned by a partner from a partnership interest where no personal services are performed).

In some families both spouses are employed. Each spouse can establish and contribute to their own IRA. A separate $2,000 or 100% of compensation limitation applies to each spouse, thus permitting a maximum $4,000 contribution by a husband and wife. If only one spouse is employed, the working spouse can establish a separate IRA for the nonworking spouse. The dollar limitation for total payments into both accounts is the lesser of $2,250 or 100% of compensation. The contributions can be divided between the two plans in whatever manner the two parties choose, except that no more than $2,000 can be placed in either plan account.

Individuals may deposit more to an IRA than their individual limitation, but a nondeductible 6% excise tax is imposed on the excess contribution unless it is withdrawn by the due date for the tax returns. This penalty is imposed each year until the excess contribution is withdrawn.

### Distributions from an IRA

Distributions from an IRA are taxable as ordinary income. Because the contributions to the IRA were deductible, no portion of the distribution can be excluded as a return of capital. Unlike the qualified pension plan, no special averaging provisions are available, except for the regular five-year income averaging provisions.

Distributions from an IRA must start by the end of the year in which an individual reaches age 70½ or a nondeductible 10% excise tax is imposed. Amounts that are withdrawn from an IRA before an individual reaches age 59½ are considered to be "premature." A nondeductible 10% excise tax is imposed on premature distributions except where they are made as a result of death, disability, or certain other limited exceptions. This penalty for premature withdrawals is used to encourage individuals to use IRAs as a long-term investment device that is directed towards retirement.

## SIMPLIFIED EMPLOYEE
## PENSION (SEP) PLANS

A simplified employee pension plan represents a combination of a qualified pension plan and an IRA. Under a SEP the employer makes contributions to each employee's IRA instead of creating and maintaining a qualified pension plan to receive the contributions. For small- to medium-sized employers this reduces the administrative cost of a pension plan.

A SEP requires that employer contributions be made on behalf of each employer who is at least 25 years of age and who has performed services for the employer in at least three of the five preceding calendar years. The employee's rights under the plan must be 100% vested, and the plan must not discriminate in favor of highly compensated individuals or shareholders.

Amounts paid to an SEP are taxed to the individual employee. A deduction can be claimed by both the individual employee and the employer for the contributions made to the SEP. The limit on the deduction is the same as for a qualified plan—the lesser of $30,000 (in 1985) or 15% of the employee's compensation. An individual can be a participant in a SEP as well as an H.R. 10 plan or a qualified pension plan. Contributions made to the SEP reduce the dollar limitations for contributions to these other plans. Contributions made to a SEP do not preclude an employee from making a voluntary contribution to an IRA of up to an additional $2,000/$2,250. As with an IRA, contributions to a SEP can be made after year-end.

The IRA rules regarding the taxability of distributions govern withdrawals of employer contributions to a SEP. The IRA rules regarding premature withdrawals, penalties and rollovers, also apply to employer contributions to a SEP.

## EQUITY-ORIENTED COMPENSATION PLANS

A number of compensation plans are based on the performance of the employer's stock. Most of these plans are based upon the actual ownership of the stock or of stock equivalents. The tax consequences of a variety of equity-based plans are examined within this chapter. (You should not overlook the financial accounting reporting requirements and federal and state securities law requirements when evaluating these plans.)

### Incentive Stock Options (ISOs)

Incentive stock option plans must satisfy a series of tax law requirements to receive preferential tax treatment. Properly structured,

ISOs can provide the employee with a tax exclusion at the time the option is received and when it is exercised. If the minimum holding period requirements are met, the employee realizes his entire profit at preferential capital gains rates.

### ISO Requirements

The following requirements must be satisfied for a stock option to qualify as an ISO:

1. The ISO must be granted to an individual as a result of his employment by a corporation, and provide the right to purchase stock of the employer corporation, or its parent or subsidiary corporation.

2. The ISO plan must specify the maximum number of shares that may be issued under the options and the employees eligible to receive the options.

3. The ISO plan must be approved by the shareholders within 12 months of the plan's adoption date.

4. The options must be granted within 10 years of the earlier of the date the plan is adopted or the date the shareholders approve the plan.

5. The option term can not exceed 10 years.

6. The option price must be at least the fair market value of the stock on the date the option is granted.

7. The option must be transferable only at death. (During the employee's lifetime the option can only be exercisable by the employee.)

8. The employee must not own more than 10% of the granting corporation's voting stock (or the stock of either a parent corporation or a subsidiary corporation of the granting corporation) at the time the option is granted.

9. The option must not be exercised at a time while an ISO granted to the employee at an earlier date is still outstanding.

10. The ISOs granted in any calendar year under the plan can not exceed $100,000. (One-half of any amount granted in excess of the $100,000 limit can be carried over for 3 years.)

## Tax Consequences for the Employee

No income is reported when the option is granted to the employee, or when the employee exercises the option. The individual's basis in the acquired shares equals the exercise price. The excess of the fair market value of the stock, over the exercise price on the date that the option is exercised, is a tax preference item for the alternative minimum tax.

The profit reported when the option shares are disposed of is a capital gain if the following two requirements are met:

1. The disposition occurs more than two years after the granting of the option *and* more than one year after the exercise of the option.

2. The individual is an employee of the corporation granting the option (or either a parent corporation or a subsidiary corporation of the granting corporation) at all times, from the date the option is granted until three months before the exercise date.

The application of these rules is illustrated by the following example:

EXAMPLE **10-6.** Very Public Corporation (VPC) grants an ISO to Tax A. Voider for 1,000 shares of its stock on July 1, 19X4. The terms of the plan meet all of the ISO requirements. The exercise price is $60. The tax consequences of exercising the option on August 15, 19X7 when VPC stock is selling for $120 is illustrated for two alternative sale situations.

|  | Situation Number | |
| --- | --- | --- |
|  | 1 | 2 |
| Sale date | December 1, 19X8 | January 1, 19X8 |
| Sale price per share | $150 | $150 |
| Less: Basis of stock | (60) | (60) |
| Equals: Realized gain | $ 90 | $ 90 |
| Income recognized on August 15, 19X7 exercise date (per share): | 0 | 0 |
| Income recognized at time of sale (per share): | | |
|    Ordinary income | 0 | 60 ($120–$60) |
|    Short-term capital gain | 0 | 30 ($150–$120) |
|    Long-term capital gain | 90 ($150 − $60) | 0 |

Since Tax A. Voider met the two holding period requirements, the entire gain on Situation No. 1 receives long-term capital gain treatment. In Situation No. 2 the failure to hold the stock for 1 year after the exercise date converts the "spread" at the exercise date into ordinary income and the capital gain into short-term capital gain.

**EXAMPLE 10-7.**   Assume the facts remain the same as in the preceding example except that Tax A. Voider terminates his VPC employment on January 1, 19X7. Tax A. Voider recognizes $60,000 [($120–$60) × 1,000] of ordinary income when the options are exercised on August 15, 19X7. The $30 ($150–$120) difference between the selling price and Tax A. Voider's basis is short-term or long-term capital gain, depending upon the length of his holding period for the shares.

One of the major drawbacks of ISOs can be the need to accumulate enough cash to be able to exercise the option. The tax laws and some ISO plans permit stock swaps to take place whereby the ISO can be exercised by using stock of the employer corporation as the consideration exchanged to exercise the ISO.

### Tax Consequences for the Employer

The employer corporation claims a deduction for the portion of the employee's profit taxed as ordinary income. Thus, in Situation No. 2 of Example 10-6, Tax A. Voider's failure to satisfy the holding period requirements grants TAV Corporation a $30,000 [($90–$60) × 1,000] compensation deduction when the shares are sold. A similar deduction is available at the exercise date in Example 10-7 because Tax A. Voider failed to meet the employee requirement.

### Nonqualified Stock Options

Nonqualified stock options are those options that do not satisfy the ISO requirements. Quite often the employer corporation intentionally fails the ISO requirements of (1) having the exercise price at least equal the market value of the stock on the grant date, or (2) issuing only $100,000 of ISOs in a given calendar year in order to make the option package more attractive and lucrative to the employee. The tax treatment for a nonqualified stock option depends upon whether the option has an ascertainable market value when it is granted. If the option can be valued, the fair market value of the option is ordinary income when the option is granted. If the option can not be valued, the excess of the stock's fair market value over the option price is ordinary income at the exercise date. The taxpayer's capital gain equals the sales price minus the sum of the exercise price plus the ordinary income that is recognized. The employer corporation claims a deduction equal to the employee's ordinary income at the time that the employee recognizes this income.

**EXAMPLE 10-8.** Assume the facts remain the same as in Situation No. 1 of Example 10-6 except that the exercise price is instead $40. The options are granted at a time when an option is selling for $20. Since the value of the option is ascertainable, Tax A. Voider recognizes $20,000 (1,000 × $20) of ordinary income on the grant date. No income is recognized when the option is exercised. A $90,000 [($150 × 1,000) − ((1,000 × $40) + $20,000)] long-term capital gain is recognized when the stock is sold. The capital gain portion of the two examples remains the same. The additional ordinary income that must be recognized occurs because Tax A. Voider receives increased compensation from the reduction in the option's exercise price.

### Stock Appreciation Rights (SARs)

SARs are issued to an employee as part of a nonqualified stock option plan. The employee receives a stock option for a given number of shares of the employer corporation stock and a SAR covering a similar amount of stock. If the option is exercised, the employee receives the actual shares. The number of shares covered by the SAR is reduced by the shares acquired through exercise of the option. If the SAR is exercised, the employee does not have to come up with cash and/or stock equal to the exercise price. Instead, he receives cash and/or property equal to the difference between the stock's market value at the exercise date and the option's exercise price times the number of shares covered by the SAR that he exercised. The number of shares covered by the stock option is reduced by the shares "acquired" through the exercise of the SAR. The SAR has an advantage in that the employee does not bear any economic risk from having capital tied up in the employer's stock (of course, he still bears a risk that the SARs will be worthless if the stock price drops below the option's exercise price). Since the SAR does not provide ownership of the stock, the income realized from exercise of the SAR is ordinary income. The employer can claim a deduction equal to the ordinary income recognized by the employee.

## REASONABLENESS OF COMPENSATION

A deduction is available for salaries or other compensation for personal services only if the payment is reasonable in amount. The reasonableness of a compensation payment is determined on a case-by-case basis. A high, absolute dollar amount of compensation may be determined to be reasonable. For example, the $1,662,000 salary payment made to the Chairman of a New York Stock Exchange Company in a recent year is not likely to be considered unreasonable. Most often one will see the unreasonable compensation question raised by the IRS in connection with a shareholder-employee of a closely held corporation. The factors cited by one court in determining whether a compensation payment is reasonable in amount include:

1. The employee's qualifications.
2. The nature, extent, and scope of the employee's work.
3. The size of the business.
4. The complexities of the business.
5. A comparison of the salaries paid with the gross and net income amounts.
6. The prevailing rates of compensation for comparable positions in comparable concerns.

Not all of these factors carry an equal weighting. The weight that the IRS or a court will apply to a single (or group of) factor(s) will vary from situation to situation.

All compensation, whether it is taxable or nontaxable to the employee, is tested to determine whether an employee's rewards are unreasonable. If the payment is unreasonable, the corporation loses its deduction for the portion of the compensation payment that is excessive. When the unreasonable compensation is paid to a shareholder-employee, the payment is nearly always recharacterized as a dividend.

## NOTES

1. A deferred compensation plan can also involve the receipt of property for services (e.g., stock of the employer company) over a period of time as a series of restrictions lapses (e.g., 20% of the total number of shares of the employer company's stock that were awarded as a bonus, are released to an employee each year that he/she remains in the firm's employment). Alternatively, one can think of a pension or profit-sharing plan that provides for payments to the employee, commencing at some future date, as a deferred compensation plan.

# ───────11

# NONLIQUIDATING DISTRIBUTIONS BY A BUSINESS ENTITY

Nonliquidating distributions made by a corporation fall into four categories. The first category consists of distributions in which property is distributed to the shareholder and the shareholder does not surrender any of his stock interest. These distributions are generally taxable as dividends. The second category consists of stock redemptions where a property distribution is made to the shareholder and the shareholder surrenders part of his stock interest. These distributions are taxable as dividends unless one of the five capital gain exceptions applies. The third category consists of distributions of additional shares of the distributing corporation's stock, or rights to acquire additional shares of the distributing corporation's stock. Ordinarily, these distributions are tax-free since they do not constitute a property distribution. The fourth category consists of the stock of a subsidiary corporation. This stock can be distributed tax-free if a series of requirements are met.

Slightly different rules apply to distributions made by S corporations. These distributions generally do not represent income to the shareholder since the S corporation's income has previously been taxed to the shareholder. Instead, they are treated as a return of the shareholder's capital investment. Distributions made after the shareholder's capital investment has been fully recovered are taxable.

Distributions of a partnership's current profits, and current distributions that reduce but do not eliminate the partner's interest in the partnership, are treated identically. These distributions reduce the partner's basis for his partnership interest, and gain is recognized only if the amount of cash distributed exceeds the partner's adjusted basis for his partnership interest. Gain may also be recognized if the distribution involves unrealized receivables or substantially appreciated inventory. Further discussions of the nonliquidating distributions made by each of these three entities are presented below.

## NONLIQUIDATING
## CORPORATE DISTRIBUTIONS

### Dividend Distributions

The tax consequences of a dividend distribution to the shareholder and to the distributing corporation must be considered. The following five questions must be answered in order to determine the tax consequences of the distribution to the shareholder:

1. Is the distribution a dividend?
2. What amount of income does the shareholder recognize?
3. Is the distribution eligible for any special tax benefits?
4. What is the basis for any property received?
5. When does the holding period for the property commence?

Each of the five questions is examined below.

### Dividend Definition

The tax laws define a dividend as a distribution of *property* made by a corporation to its shareholders out of its *earnings and profits* for the current taxable year, or out of its earnings and profits accumulated in preceding taxable years after February 28, 1913. The term "property" includes money, securities, and any other property; however, the term does not include stock or stock rights of the distributing corporation. The "earnings and profits" concept differs from both the financial accounting concept of net income and the tax concept of taxable income, so it is impossible to review the corporation's balance sheet or its tax return and determine the taxability of a property distribution with absolute certainty.

Current earnings and profits (E & P) is determined as follows:

|         | Taxable income |
|---------|----------------|
| Plus:   | Income earned by the corporation but not included in determining taxable income |
| Minus:  | Deductions and losses incurred by the corporation but not deducted in determining taxable income |
| Plus:   | Deductions included in determining taxable income but which do not require an economic outlay (special deductions) |
| Plus:   | Special adjustments for "excess" depreciation, capital recovery allowances, or depletion deductions claimed by the corporation |
| Equals: | Current E & P |
| Less:   | Distributions made out of current E & P |
| Equals: | Addition to accumulated E & P |

All distributions are considered to come first out of current E & P, and then out of accumulated E & P.

EXAMPLE **11-1.** Tax A. Voider owns all of the ABC Corporation stock. ABC has current and accumulated E & P of $9,000 and $7,000, respectively. A $12,000 distribution made to Tax A. Voider during the current year is treated as coming $9,000 out of current E & P and $3,000 out of accumulated E & P. The full $12,000 distribution is a dividend.

### Income Recognized

Dividend income recognized by a noncorporate shareholder equals the money distributed, plus the fair market value of all noncash property distributed. Any liabilities of the distributing corporation that are assumed or acquired by the shareholder reduce the amount of dividend income recognized. This amount is taken into gross income on the day the shareholder receives the distribution.

The dividend income recognized by a corporate shareholder is determined by using a two-part rule. The income amount equals the money distributed, plus the lesser of (1) the fair market value of the nonmoney property distributed; or (2) the sum of the adjusted basis (in the distributing corporation's hands) of the nonmoney property distributed *plus* the amount of gain (if any) recognized by the distributing corporation on the distribution. As with the noncorporate shareholder, the amount of the distribution is reduced by liabilities of the distributing corporation that are assumed or acquired by the corporate shareholder.

EXAMPLE **11-2.**   Tax A. Voider owns all of the DEF Corporation stock. DEF's current and accumulated E & P totals $40,000. DEF distributes to Tax A. Voider $10,000 cash and XYZ Corporation stock having a fair market value and adjusted basis of $15,000 and $7,000, respectively. An $8,000 ($15,000 − $7,000) gain is recognized by DEF on the distribution. Tax A. Voider has received a $25,000 ($10,000 + $15,000) dividend. Had the distribution instead been received by a corporate shareholder, the corporation would also report $25,000 ($10,000 + $7,000 + $8,000) of dividend income.

Distributions made in excess of the distributing corporation's E & P balance represent a tax-free return of the shareholder's capital investment. As such, they reduce the shareholder's basis for his stock. Once this basis has been reduced to zero, any additional amounts received are treated as gain from the sale or exchange of the stock. Ordinarily, these amounts represent capital gain.

EXAMPLE **11-3.**   Tax A. Voider owns all of the GHI Corporation stock. GHI's current and accumulated E & P total $15,000. Tax A.

Voider's basis for the GHI stock is $25,000. A $35,000 distribution made by GHI would represent $15,000 of dividend income and a $20,000 tax-free recovery of the capital investment. Tax A. Voider's adjusted basis for his GHI stock is $5,000 after the distribution.

### Special Tax Benefits for Dividends

An individual shareholder can exclude $100 ($200 if a joint return is filed) of dividend distributions received from a domestic corporation. The increased exclusion is available for joint return filers without regard to which spouse owns the stock investment. This exclusion is not available for distributions representing a return of the shareholder's capital investment, distributions eligible for capital gain treatment, or most distributions made by an S corporation.

A corporate shareholder can claim a special dividends-received deduction. This deduction is intended to mitigate the effects of double taxation that occurs when the income is taxed to the distributing corporation at the time it is earned and again to the shareholder corporation at the time it is distributed. This deduction is not available for distributions which represent a return of the shareholder's capital investment, distributions eligible for capital gain treatment, or distributions made by most foreign corporations. The dividends-received deduction equals 85% of the amount that has been taken into gross income. The dividends-received deduction percentage is reduced below 85% where the corporate shareholder owns a non-controlling interest in the distributing corporation and the investment is partially or totally financed with borrowed funds. This prevents the taxpayer from obtaining an interest deduction for the interest payment and a dividends-received deduction that makes most of the dividend payment tax exempt.

**EXAMPLE 11-4.** Assume the facts remain the same as in the portion of Example 11-2 where the distribution was received by the corporate shareholder. The dividends-received deduction equals 85% of the $25,000 gross income amount, or $21,250.

The 85% dividends-received deduction is limited to 85% times the shareholder corporation's taxable income. Taxable income, for this purpose, does not include capital loss carrybacks to the taxable year, the 85% dividends-received deduction, or the net operating loss deduction. The limitation does not apply if the shareholder corporation reports a net operating loss for the taxable year after claiming the 85% dividends-received deduction.

**EXAMPLE 11-5.** JKL Corporation reported the results shown in the following three independent situations:

|  | Situation Number | | |
| --- | --- | --- | --- |
|  | 1 | 2 | 3 |
| Dividend income | $1,000,000 | $1,000,000 | $1,000,000 |
| Operating income (loss) | –0– | (150,000) | (150,001) |
| Taxable income before dividends-received deduction | $1,000,000 | $ 850,000 | $ 849,999 |
| Dividends-received deduction | | | |
| Lesser of: | | | |
| (1)  85% × $1,000,000 or | | | |
| (2)  85% × taxable income (before dividends-received deduction) | (850,000) | (722,500) | (850,000) |
| Taxable income | $ 150,000 | $ 127,500 | $ (1) |

The limitation does not reduce the amount of the dividends-received deduction in Situation No. 1. However, in Situation No. 2, the limitation reduces the dividends-received deduction claimed from $850,000 to $722,500. Since a net operating loss is created in Situation No. 3, the full deduction can be claimed. The additional $1 of operating expenses reduces taxable income by $127,501. In Situation No. 3, the IRS may attempt to reallocate income from other years to the current year, or to reallocate expenses from the current year to other years to avoid the creation of the loss.

Members of a group of related corporations that file separate tax returns and that receive dividend distributions from other group members can elect to claim a 100% dividends-received deduction, with respect to these distributions. The related group (known as an affiliated group) includes a common parent corporation and each subsidiary corporation having at least 80% of its voting power and

80% of each class of nonvoting stock owned by the parent corporation or by another group member. (Starting in 1985 the second requirement becomes 80% of the value of the outstanding stock). The earnings must be accumulated and distributed while both the distributing and shareholder corporations are members of the affiliated group. This election provides one of the major benefits of filing a consolidated tax return, without requiring the corporations to engage in the additional recordkeeping required when such an election is made.

### Basis of Property Received

The basis of property received by a noncorporate shareholder equals the amount of money or the fair market value of the nonmoney property that is received. The basis of property received by a corporate shareholder equals the amount of money received or the lesser of (1) the fair market value of the nonmoney property received, or (2) the sum of the adjusted basis of the nonmoney property (in the hands of the distributing corporation) received, plus the amount of gain recognized by the distributing corporation on the distribution.

### Holding Period for Property Received

The holding period for property received by a noncorporate shareholder begins on the distribution date. The date for commencing the holding period for a corporate shareholder depends upon whether the distributing corporation recognizes a gain on the distribution. If gain was recognized, the holding period commences on the distribution date. If no gain was recognized by the distributing corporation and a carryover basis is used, the holding period begins on the later of the date the property or the stock was acquired. If property that has declined in value was distributed, the holding period commences on the distribution date.

### Recognition of Gain by the Distributing Corporation

In general, the distributing corporation recognizes gain (but not loss) when it distributes property to its shareholders. The amount and character of the gain is determined as if the property had been sold at the time of the distribution. A number of exceptions to this general rule exist which permit the gain to go unrecognized. These exceptions are listed below:

1.  A distribution of an obligation of the distributing corporation.
2.  A distribution that is a "qualified dividend" and which is made with respect to qualified stock.
3.  A distribution of stock or an obligation of a controlled corporation.

A qualified dividend is a distribution of property (other than inventory, accounts receivable, or notes receivable) to a noncorporate shareholder where the property was used by the distributing corporation in the active conduct of a trade or business. The trade or business must have been conducted during the 5-year period ending on the distribution date and not have been acquired in a tax-free transaction. The noncorporate shareholder must have held at least 10 percent of the distributing corporation's outstanding stock at all times during the shorter of the 5-year period ending on the date of the distribution or the corporation's entire existence.

The above rules apply to distributions made after June 14, 1984. They replace a more liberal set of rules which did not require the recognition of gain when a property distribution was paid except in the case of LIFO inventory, property subject to a liability in excess of its adjusted basis, installment obligations, and recapture property that was distributed.

### Constructive Distributions

Some dividend payments are never formally authorized by the board of directors. Instead, they represent constructive dividends, or disguised dividends, that result because the taxing authorities are unwilling to accept a transaction as it was originally reported by the corporation or the shareholder. Transactions that can result in a constructive dividend, and the amount of dividend income that is recognized, are indicated as follows:

| Transaction | Constructive Dividend Amount |
|---|---|
| 1. Unreasonable compensation paid to shareholder-employee. | 1. Amount of compensation paid in excess of a reasonable allowance for services rendered. |
| 2. Unreasonable rentals, interest, or royalties paid for the use of property. | 2. Amount of compensation paid in excess of reasonable allowance for property used. |
| 3. Sale of property to corporation at an excessive price. | 3. Amount paid for property in excess of reasonable price. |
| 4. Sale of property to shareholder at a bargain price. | 4. Excess of the fair market value of the property over the sale price to the shareholder. |
| 5. Corporate advances to shareholder. | 5. Amount of the advances that cannot be classified as a loan. |
| 6. Corporate payments on a debt issue that is reclassified as an equity issue. | 6. Interest payments are reclassified as dividend payments and principal payments are reclassified as stock redemptions. |
| 7. Corporate payment for shareholder's benefit (e.g., payment of a shareholder expense). | 7. Amount of the payment for which it can be shown that the shareholder derived a direct or indirect economic benefit. |

The reasonableness of a corporate payment is determined by the facts and circumstances of the situation.

### Stock Dividends

A stock dividend can be either taxable or tax-free, but most stock dividends are tax-free. The tax-free nature of the distribution originates from the fact that the distributing corporation's stock does not constitute "property" for dividend purposes. No part of the distribution is included in gross income. A portion of the basis of the shares with respect to which the distribution was made (known as the underlying shares) must be allocated to the dividend shares.

EXAMPLE 11-6.    Tax A. Voider owns two blocks of ABC Corporation stock. Each block contains 100 shares of common stock and the blocks were purchased at prices of $40 and $60 per share. On December 1, 19X1, ABC pays a stock dividend of one share of additional common stock (selling for $80 per share), for each ten shares that are held. The basis for the 200 shares of common stock already held and the 20 dividend shares that are received is determined as follows.

| Block No. | Number of Shares | Adjusted Basis | Dividend Shares | Total Shares | Post-Dividend Per Share Adjusted Basis |
|---|---|---|---|---|---|
| 1 | 100 | $4,000 | 10 | 110 | $36.364[a] |
| 2 | 100 | 6,000 | 10 | 110 | 54.545[b] |

[a] $\dfrac{\$4,000}{100 + 10} = \$36.3636$        [b] $\dfrac{\$6,000}{100 + 10} = \$54.5454$

The holding period for the dividend shares commences on the original acquisition date for the underlying stock. If Tax A. Voider decides to sell his 20 "dividend" shares, he should select shares from Block No. 2 since this results in a smaller capital gain being recognized. If the Block No. 2 shares have been held at least 6 months (for underlying stock purchased after June 22, 1984), then the capital gain that is recognized will be long-term.

Some stock dividends are taxable. Examples of taxable stock dividends include distributions where:

1.  A shareholder can elect to receive stock of the distributing corporation or property (e.g., money).

2.  Some shareholders receive property and other shareholders receive an increase in their proportionate interest in the distributing corporation's assets or earnings.

3.  Some holders of common stock receive preferred stock and other common stock holders receive additional common stock.

Included in the first category of taxable stock dividends are some of the dividend reinvestment plans in which the shareholder can elect to receive a cash payment or have the dividend payment used to purchase additional stock of the distributing corporation. In the case of all taxable stock dividends, corporate and noncorporate shareholders include the fair market value of the stock or stock rights that are received in their gross income.

A special exception to the taxable stock dividend rules applies to qualified reinvestment plans of public utility companies.

### Stock Rights

Stock rights can be distributed tax-free to shareholders. If the stock rights are exercised or sold, a basis allocation between the underlying stock and the rights themselves must occur if the fair market value of the rights on the distribution date is at least 15% of the fair market value of the underlying stock. The basis allocation is elective if the fair market value of the rights is less than 15% of the fair market value of the underlying stock. No basis allocation can be made if the stock rights are allowed to lapse. The basis allocation is based on the relative market values of the underlying stock and the stock rights on the distribution date. If the stock rights are exercised, the basis for the acquired stock equals the cash outlay made plus the amount of the basis (if any) allocated to the rights. An allocation of basis to the stock rights reduces the gain recognized when the stock rights are sold or when the stock rights are exercised and the stock so acquired is subsequently sold.

EXAMPLE **11-7.**   Tax A. Voider receives a tax-free distribution of stock rights. On the distribution date, the market values of the rights and the underlying stock are $1,250 and $10,000, respectively. The basis of the underlying stock is $6,000. An election to allocate part of the basis of the stock to the stock rights results in the rights having a $667 [$6,000 × ($1,250/($1,250 + $10,000) )] basis. By making this allocation, the gain recognized on an immediate sale of the rights for their market value is reduced from $1,250 to $583 ($1,250 − $667).

## DISTRIBUTIONS OF STOCK OF A CONTROLLED CORPORATION

Stock of a controlled subsidiary corporation can be distributed tax-free if certain requirements are satisfied. This type of tax-free transaction can be used to convert a parent-subsidiary group of corpora-

**FIGURE 11-1**   Distribution of stock of a controlled corporation.

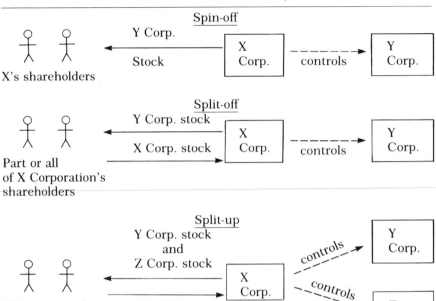

tions into a brother-sister group of corporations (spin-off), or to divide up two corporations so that one shareholder group ends up
owning one corporation, and a second shareholder group ends up
owning the second corporation (split-off or split-up). The three
forms that the distribution can take are illustrated in Figure 11-1.

### Requirements

The following six requirements must be satisfied to have a corporate
division:

1.   The distributing corporation must distribute stock or se-
     curities of a corporation that it controls immediately before
     the distribution. Control is defined here as owning at least
     80% of the voting stock and at least 80% of each class of
     nonvoting stock.

2. The distributing corporation must distribute all the stock and securities of the controlled corporation that it holds immediately before the distribution, or a sufficient amount of stock to constitute control.

3. The distribution must not represent a device to distribute the E & P of the distributing corporation, the controlled corporation, or both.

4. Both the distributing corporation and the controlled corporation must be engaged in the active conduct of a trade or business immediately after the exchange. Each trade or business activity must have been conducted during the entire five-year period preceding the distribution, or have been acquired during this period in a transaction in which no gain or loss was recognized.

5. A business purpose must exist at the corporate level for making the distribution.

6. Immediately after the exchange the shareholders of the distributing corporation must maintain a continuing equity interest in the distributing corporation, the controlled corporation, or both.

### Tax Consequences

No income is recognized by the shareholder if all six requirements are satisfied. In a spin-off transaction, the basis of the shares already held is allocated (based on relative market values) between the shares of both corporations held immediately after the distribution. In a split-off or split-up transaction the basis of the shares redeemed carries over to the shares that are received. If the transaction fails to meet one or more of the requirements, income must be recognized. In this situation the spin-off is treated like a dividend distribution, the split-off is treated like a stock redemption, and the split-up like a corporate liquidation.

If property other than stock of a qualifying corporation is received (boot), the shareholder recognizes income equal to the lesser of his realized gain or the amount of boot received. The character of the boot received in a spin-off is dividend income. In a split-off or split-up the stock redemption rules described in a later section are used to determine whether or not the boot qualifies for capital gain treatment. The basis of any boot property received is its fair market value.

No gain or loss is recognized by the distributing corporation when stock of the controlled corporation is distributed. The distribution of boot property triggers the recognition of gain by the distributing corporation according to the rules outlined for a dividend or stock redemption.

**EXAMPLE 11-8.** TAV Corporation is owned 70% by Tax A. Voider and 30% by individual A. TAV Corporation is valued at $2,500,000. Tax A. Voider and A decide to go their separate ways and no longer want to continue to jointly own TAV Corporation. They agree that TAV Corporation will distribute its JKL Corporation stock, that is worth $650,000 and $100,000 of cash in exchange for all of A's TAV stock. A's basis for the TAV stock is $200,000. The transaction is assumed to meet all of the requirements for a tax-free distribution of the stock of a controlled corporation. A realizes a $550,000 [($650,000 + $100,000) − $200,000] gain on the exchange. Only $100,000 of the gain is recognized. The gain is treated as a capital gain since a hypothetical redemption of TAV stock for the $100,000 cash payment would have received capital gain treatment under the not essentially equivalent to a dividend exception to the stock redemption rules. A's basis for the JKL stock carries over from the TAV stock and is $200,000.

## S CORPORATION
## DISTRIBUTIONS

Distributions made by an S corporation are generally tax-free returns of the shareholder's capital investment. In limited circumstances, the distribution is taxable. Two sets of rules exist regarding an S corporation's distributions, depending upon whether the corporation has an E & P balance that arose (1) in a taxable year in which the corporation was *not* taxed under the rules of Subchapter S or (2) in a pre-1983 taxable year in which the "old" Subchapter S rules were in effect.

If no such E & P balances exist, then money distributions made by an S corporation are tax-free and reduce the shareholder's basis for his stock investment. Any amount received in excess of the shareholder's basis for the stock investment is treated as a gain from the sale or exchange of the investment. Ordinarily, this results in a capital gain.

**EXAMPLE 11-9.** Tax A. Voider owns all the stock of JVB Corporation. The stock, which is a capital asset, has a basis of $60,000. A $40,000 cash distribution made by JVB to Tax A. Voider is tax-free and reduces the basis of the investment to $20,000. If a $70,000 cash distribution were instead made by JVB, the distribution would exhaust Tax A. Voider's basis and require her to recognize a $10,000 capital gain.

A nonmoney "dividend" distribution made by an S corporation is slightly more complicated. The corporation must include in its income the excess of the property's fair market value over its basis as if the property had been sold by the corporation. The fair market value of the property also reduces the recipient shareholder's basis in his stock investment. As with a money distribution, any amount of property distribution in excess of the shareholder's basis for his stock investment is treated as a gain from the sale or exchange of the stock. The shareholder's basis for the property that is received equals its fair market value.

A slightly different procedure is followed if the corporation has an accumulated E & P balance. Distributions first come out of the S corporation's post–1982 accumulated earnings until they are exhausted. Additional money distributions (but not property distributions) can be made tax-free out of pre–1983 earnings of the corporation that were taxed under the Subchapter S rules (known as "previously taxed income"). Both categories of earnings can be distributed tax-free unless they exceed the basis of the stock. Distributions in excess of the basis of the investment result in the recognition of gain from the sale or exchange of the stock. Any further money or nonmoney distributions come out of the S corporation's E & P balance. These distributions are taxable according to the ordinary distribution rules previously outlined and do not reduce the shareholder's basis for his investment. Any distributions made after the E & P balances are exhausted are tax-free and reduce the shareholder's basis for his stock investment until it is exhausted, and then result in a gain being recognized from the sale or exchange of the stock.

## STOCK REDEMPTIONS

A stock redemption represents the acquisition by a corporation of its own stock in exchange for property. As with ordinary distributions, the term "property" represents money, securities, and any other nonmoney property that the corporation uses to make the acquisition.

### General Rule

The general rule is that a stock redemption is treated as a dividend. Capital gain treatment is available only if the stock redemption is: not essentially equivalent to a dividend; substantially disproportionate; a complete termination of the shareholder's interest; a partial liquidation involving the redemption of a noncorporate shareholder's stock; or made in order to pay death taxes. Each of these five exceptions to the general rule is explained later.

A stock redemption is treated as a dividend because it is not thought to be equivalent to a sale or exchange. Both corporate and noncorporate shareholders recognize dividend income and take a basis for the property received according to the rules for ordinary distributions. The basis of the redeemed shares is added to the basis of the stock that the shareholder continues to hold.

EXAMPLE 11-10.   Tax A. Voider holds 1,000 shares of HPS Corporation stock. All shares have a basis of $20. HPS distributes $4,000 to Tax A. Voider in exchange for 50 shares of its stock. If the stock redemption does not satisfy the requirements of one of the capital gain exceptions, Tax A. Voider recognizes $4,000 of dividend income and his remaining 950 shares take a basis of $20,000, or $21.05 per share. If one of the capital gain exceptions can apply to the transaction, Tax A. Voider recognizes a $3,000 capital gain [50 × ($80 − $20)]. The basis of the remaining shares is $20 per share.

Tax planning in this area is aimed at obtaining capital gain treatment so that a shareholder can withdraw funds from a business activity at preferential capital gains rates. Most tax planning actions center upon structuring the redemption so that it satisfies the requirements of one of the capital gain exceptions.

### Substantially Disproportionate Redemption

A substantially disporportionate redemption is one that meets the following three requirements:

1. The shareholder must own less than 50% of the voting stock immediately after the redemption.
2. The ratio of the shareholder's holdings of voting stock to all voting stock that is outstanding immediately after the redemption must be less than 80% of the same ratio before the redemption.
3. The ratio of the shareholder's holdings of common stock to all common stock that is outstanding immediately after the redemption must be less than 80% of the same ratio before the redemption.

The second and third tests when combined prevent a redemption of solely nonvoting stock from being a substantially disproportionate redemption.

A special set of stock attribution rules is used to determine if the various stock redemption requirements have been satisfied. Four types of stock ownership are attributed between related parties:

1. *Family Attribution.* A shareholder is considered to own all the stock owned by his spouse, children, grandchildren and parents. Stock attributed from one family member to a second family member

under the family attribution rules cannot be reattributed to a third family member.

2. *Attribution From an Entity to an Owner or Beneficiary.* Stock owned, directly or indirectly, by a partnership, S corporation, estate, or trust is considered to be owned proportionately by the partners, shareholders, or beneficiaries. Stock owned, directly or indirectly, by a regular corporation is considered to be owned proportionately by any shareholder owning at least 50% of the value of its stock.

3. *Attribution From an Owner or Beneficiary to an Entity.* Stock owned, directly or indirectly, by a partner, shareholder, or beneficiary is considered to be owned by the partnership, S corporation, trust, or estate. Stock owned, directly or indirectly, by a shareholder owning at least 50% of the value of a regular corporation's stock is considered to be owned by the corporation. Stock attributed from an owner or beneficiary to an entity cannot be reattributed from an entity to another owner or beneficiary.

4. *Option Attribution.* An individual or entity having an option to purchase stock is considered to own the stock.

**EXAMPLE 11-11.** Tax A. Voider owns 40 of the 100 outstanding shares of DAS Corporation's single class of stock. Her basis in these shares is $60 per share. DAS redeems 10 of Tax A. Voider's shares for $2,500. The redemption is treated as a dividend to Tax A. Voider since she does not satisfy the requirements for a substantially disproportionate redemption. Her ownership interest needs to decline from 40% to less than 32% as a result of the redemption in order to be substantially disproportionate. Immediately after the redemption, Tax A. Voider holds 33.33% (30 out of 90) of the DAS shares.

**EXAMPLE 11-12.** Assume the facts remain the same as in the preceding example except that the 60 shares not owned by Tax A. Voider were owned by her spouse. The redemption could not qualify as being substantially disproportionate, since after applying the family attribution rules Tax A. Voider owns all of the DAS stock both before and after the redemption.

### Termination of a Shareholder's Interest

Capital gain treatment is provided for a stock redemption if the redemption results in a complete termination of a shareholder's stock interest. The complete termination rules offer an additional route to capital gain treatment where (1) the stock attribution rules would preclude a shareholder from obtaining capital gain treatment under the "substantially disproportionate" redemption rules, or (2) a shareholder owns only nonvoting stock in a corporation.

Under these rules, a shareholder can waive the family attribution rules. This waiver permits the shareholder to be treated as owning no stock in the redeeming corporation even though other family members may own such stock. With a limited exception, the other three types of attribution rules cannot be waived.

### Not Essentially Equivalent to a Dividend

Whether or not a stock redemption satisfies this requirement depends on the facts and circumstances. A redemption satisfies the requirements when it results in a "meaningful reduction in the shareholder's proportionate interest in the business." Three shareholder rights are generally examined to determine if a meaningful reduction has occurred: (1) the right to vote and exercise control; (2) the right to share in earnings; and (3) the right to share in liquidation proceeds. Examples of stock redemptions that qualify as being "not essentially equivalent to a dividend" include the following:

1. A reduction in a shareholder's interest from 57 to 50% where the remaining stock is held by a single, unrelated shareholder.

2. Redemption of voting stock of a minority shareholder that fails to qualify as substantially disproportionate, or as a complete termination.

3. Redemption of one-half of the preferred stock of a shareholder who owns none of the corporation's voting stock.

Tax planners always test a stock redemption that fails to qualify under one of the other capital gains standards against the "not essentially equivalent to a dividend" standard to see if it can be used to avoid the dividend income treatment. A number of IRS administrative rulings have been issued interpreting this standard and may be helpful.

### Partial Liquidation

Whether a transaction is a partial liquidation is determined at a corporate level. A partial liquidation has occurred if:

1. A distribution is "not essentially equivalent to a dividend" and occurs in the taxable year in which a plan of partial liquidation is adopted, or the next taxable year.

2. A distribution is attributable to a corporation's termination of one of its businesses where the business has been actively conducted by the corporation for at least 5 years preceding the distribution, *and* where the corporation continues to conduct a business that it has actively conducted for the past 5 years.

In the first case, the standard that most often is applied requires that a bona fide contraction of the corporation's business must have occurred.

A stock redemption that occurs as part of a partial liquidation is treated as an exchange transaction for an individual shareholder and usually results in a capital gain or loss being recognized. A corporate shareholder, on the other hand, must qualify for exchange treatment under either the substantially disproportionate, complete termination of an interest, or not essentially equivalent to a dividend exceptions. If one of these exceptions does not apply, the corporate shareholder must report the redemption as a dividend.

**EXAMPLE 11-13.** Tax A. Voider owns 80 of the 300 outstanding shares of the DPH Corporation stock. This stock is a capital asset. A partial liquidation of DPH occurs resulting in 35 of Tax A. Voider's shares being redeemed. Tax A. Voider receives capital gain treatment for the redemption whether the distribution is pro rata or not among the corporation's shareholders.

### Redemption to Pay Death Taxes

When stock of a corporation represents a substantial proportion of a decedent's estate, a stock redemption may take place under a special exception which permits earnings to be withdrawn from the corporation by an estate or beneficiary at capital gains rates. These withdrawn funds can be used to add liquidity to the decedent's estate. This special exception applies only if the value of the corporation's stock included in the decedent's gross estate exceeds 35% of the total gross estate (less the deductions available for funeral and administrative expenses, the estate's liabilities, and deductible casualties). Special rules exist for aggregating the holdings of two or more corporations' stocks. The maximum distribution that can be received at capital gains rates under this exception is the sum of all state and federal estate and inheritance taxes, any interest due on these taxes, and the deductible funeral and administrative expenses.

This provision is most beneficial because it permit earnings to be withdrawn from a corporation at capital gains rates; however, the funds do not have to be used by the estate or the beneficiary to pay the death taxes or funeral and administrative expenses. Accordingly, these rules should be carefully examined to determine if they can be used by the corporation to avoid the payment of dividends.

### Related Party Redemptions

A shareholder (or group of shareholders) can attempt to withdraw funds out of a controlled corporation by selling his stock to a second corporation that he also controls and having the gain on the sale taxed at capital gains rates. However, the tax laws treat the "sale" transaction as a stock redemption involving the stock of the second corporation. The stock redemption generally results in dividend income for the controlling shareholder, to the extent of the lesser of the amount distributed or the combined E & P balances of the two corporations. Exchange treatment is available if the requirements for one of the capital gains exceptions to the stock redemption rules can be satisfied. Because the stock is acquired by a related corporation, the stock attribution rules usually prevent the shareholder from achieving capital gain treatment.

A similar set of rules applies when a controlling shareholder sells the stock of a parent corporation to one of its subsidiary corporations. In such a case, the sale is treated as a redemption by the parent corporation of its own stock. Generally this results in dividend income to the controlling shareholder to the extent of the lesser of the amount distributed or the combined E & P balances of the two corporations. It is likely that the stock attribution rules will also apply here to prevent one of the capital gains exceptions from applying.

### Preferred Stock Bailouts

A preferred stock bailout represented an attempt to combine a tax-free stock dividend and a sale, exchange, or redemption of the dividend shares to withdraw earnings from a corporation at capital gain rates. The plan worked like this: First, preferred stock was distributed tax-free as a stock dividend. Part of the basis of the underlying stock was allocated to the dividend shares and the dividend shares assumed the holding period of the underlying shares. If the underlying shares had been held long-term, the dividend shares could immediately be sold to an unrelated party and the recognized gain would be eligible for long-term capital gain treatment. The distributing corporation would then redeem the unrelated party's stock holdings in a complete termination of his interest.

The antipreferred stock bailout rules prevent this type of tax planning. Under these rules, a sale or exchange of the dividend shares results in the recognition of the ordinary income that the shareholder would have had if the distributing corporation had made a cash distribution in lieu of the stock dividend. Any additional amounts received are treated as a recovery of the shareholder's capital investment. Once this basis has been fully recovered, only then can any subsequent amounts represent gain from the sale or exchange of the investment. A redemption of the preferred stock, on the other hand, is treated as a dividend equal to the lesser of the amount distributed or the distributing corporation's E & P balance at the time of the redemption. The conversion of capital gain into ordinary income can be avoided by a series of exceptions. Some of these exceptions include all of a shareholder's stock being sold, exchanged, or redeemed in a complete termination of his interest; the stock of an individual shareholder being redeemed in a partial liquidation; the corporation being completely liquidated; or the stock being transferred in a transaction where the realized gain goes unrecognized.

### Distributing Corporation's Gain or Loss

The distributing corporation must recognize income or gain when it uses appreciated property to redeem its stock. Three major exceptions to this gain recognition rule exist as follows:

1.  A distribution made to an individual shareholder in redemption of part or all of his stock holdings that is treated as a "qualified dividend," or as a partial liquidation, provided the redeeming shareholder has held at least 10% of the distributing corporation's outstanding stock at all times during the shorter of the 5-year period preceding the distribution or the time the corporation has been in existence.

2.  A distribution of the stock or obligations of a 50% owned subsidiary corporation.

3.  A distribution qualifying under the "redemption to pay death taxes" exception.

**EXAMPLE 11-14.**    Assume the facts remain the same as in the preceding example. By having the redemption occur as part of a partial liquidation, appreciated property can be used to redeem Tax A. Voider's stock without requiring DPH Corporation to recognize gain (as long as the shareholder's stock holdings have not dropped below 10% of the outstanding stock during the 5-year period preceding the distribution). DPH Corporation must recognize the gain if the redemption fails to qualify under the partial liquidation exception, or the property used to redeem the stock is "recapture" property (e.g., Section 1245 property).

### Bootstrap Acquisitions

Bootstrap acquisitions involve using a portion of a corporation's assets to acquire its own stock. These transactions are most often found in connection with the acquisition of a closely held corporation, where the purchaser does not have sufficient cash to acquire all of the outstanding stock. A bootstrap acquisition will usually involve two steps. In the first step the seller sells part of his stock to the purchaser for cash or cash plus a note. The second step is the seller inducing the corporation to redeem his remaining stock for cash or cash and property. The courts have held that both the sale transaction and the stock redemption provide the seller with capital gain treatment when they take place as part of an integrated plan, regardless of which step takes place first.

**EXAMPLE 11-15.** Tax A. Voider wants to purchase all of the stock of TDE Corporation. A sales price of $600,000—$200,000 in cash and $400,000 in a series of installment obligations—is agreed upon for 600 of the 1,000 outstanding TDE shares. TDE is to redeem the remaining 400 shares from the selling shareholder for $400,000. The sale receives capital gain treatment and is reported by using the installment method of accounting. The redemption qualifies as a complete termination of the seller's interest and receives capital gain treatment. A caveat is appropriate here. The purchaser will have a constructive dividend if she uses corporate funds to satisfy the installment obligations incurred to purchase the 600 shares.

### Buy-Sell Agreements

Buy-sell agreements are arrangements in which the owners of a closely held corporation have their interest in the business purchased by the business itself or the other owners of the business. Two common situations when buy-sell agreements are used are (1) when an owner desires to terminate his entire interest in a business or (2) when one of the owners of a business dies. The buy-sell agreements may call for a specific formula to be used to value the interest in the business or may require an appraisal of the business to ascertain the value of the interest.

When an owner dies, the proceeds of a life insurance policy may be used to make the purchase. Some buy-sell agreements call for the business to maintain insurance policies on each of the owners. The company pays the premiums on the policies and receives the insurance proceeds upon the death of an owner. These funds are then used by the corporation to redeem the stock held by the decedent's estate. Alternatively, each of the owners could maintain separate insurance policies on the other owners. The shareholders pay the premiums on the policies and receive the proceeds upon the death of an owner. These funds are then used by the remaining owners to purchase the stock held by the decedent's estate. In either case, the decedent's estate receives capital gain treatment for its disposition of the shares (either under the redemption to pay death taxes exception or the complete termination exception).

## NONLIQUIDATING PARTNERSHIP DISTRIBUTIONS

Nonliquidating distributions from a partnership (also known as current distributions) are generally not as complex as similar distributions from a corporation. The same rules apply for current partnership distributions regardless of whether all partners get a distribution or only one gets a distribution, or whether the partner maintains his ownership interest intact or reduces (but does not eliminate) it with the distribution. Complications in partnership nonliquidating distributions arise only if the partner gets a disproportionate change in his ownership of so called "Section 751 assets." Because of the complexity of such a disproportionate distribution, we will discuss it only after the more basic rules are explained. Until then, we will assume that the Section 751 rules do not apply in any of our discussions.

### Distributions Without Section 751

In general, all income earned by a partnership is reported by and taxed to the partners. Income on which the partner has already paid the tax increases the partner's basis as was discussed in Chapter 6. Since the partner has already paid tax on the partnership's earnings, most current distributions represent only the partner's receipt of income that has already been taxed to him. Accordingly, the distributions are tax-free to him. Gain is recognized only if the partner receives cash in excess of his basis in his partnership interest. Under no conditions can a loss be recognized on a nonliquidating distribution. These rules hold even if an economic gain (or very rarely a loss) has occurred.

**EXAMPLE 11-16.**    Tax A. Voider has a partnership interest with a $4,000 adjusted basis. In a current distribution, he receives property having a fair market value of $7,000. Clearly he has recognized an economic gain, since he now has both his partnership interest and property worth $7,000. However, he recognizes no gain since the distribution did not result in his receiving cash in excess of his basis in the partnership interest.

One item must be remembered in calculating the gain to be recognized. A reduction in a partner's share of partnership liabilities is treated as a distribution of cash for all purposes. Accordingly, a reduction in a partner's share of liabilities can cause him to recognize gain on a current distribution even though no actual distribution takes place. This rule is unlikely to cause gain recognition in an operating partnership, but it could trigger gain under certain arrangements that are relatively common in tax shelter partnerships.

**EXAMPLE 11-17.**    Tax A. Voider is a limited partner in a real estate partnership. Under the terms of the partnership agreement, Tax A. Voider has a 50% profits and loss interest until certain conditions are met. Once they are met, her interest is reduced to 20%. If Tax A. Voider has a $250,000 basis for the partnership interest and the partnership has $1,000,000 in liabilities at the time her interest is reduced, Tax A. Voider is deemed to have a $300,000 cash distribution (a reduction from 50 to 20% in her share of the $1,000,000 in liabilities). Therefore, Tax A. Voider must recognize a $50,000 gain even though she has not actually received any cash.

If gain is recognized on a current distribution, it is normally treated as gain from the sale of a partnership interest and is a capital gain.

Only if Section 751 comes into play will any gain on a current distribution be treated as ordinary income.

### Basis of Property Received

If a current distribution includes any property other than money, the question of the property's basis in the partner's hands must be considered. The general rule is that property received in a current distribution takes a carryover basis from the partnership.

**EXAMPLE 11-18.** Tax A. Voider has a $20,000 basis in his partnership interest, before receiving a current distribution of inventory having a basis to the partnership of $6,000 and a fair market value of $6,500. Tax A. Voider's basis for the inventory is the same as the partnership's basis, or $6,000.

The only condition, under which property received in a current distribution does not take a carryover basis, occurs when the carryover basis of property received exceeds the partner's basis in his partnership interest before the distribution. In that case, the basis of the property received is limited to the partner's basis in his partnership interest.

**EXAMPLE 11-19.** Tax A. Voider has a $15,000 basis in her partnership interest before a current distribution of land having an adjusted basis of $20,000 in the partnership's hands. The land's basis to Tax A. Voider is limited to $15,000.

When a partner receives more than one piece of property in a current distribution, no allocation problem exists as long as the total of all the carryover bases is less than the partner's adjusted basis in his partnership interest. However, when the sum of the carryover bases exceeds the partner's basis in his partnership interest, additional rules must be applied.

In order to understand these rules we must first define the term "unrealized receivables." For purposes of the distribution rules, unrealized receivables are rights to payments for goods or services which have not been included in income under the partnership's method of accounting. The most common example of unrealized receivables is the accounts receivable of a cash-basis partnership (e.g., income from sales is not recognized until the cash is received). With this definition in mind, we can continue with the rules for current distributions, where the sum of the carryover bases of property received plus the amount of cash received exceeds the partner's basis in his partnership interest.

First, cash distributions (or deemed cash distributions from the reduction of liabilities) are used to reduce the partner's basis in the partnership interest. Any remaining basis is then used to provide a carryover basis for inventory items and unrealized receivables. If the remaining basis in the partnership interest is insufficient to provide a carryover basis for these two items, the partner's remaining basis is allocated among all inventory items and unrealized receivables based on their relative adjusted bases. If any basis remains in the partnership interest after the basis has been reduced by cash distributions and the carryover bases assigned to the inventory items and unrealized receivables, the remaining basis is allocated among all other property distributed based on their relative adjusted bases on the partnership's books. An example will illustrate these rules.

**EXAMPLE 11-20.**    Tax A. Voider has a $15,000 basis in his partnership interest before receiving a current distribution of $6,000 cash, inventory with a basis (to the partnership) of $4,000, unrealized receivables with a basis of $3,000, and land with a basis of $3,500. Tax A. Voider must first reduce his basis for the partnership interest·by the $6,000 cash received. His remaining basis of $9,000 must then be allocated to inventory ($4,000) and unrealized receivables ($3,000) up to the full amount of their carryover basis from the partnership. The $2,000 remaining basis in the partnership interest [$15,000 − ($6,000 + $4,000 + $3,000)] is allocated to the land.

### Holding Period of Property Received

The holding period for property received by a partner in a current distribution includes the holding period of the partnership. Special rules apply to the current (or liquidating) distribution of inventory or unrealized receivables that serve to preserve the ordinary income character of these items. Any gain or loss recognized by a distributee partner on a later sale or disposition of unrealized receivables is always characterized as ordinary income. Any gain or loss recognized by a distributee partner on a later sale (or other disposition) of items that were inventory to the partnership is characterized as ordinary income if the sale occurs within five years of their distribution to the partner. After the partner holds the inventory items for five years, the character of any gain or loss recognized is determined by the character of the item in the partner's hands. If he holds the item as an investment, a capital gain or loss could be recognized. If the partner holds the item as inventory in his own business, any gain or loss is, of course, ordinary in nature regardless of whether he has held the property for more or less than five years.

### Remaining Basis in the Partnership Interest

Remember that a partner's basis in his partnership interest is adjusted to reflect his distributive share of partnership income, gain or loss. The partner's basis is reduced when he receives a distribution from the partnership by the amount of cash (or liability reduction deemed to be cash) distributed plus the distributed property's basis in the partner's hands.

EXAMPLE **11-21.** Tax A. Voider has a $25,000 basis in his partnership interest before he receives a current distribution of $4,000 cash and land having a fair market value of $10,000 and a basis of $8,000. These distributions reduce the basis of the partnership interest to $13,000 [$25,000 − ($4,000 + $8,000)].

A partner's basis in his partnership interest cannot be reduced below zero by a distribution. If cash is received in excess of the partner's basis in his partnership interest, the basis of the partnership interest is reduced to zero. And as we discussed earlier, gain is recognized if the amount of the cash distribution exceeds the partner's basis. If the distribution includes cash and property which in total has an adjusted basis in excess of the partner's remaining adjusted basis in his partnership interest, application of the normal procedure outlined will also result in a zero basis for the partnership interest.

**EXAMPLE 11-22.**    Assume the same facts as in Example 11-20. The basis for Tax A. Voider's partnership interest after the distribution is determined as shown below.

|        | Basis in partnership interest before distribution | $15,000 |
|--------|----------------------------------------------------|---------|
| Less:  | Cash received                                      | (6,000) |
|        |                                                    | $ 9,000 |
| Less:  | Adjusted basis to Tax A. Voider of property received ($4,000 + $3,000 + $2,000) | (9,000) |
| Equals: | Basis in partnership interest after the distribution | 0 |

It should be clearly understood that a zero basis in a partnership interest is not the same as no longer having an ownership interest in the partnership. The zero basis simply signifies that the partner has recognized a loss and/or received distributions which equal his basis in his original investment plus any income or gain which has accrued to him. A current distribution, by definition, is one which does not liquidate a partnership interest but it may reduce the basis in a partnership interest to zero.

### Section 751 and Current Distributions

Application of Section 751 to current distributions is one of the most difficult and complex areas of partnership taxation. The explanations that follow only scratch the surface of this exceedingly complex area. Good tax advice from a competent tax accountant or tax lawyer is essential when a Section 751 distribution is made. With this caveat in the forefront of your mind, let us continue with the basics of Section 751.

Section 751 assets, or "hot assets" as they sometimes are called, are assets which if sold by the partnership would generate ordinary income. The purpose of Section 751 is to insure that any partner who gives up part of his ownership interest in these Section 751 assets must recognize his share of ordinary income. Accordingly, there are two requirements which must be met before Section 751 applies to a current distribution. They are as follows:

1.  The partnership must have Section 751 assets.
2.  Some partner(s) must be giving up some of their proportionate ownership of these Section 751 assets.

**EXAMPLE 11-23.**   Tax A. Voider had a 50% interest in a partnership which had Section 751 assets. Tax A. Voider received $20,000 in a current distribution which reduced her partnership interest to 40%. Section 751 applies to this distribution because Tax A. Voider's interest in the Section 751 assets has been reduced from 50 to 40%.

What are Section 751 assets? There are two categories of hot assets: unrealized receivables and substantially appreciated inventory. For purposes of Section 751, unrealized receivables has a broader definition than the one provided above for distributions in general. Unrealized receivables in this context also includes the amount of income that would be recaptured as ordinary income under Sections 1245, 1250 and other similar recapture sections. This means that any business which, for example, owns its own office equipment has an unrealized receivable equal to the amount which would be recaptured as ordinary income under Section 1245 if the equipment were sold for its fair market value. Because of the breadth of this definition, virtually every partnership has some Section 751 assets.

Substantially appreciated inventory is inventory which meets two mechanical tests. The inventory is substantially appreciated if its fair market value exceeds the following two conditions:

1.  120% of the partnership's basis for the inventory.
2.  10% of the fair market value of all partnership property other than cash.

For purposes of this test only, unrealized receivables must be considered inventory. Because the tests are purely mechanical, it is not especially difficult for partnerships to manipulate the results. For example, a partnership which did not want to have substantially appreciated inventory could buy significant amounts of inventory. Presumably, this new inventory would have a basis equal to its fair market value and the first test could be failed. Another simple way to fail the test of substantially appreciated inventory would be to invest cash reserves in marketable securities. Cash is not used to calculate the 10% of fair market value test, but marketable securities are. These are only two of a wide variety of ideas. A nimble-minded manager could develop several other similar strategies to avoid having substantially appreciated inventory at the time of a distribution.

Now, we must examine the tax effect of a current distribution which does involve Section 751. As pointed out earlier, such distributions can be extremely complex so only the simplest one will be illustrated in which a partner receives cash. The tax treatment for a partner who receives cash in a current distribution that reduces his ownership interest requires a bifurcation of the transaction into a Section 751 transaction and a regular current distribution. In the Section 751 transaction, it is assumed that the partner first receives the share of hot assets which he is giving up in a current distribution. Then it is assumed that the partner sold these hot assets back to the partnership for cash. Under this fiction, the partner recognizes ordinary income on the "sale" and the partnership receives a basis in the hot assets equal to the purchase price. After the Section 751 transaction is accounted for, any other cash received in this distribution is treated as a normal current distribution. An example will help illustrate the calculations.

**EXAMPLE 11-24.**   Tax A. Voider receives $20,000 in a current distribution which reduces her interest in a partnership from 50 to 40%. Before the distribution her basis in the partnership interest is $50,000. The partnership's balance sheet immediately preceding the distribution is as follows:

|  | Assets | |
|---|---|---|
|  | Basis | Fair Market Value |
| Cash | $ 30,000 | $ 30,000 |
| Inventory | 10,000 | 40,000 |
| Land | 60,000 | 130,000 |
| Total | $100,000 | $200,000 |

|  | Equities | |
|---|---|---|
|  | Basis | Fair Market Value |
| Tax A. Voider's capital | $ 50,000 | $100,000 |
| Other partner's capital | 50,000 | 100,000 |
| Total | $100,000 | $200,000 |

The first step is to determine if there are Section 751 assets. The inventory has a fair market value which is greater than 10% of all noncash assets, and the fair market value of the inventory exceeds 120% of its basis. Therefore, the inventory is substantially appreciated and Section 751 does apply.

The next step is to determine what portion of the inventory that Tax A. Voider is giving up.

|  |  | Basis | Fair Market Value |
|---|---|---|---|
|  | Ownership of inventory before distribution (50%) | $5,000 | $20,000 |
| Less: | Ownership of inventory after distribution (40%) | (4,000) | (16,000) |
| Equals: | Inventory being given up | $1,000 | $ 4,000 |

First, Tax A. Voider is assumed to receive the inventory she is giving up in a current distribution. She takes a $1,000 carryover basis in this inventory. Then it is assumed that Tax A. Voider is paid the fair market value for the inventory. Thus, $4,000 of the $20,000 cash distribution represents the payment for the inventory. Tax A. Voider calculates her gain on the hypothetical "sale" as shown below.

|  | Amount realized | $4,000 |
|---|---|---|
| Less: | Basis of inventory | (1,000) |
| Equals: | Ordinary income on "sale" | $3,000 |

The partnership basis for the inventory is first reduced by $1,000 to reflect the deemed distribution of inventory to Tax A. Voider and then increased by $4,000 to reflect the deemed purchase. This results in a $13,000 partnership basis for the inventory [$10,000 (basis) − $1,000 (distribution) + $4,000 (purchase)]. Now that the Section 751 distribution is accounted for, the remaining $16,000 [$20,000 (distribution) − $4,000 (Sec. 751 payment)] is treated as a regular current distribution. No gain will be recognized on the $16,000 distribution, but rather it reduces Tax A. Voider's basis in her partnership interest to $33,000 ($50,000 − $1,000 − $16,000).

As you can see even the simplest Section 751 distribution is far from easy. Distributions which involve property and/or changes in partners' liability shares are far more complicated. Clearly a tax advisor should be consulted before any distribution is made which changes a partner's interest in hot assets.

### Tax Planning with Current Distributions from Partnerships

The rules for current distributions provide some interesting potential for tax planning. It is possible for the timing of distributions of cash and property to result in a taxpayer recognizing a capital gain or permitting deferral of a gain. If cash and property are distributed at the same time, the cash is first used to reduce the partner's basis in his partnership interest and the property will receive a carryover basis from the partnership up to the partner's remaining basis. However, if the property is distributed first and the cash is distributed later, gain is recognized on the cash distribution to the extent it exceeds the basis in the partnership interest.

EXAMPLE 11-25.   Tax A. Voider has a $10,000 basis in his partnership interest at the time the partnership wants to distribute cash of $5,000 and land having a basis of $7,000. The partnership is making proportionate distributions of cash and land to all partners, so Section 751 does not apply.

If the partnership distributes cash and land at the same time, the result is as follows:

|         | Beginning basis in partnership interest | $10,000 |
|---------|------------------------------------------|---------|
| Less:   | Cash received                            | (5,000) |
| Equals: | Remaining basis in partnership interest  | $ 5,000 |
| Less:   | Carryover basis in land (limited to remaining basis in partnership interest) | (5,000) |
| Equals: | Basis in partnership interest after distribution | 0 |

No gain is recognized on this distribution since the cash received did not exceed Tax A. Voider's basis in his partnership interest.

If the property is distributed first and the cash is distributed in a later, separate distribution, the result is significantly different. The property distribution has the following result:

|  | Beginning basis in partnership interest | $10,000 |
|---|---|---|
| Less: | Carryover basis in land | (7,000) |
| Equals: | Remaining basis in partnership | $ 3,000 |

Then, when the $5,000 cash is distributed, the partner will recognize a $2,000 capital gain since the cash distribution exceeds the partner's basis in his partnership interest.

Such a strategy could be very useful in a situation where a partner has a capital loss which he needs to offset with a capital gain. However, the two distributions must clearly be separate for such a strategy to work. At a minimum the two distributions must be separated by more than a few days. If the distributions occur too close in time, the IRS can be expected to collapse them into a single transaction and deny the capital gain. However, there is no magic number of days or weeks that will guarantee separate treatment, and a tax advisor's input should be sought before such a strategy is implemented.

### Liquidating Distributions from a Continuing Partnership

There are two kinds of liquidating distributions in a partnership setting; distributions which terminate a single partner's interest in a continuing partnership, and distributions made on the termination of the partnership itself. While many of the rules for the two situations are the same, there are enough differences so that we will discuss them separately. In this chapter we will discuss only the distributions from a continuing partnership. Distributions resulting from the termination of a partnership are discussed in Chapter 12. In order to discuss liquidating distributions from a continuing partnership, we must consider two kinds of payments; payments for a partner's interest in partnership assets, and all other payments made by the partnership.

#### Payments for Partnership Assets

Distributions which represent payments to a partner for his share of partnership assets are treated very similarly to current distributions. (However, it should be noted that payments to a partner for his share of unrealized receivables are not considered payments for assets but rather generate ordinary income under rules to be explained later.) The distributions are treated as a return of capital up to the partner's basis in his partnership interest. Gain is recognized only if cash (or deemed cash resulting from a liability reduction) exceeds the partner's basis. A loss can be recognized on a liquidating distribution only if the retiring partner receives no assets other than cash, inventory, and unrealized receivables. Inventory and unrealized receivables can never have a basis to the partner greater than their basis to the partnership. If a partner's basis in his partnership interest is greater than the amount of cash received plus the basis of any inventory and unrealized receivables, and he receives no other property, he recognizes a loss equal to the amount of his unrecovered basis.

**EXAMPLE 11-26.**    Tax A. Voider has a basis in her partnership interest of $23,000 before she receives a liquidating distribution. The distribution consists of $10,000 cash and inventory having a basis to the partnership of $4,000. Tax A. Voider will recognize a loss of $9,000 determined as follows:

|         | Beginning basis in partnership interest | $23,000 |
|---------|------------------------------------------|---------|
| Less:   | Cash received                            | (10,000) |
|         | Basis of inventory                       | ( 4,000) |
| Equals: | Loss to be recognized                    | $ 9,000 |

The basis rules for property received by a partner in a liquidating distribution are similar to the rules for a current distribution. As in a current distribution, the basis for inventory and unrealized receivables is carried over from the partnership provided that the partner's basis in his partnership interest is at least that large. After reducing the partner's basis in his partnership interest for cash received and the basis of the inventory and unrealized receivables, the remaining basis is allocated to the other property received based on their relative basis amounts. If no gain or loss is recognized, the sum of cash received plus the basis allocated to the inventory and other property must equal the basis of the partner's interest in the partnership before the distribution. An example will help clarify the rules.

**EXAMPLE 11-27.**    Tax A. Voider had a $26,000 basis in his partnership interest before he received a liquidating distribution. The distribution consisted of $4,000 cash, inventory having an adjusted basis to the partnership of $12,000, and one piece of land. The basis of the land to Tax A. Voider is determined as follows:

|        |                                         |            |
| ------ | --------------------------------------- | ---------- |
|        | Beginning basis in partnership interest | $26,000    |
| Less:  | Cash received                           | ( 4,000)   |
|        | Adjusted basis of inventory             | (12,000)   |
| Equals:| Basis allocated to the land             | $10,000    |

Tax A. Voider's basis in the land is $10,000 in this situation regardless of whether its basis to the partnership was as small as zero or as large as $1,000,000.

These rules provide interesting opportunities for tax planning. For example, a partner who is going to have an economic loss on the dissolution of the partnership can recognize at least some of it by accepting only cash and/or inventory as his liquidating distribution. If it would be more beneficial to recognize the loss in another tax year, he can arrange this by taking cash and/or inventory, and some other property. The other property will receive a basis in excess of its market value and his loss will be recognized at a later date when he sells the property.

### Other Payments to a Retiring Partner

All payments for unrealized receivables and goodwill (unless the partnership agreement specifically provides for payments for goodwill), as well as any other payment which is not compensation for partnership assets, will generate ordinary income to the liquidating partner. When the partner recognizes ordinary income, the partnership will be able to take a deduction for an equal amount.

Clearly, the partnership prefers that payments to a retiring partner be deductible, but the retiring partner will generally prefer payments for partnership assets which are likely to generate no taxable gain or a capital gain. The tax law provides the partner and the partnership significant flexibility in determining the character of the payment since the two parties generally will favor opposite results. The agreement entered into by the parties as to what payments are for partnership assets and what payments are "other payments" (deductible by the partnership) will normally be accepted. Accordingly, all parties should sit down with a finely-sharpened pencil to determine the most advantageous division of payments for all parties involved. A retiring partner will normally take a smaller payment if all of the payment can be categorized as being made for partnership assets. However, an intelligent retiring partner will insist on a payment greater than fair market value if much of the payment will be taxed as ordinary income. In order to get a deductible payment, the continuing partners will frequently find it advantageous to pay a slightly higher total amount.

# ━━━━━12

# LIQUIDATING DISTRIBUTIONS BY A BUSINESS ENTITY

At some time in the life of a business entity, the decision may be made to liquidate the business. If the corporate form is used to conduct the activities, the liquidation is generally a taxable event for the shareholders and tax-exempt for the corporation being liquidated. Special nonrecognition rules can permit (1) a parent corporation to liquidate a subsidiary corporation without recognizing any gain or loss, or (2) individual and corporate shareholders to liquidate a corporation within a 1-month period and avoid recognizing part or all of the realized gain. A liquidating corporation may recognize a gain on the liquidation when it distributes certain forms of property (e.g., Section 1245 property) or sells its assets. Special nonrecognition rules permit a corporation to sell some or all of its assets and liquidate within a 12-month period, and avoid recognizing part or all of the gain from the sale.

Liquidation of a partnership is generally a tax-free event at both the partnership and partner level. Gain is recognized by a partner only when cash or cash equivalents that are received exceed the basis for the partnership interest. This excess amount ordinarily is taxed as a capital gain. A loss can be recognized on the liquidation of a partnership only if (1) the distributee partner receives only money, unrealized receivables, and inventory from the partnership and (2) the basis for the partnership interest exceeds the partnership's basis for the properties distributed. No gain or loss is ordinarily recognized by the partnership on the distribution of its properties, but a gain or loss must be recognized when its properties are sold as part of the liquidation.

## CORPORATE LIQUIDATION

A sample corporate liquidation transaction is illustrated in Figure 12-1. The following four questions usually must be answered regarding the tax consequences of the liquidation to the shareholder:

1. What amount of gain or loss is recognized as a result of the liquidation?
2. What is the character of the recognized gain or loss?
3. What is the basis of the property received by the shareholder?
4. When does the shareholder's holding period for the property received in the liquidation begin?

Three additional questions must be answered with respect to the corporation being liquidated. They are as follows:

1. What amount of gain or loss is recognized as a result of the liquidation?
2. What is the character of the realized gain or loss?
3. What is the effect of the liquidation on the distributing corporation's tax attributes?

**FIGURE 12-1** Liquidation of a business entity.

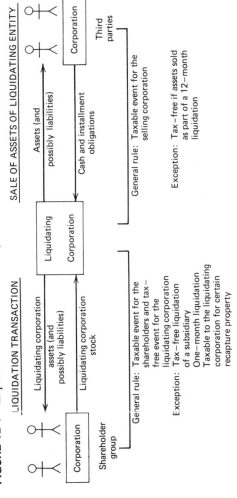

LIQUIDATION TRANSACTION

SALE OF ASSETS OF LIQUIDATING ENTITY

Shareholder group

Liquidating corporation assets (and possibly liabilities)

Liquidating corporation stock

General rule: Taxable event for the shareholders and tax–free event for the liquidating corporation

Exception: Tax–free liquidation of a subsidiary
One–month liquidation
Taxable to the liquidating corporation for certain recapture property

Assets (and possibly liabilities)

Cash and installment obligations

Third parties

General rule: Taxable event for the selling corporation

Exception: Tax–free if assets sold as part of a 12–month liquidation

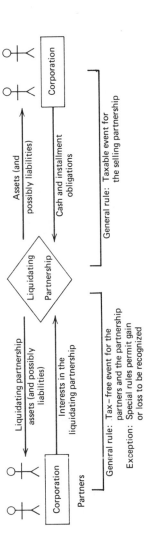

Partners

Liquidating partnership assets (and possibly liabilities)

Interests in the liquidating partnership

General rule: Tax–free event for the partners and the partnership

Exception: Special rules permit gain or loss to be recognized

Assets (and possibly liabilities)

Cash and installment obligations

General rule: Taxable event for the selling partnership

305

### General Rule

*Shareholder Gain or Loss*

A status of liquidation exists when the corporation ceases to be a going concern and its activities are being conducted in order to wind up its affairs, pay its debts, and distribute any properties that remain to its shareholders. A corporation may be liquidated prior to its actual dissolution under state law. The importance of the liquidation status arises from the fact that the shareholder treats any property distributed in complete liquidation of the corporation as received in exchange for his stock. Nonliquidating distributions, on the other hand, ordinarily are treated as dividends.

The shareholder's realized gain is determined as follows:

|  | Money received |
|---|---|
| Plus: | Fair market value of nonmoney property received |
| Less: | Liabilities of the liquidating corporation assumed or acquired by the shareholder |
| Less: | Basis for the stock redeemed |
| Equals: | Realized gain (or loss) |

The realized gain (or loss) must be recognized by the shareholder, unless one of the nonrecognition rules described below applies. The recognized gain or loss generally is a capital gain or loss. As is described below, a long-term capital gain arising from a liquidation transaction may be converted into ordinary income by the collapsible corporation rules. Similarly, the Section 1244 small business corporation stock provisions may convert a capital loss on a liquidation transaction into an ordinary loss for an individual or partnership.

Liquidation may take place by having a series of liquidating distributions made to the shareholders. Each distribution is treated as a recovery of the shareholder's basis for the individual share of stock (or block of stock) in question. Once the basis for a share (or block of stock) has been fully recovered, any excess amounts received result in a gain being recognized by the shareholder. No losses are recognized on the distribution until the final liquidating distribution is received.

### Basis and Holding Period for Property Received

The shareholder takes the property's fair market value at the time of the liquidation as his basis. The holding period for the property commences on the day following the day of the liquidating distribution.

### Distributing Corporation's Gains and Losses

As a general rule, the liquidating corporation does not recognize gain or loss when it distributes property pursuant to a complete liquidation. A number of exceptions to this general rule exist. First, the liquidating corporation must recognize ordinary income when it distributes inventory accounted for under the last-in, first-out (LIFO) method to the extent that the inventory's basis under a non-LIFO valuation method (e.g., first-in, first-out) would exceed its LIFO basis. Second, the excess of the fair market value of any installment obligations that are distributed, over their basis to the corporation, is recognized as a gain by the distributing corporation. The nature of this gain depends upon the character of the property sold in the original installment sale. Third, the various "recapture" provisions (e.g., Sections 1245 or 1250) over-ride the nonrecognition rules. Thus, the excess of the fair market value (on the distribution date) of any recapture properties that are distributed over their basis (but not more than the recapture amount) must be recognized as gain by the liquidating corporation. Fourth, the fair market value of any previously expensed properties (e.g., supplies expensed when purchased) that are distributed to the shareholders must be recognized as ordinary income by the liquidating corporation under the "tax benefit" rule. This "recapture" occurs because the corporation claimed a deduction with respect to an outlay which has a current value, as is evidenced by its distribution to the shareholders. Finally, although not part of the gain or loss rules, the amount of any previously claimed investment tax credits on property (which has not been held until the end of its recovery period) and any other credits recovered under the "tax benefit" rule must be recaptured by increasing the liquidating corporation's federal income tax liability.

### Tax Attributes

All of the tax attributes of the liquidating corporation disappear at the time liquidation occurs. Thus, any unused net operating loss carryovers, capital loss carryovers, or earnings and profit balances disappear when liquidation occurs.

**EXAMPLE 12-1.**  Tax A. Voider owns 25% of the stock of RLG Manufacturing Corporation which is in the process of liquidating. His basis for the stock, which is a capital asset, is $62,500. The corporation's balance sheet immediately preceding the liquidating distribution is as follows:

| | Assets | | Equities | |
|---|---|---|---|---|
| | Adjusted Basis | Fair Market Value | | Amount |
| Cash | $ 350,000 | $ 350,000 | Mortgages payable | $ 150,000 |
| Marketable securities | 25,000 | 22,000 | Paid-in capital | 250,000 |
| Inventory (LIFO) | 40,000 | 98,000[a] | | |
| Land | 25,000 | 40,000 | Retained earnings | 600,000 |
| Building (net of $100,000 ACRS capital recovery allowances) | 160,000 | 280,000 | | |
| Equipment (net of $200,000 ACRS capital recovery allowances) | 400,000 | 610,000 | | |
| Total | $1,000,000 | $1,400,000 | Total | $1,000,000 |

[a] The FIFO valuation for the inventory would be $84,000.

RLG recognizes the following gains when it liquidates: inventory, $44,000 ($84,000 − $40,000); building, $100,000 (recapture amount); and equipment, $200,000 (recapture amount). The inventory gain is ordinary income under the LIFO inventory recapture rules and the building and equipment gains are ordinary income under the Section 1245 depreciation recapture rules.

The corporation's tax liability on this gain (at a 46% tax rate) is $158,240. Tax A. Voider receives one-fourth of RLG's assets and liabilities. His realized and recognized gain is $210,440 [0.25 ($1,400,000 − $150,000 − $158,240) − $62,500]. His gain is a capital gain. Tax A. Voider's basis for the assets that he receives are: cash, $47,940 [0.25 × ($350,000 − $158,240)]; marketable securities, $5,500; inventory, $24,500; land $10,000; building, $70,000; and equipment, $152,500. None of the loss from the decline in the value of the marketable securities can be recognized by either the corporation or its shareholders. The shareholders compute their gain or loss on a subsequent disposition of the securities based on the property's fair market value on the distribution date. The liquidated corporation may have to recapture previously claimed investment tax credits which will increase the tax liability shown in its final tax return. RLG's tax attributes (e.g., the E & P balance) disappear at the time of the liquidation.

## Liquidation of a Subsidiary Corporation

### Shareholder Gain or Loss

The liquidation of a subsidiary corporation can occur tax-free to the parent corporation, provided the following four requirements are met:

1. The parent corporation must own at least 80% of the voting stock and at least 80% of the nonvoting stock (other than nonvoting, preferred stock).

2. A complete cancellation or redemption of all of the subsidiary corporation's stock must take place pursuant to a plan of liquidation.

3. All of the subsidiary corporation's property must be transferred to the parent corporation and minority shareholders within one taxable-year (of the subsidiary corporation), if no formal plan of liquidation has been adopted. If a formal plan of

liquidation has been adopted, the liquidation must be completed not later than three years from the close of the taxable year in which the first liquidating distribution occurred.

4.  The subsidiary corporation must not be insolvent when liquidated.

If these four requirements are satisfied, then the parent corporation cannot recognize any gain or loss on the liquidation. Otherwise, the general liquidation rules described apply. Minority shareholders, on the other hand, are not covered by the nonrecognition rules. They must recognize gain or loss under the general liquidation rules described above, or the one-month liquidation rules described below. It may be to the parent corporation's advantage to fail one of the four requirements in order to recognize a loss incurred on the liquidation.

### Basis and Holding Period for Property Received

The parent corporation takes over the property's adjusted basis from the books of the subsidiary corporation. The parent corporation's use of the carryover basis occurs because the subsidiary corporation is considered to continue as part of the parent corporation (e.g., as an operating division). Unlike many tax-free transactions, the parent corporation's basis for its stock investment is ignored in determining the basis for the individual properties. This can be detrimental to the parent corporation when its acquisition cost for the stock investment is in excess of the subsidiary corporation's basis for the distributed assets. However, the deemed liquidation rules described below can solve this problem. On the other hand, it could be an advantage where the assets have declined in value and stock investment can be acquired at a cost below the total basis of the assets in question. The acquiring corporation in this case can obtain additional depreciation deductions and losses as a result of the stock acquisition and liquidation.

The parent corporation's holding period for the properties that are received includes the holding period of the subsidiary corporation.

### Distributing Corporation's Gains and Losses

The subsidiary corporation recognizes no gain or loss when making the liquidating distributions. Unlike the general rules outlined earlier, the LIFO inventory exception, the installment obligation exception, the various recapture provisions, and the tax benefit rule do not apply here, thereby allowing the liquidating corporation to avoid recognizing gain when distributing appreciated property. Similarly, the investment tax credit recapture requirements are also waived for the liquidation of a subsidiary corporation.

### Tax Attributes

All of the tax attributes of the liquidated subsidiary corporation carryover to the parent corporation. Thus, the parent corporation can use the net operating loss carryovers of the subsidiary corporation to offset its postliquidation taxable income. These carryovers cannot be used to recover taxes paid by the parent corporation on its preliquidation profits.

**EXAMPLE 12-2.** Assume that the facts remain the same as in Example 12-1 except that TAV Corporation owned 100% of the RLG stock and the basis for the investment is $250,000. The realized gain in the liquidation is $1,000,000 [ ($1,400,000 − $150,000) − $250,000]. The entire gain goes unrecognized. TAV's basis for the assets it receives is the same as they were on RLG's books, or $1,000,000. As a result of this carryover basis, TAV cannot increase its depreciation deduction over that which was being claimed by RLG. Also, the unrealized appreciation that exists at the time of the liquidation is taxed to TAV when it sells or exchanges the assets. RLG does not recognize any gain on distributing the appreciated property. The Section 1245 depreciation recapture potential and investment tax credit recapture potential carries over to TAV, along with RLG's E & P balance and other tax attributes.

### One-Month Liquidation

The one-month liquidation rules permit individual and corporate shareholders to elect to defer part or all of the gain on a corporate liquidation. These rules do not apply to losses realized on a liquidation. For these rules to apply, the following three requirements must be met:

1. The shareholder must own stock on the date the plan of liquidation is adopted.

2. The shareholder must make a timely election to have the one-month liquidation rules apply.

3. (a) Noncorporate shareholders owning at least 80% of the total voting power owned by all noncorporate shareholders must elect to come under the one-month liquidation rules.

   (b) Corporate shareholders (other than excluded corporations) owning at least 80% of the total voting power owned by all corporate shareholders (other than excluded corporations) must elect to come under the one-month liquidation rules. (An excluded corporation is any corporate shareholder that has owned 50% or more of the liquidating corporation's voting power at any time between January 1, 1954 and the date the plan of liquidation is adopted.)

Electing shareholders fall into two groups—corporate and noncorporate shareholders. If requirements 3(a) and 3(b) are satisfied, all shareholders can elect to use the one-month liquidation rules. If only one group satisfies the requirements, all members of that group can elect to use the one-month liquidation rules. All members of the other group, all nonelecting shareholders, and all excluded corporations come under the general liquidation rules or the subsidiary corporation liquidation rules previously explained.

#### Shareholder Gain or Loss

An electing shareholder recognizes gain to the extent of the greater of: (1) his pro rata share of the corporation's post–February 28, 1913 current and accumulated E & P, or (2) the total of the money received plus the fair market value of all stocks and securities received that were acquired by the corporation after December 31, 1953. A noncorporate shareholder's recognized gain is characterized as dividend income up to the amount of his pro rata share of the liquidating corporation's E & P. Any additional gain, that must be recognized because the cash and securities that are distributed exceed the shareholder's pro rata share of E & P, is capital gain. All gains recognized by corporate shareholders are capital gains.

The one-month liquidation rules can permit a total deferral of the realized gain or loss if the liquidating corporation does not distribute any liquid assets *and* it has no current or accumulated E & P. Such a result could occur where the liquidating corporation held primarily substantially appreciated properties (e.g., real estate) and capital recovery allowances and operating expenses had been sufficiently large to prevent an E & P build-up. Substantial amounts of liquid assets or E & P could produce a more costly liquidation for an individual shareholder, because of the need to characterize the recognized gain as dividend income. This detriment could cause a shareholder not to elect the one-month liquidation rules.

### Basis and Holding Period for Property Received

Because part or all of the realized gain goes unrecognized, a carryover basis that references the shareholder's basis for his stock is used for the property received. This basis is determined as follows:

|        | Basis of the stock surrendered or cancelled |
|--------|---------------------------------------------|
| Less:  | Amount of money received |
| Plus:  | Amount of gain recognized |
|        | Amount of unsecured liabilities assumed or acquired by the shareholders |
| Equals: | Total allocable basis of properties received |

This basis is allocated to the individual assets based on their net fair market values (fair market value minus any specific liabilities to which it is subject). The allocated basis for the asset is increased by any specific lien or mortgage that attaches to the property.

This carryover process ordinarily produces a basis for the individual assets which is below market value. The amount of this difference represents the allocation of the deferred gain to the individual assets. This deferred gain is recognized at a later date when the property is sold or exchanged, but the deferred gain does not automatically receive capital gain treatment as it would under the general liquidation rules. Instead its character depends on the asset's use in shareholder's hands. Thus, if some of the assets received by the shareholder are inventory and Section 1245 depreciable properties and they are subsequently sold, the deferred gain will be recognized as ordinary income. In addition, the use of the lower carryover basis reduces the amount of capital recovery deductions that would otherwise be claimed following a fully taxable liquidation.

### Distributing Corporation's Gains and Losses

The general rules regarding recognition of gain or loss and the recapture of investment tax credits apply to the one-month liquidation. Any gain that is recognized here can have three tax consequences. First, the corporation must include the gain in its taxable income and pay taxes on it. Second, the shareholder may have the amount of his recognized gain increased because the corporate gain increases its E & P balance. Third, part of the shareholder's capital gain that is recognized because of receiving money or securities may be converted into dividend income because of the increased E & P balance.

### Tax Attributes

Like the fully taxable liquidation, the tax attributes of the liquidated corporation disappear following a liquidation that comes under the one-month rules.

**Example 12-3.** Tax A. Voider owns all of the TAV Development Corporation stock. On December 10, 19X4, the corporation's balance sheet is as follows:

|  | Assets | | Equities | |
|  | Adjusted Basis | Fair Market Value | | Amount |
|---|---|---|---|---|
| Cash | $ 50,000 | $ 50,000 | Mortgages payable | $300,000 |
| Marketable securities | 50,000 | 60,000 | Paid-in capital | 100,000 |
| Land (non-inventory property) | 400,000 | 790,000 | Retained earnings | 100,000 |
| Total | $500,000 | $900,000 | Total | $500,000 |

TAV Development Corporation's E & P balance is the same as its retained earnings balance. Tax A. Voider's basis for her stock, which is a capital asset, is $100,000. The corporation adopts a plan of liquidation, Tax A. Voider makes the necessary election, and then the corporation distributes all of the properties to Tax A. Voider within one calendar month. Tax A. Voider's realized gain is $500,000 [($900,000 − $300,000) − $100,000]. Only $110,000 of this gain must be recognized. The gain is characterized as $100,000 of dividend income and $10,000 of capital gain. No gain is recognized by TAV Development when making the distribution. The basis of the cash is $50,000. The total basis of the other properties is $460,000 ($100,000 − $50,000 + $110,000 + $300,000). This is allocated as follows:

$$\text{Securities} = \frac{\$60,000}{\$790,000 + \$60,000} \times \$160,000 = \$\ 11,294$$

$$\text{Land} = \frac{\$790,000}{\$790,000 + \$60,000} \times \$160,000$$
$$+ \$300,000 \text{ (mortgage assumed)} = \frac{448,706}{\$460,000}$$

The deferred gain is allocated to both the securities and the land. The character of this gain when it is recognized depends on the nature of each individual asset in the shareholder's hands. This result can be contrasted with the general liquidation rules where

Tax A. Voider's full $500,000 realized gain would be recognized as a capital gain and the securities and land would have bases of $60,000 and $790,000, respectively.

### Twelve-Month Liquidation Rules

A sale of the corporation's assets followed by the liquidation of the corporation ordinarily would result in double taxation—once to the corporation on the sale of the assets and once to the shareholder on the exchange of his stock. To avoid this double taxation, at one time shareholders were required to liquidate a corporation and then, either individually or as a group, sell the assets. The liquidation was taxed to the shareholder at capital gains rates. Little or no tax liability was incurred by the corporation when making the liquidating distribution. Because the basis of the assets equalled their fair market value, the shareholders recognized little or no gain or loss on the later sale of the assets. Problems arose because it was difficult for the shareholders and the IRS to determine whether sufficient sales negotiations had occurred at the corporate level prior to the liquidation to deem the sale of assets as having been made by the corporation. If the corporation was, in fact, deemed to have made the sale, then double taxation occurred.

Special nonrecognition rules were enacted to prevent the double taxation. To utilize these rules, the corporation must (1) adopt a plan of liquidation and (2) distribute all of its assets (other than those retained to satisfy creditor claims) within 12 months of the date that the plan of liquidation was adopted. A corporation that satisfies both requirements cannot recognize gains or losses on sales or exchanges of its property within the period of time from the adoption of the plan of liquidation to until liquidation is completed. If the corporation fails to satisfy either requirement, then all gains and losses on the sales of corporate assets (and not just those made outside the 12-month period) must be recognized.

Corporations and shareholders can sometimes take advantage of these two requirements. First, because the nonrecognition rules are mandatory for both gains and losses if the requirements are met, shareholders may prolong the liquidation period beyond 12 months in order to fall outside the nonrecognition rules. Such plans have been accepted by the IRS, although some taxpayers have been treated by the IRS and the courts as having constructively received the liquidating distribution within the 12-month period. Alternatively, the corporation may attempt to sell its "loss" assets prior to the adoption of a plan of liquidation and its "gain" assets after a plan has been adopted. If successful, this plan permits the losses to be recognized by the corporation and the gains to be deferred. In order to prevent the loss recognition, the IRS (in some situations) has been successful in imputing the adoption of an informal plan of liquidation that predates the sale of the loss assets. This change in the date of the adoption of the plan of liquidation can also cause the 12-month requirement to be failed and require all gains and losses to be recognized.

The nonrecognition rules apply only to sales of property that occur as part of a complete liquidation. As a result, sales of property in connection with a partial liquidation, a stock redemption, or a corporate reorganization are not eligible for nonrecognition. Special exceptions also prevent these rules from applying to the tax-free liquidation of a subsidiary corporation or a corporation liquidating under the one-month liquidation rules.

The nonrecognition rules apply only to sales or exchanges of *property* that occur in qualifying transactions. The term "property" does not include inventory items, property held primarily for sale in the conduct of a trade or business, installment obligations acquired when inventory is sold, or installment obligations arising from the sale of property before the adoption of a plan of liquidation. Inventory items that are sold in a bulk sale to a single purchaser, however, do qualify as property and are eligible for nonrecognition treatment. Even though an asset may qualify as "property," some gain may be recognized or investment tax credits may be recaptured. The gain recognition rules described earlier for LIFO inventory, the recapture properties (e.g., Section 1245 or 1250 property), and previously expensed items all override the nonrecognition rules. In addition, the IRS has been successful in applying the assignment of income doctrine to prevent a corporation from selling assets (upon which income has been earned but not yet reported for tax purposes) to a third party, and exempting the gain from taxation by using these nonrecognition rules.

**Example 12-4.** Assume the facts remain the same as in Example 12-1 except that RLG Manufacturing Corporation sells its non-cash assets to a third party for $1,050,000, and uses part of the remaining cash to pay the mortgage on the building. The total realized gain or loss from the sale of the individual assets is $400,000 ($1,050,000 − $650,000). The corporation recognizes the gain on the sale of the inventory, the building, and the equipment in the same manner as in Example 12-1. (Even though a bulk sale of the inventory occurred, the LIFO inventory gain recognition rules override this exception). The tax on the $344,000 of gain at a 46% tax rate is again $158,240. The net result of the 12-month liquidation rules is that the corporation has a smaller tax liability because $56,000 of its gain on the sale is deferred. The shareholder gain is unchanged from Example 12-1, as a result of the 12-month liquidation rules.

### Stock Purchase Treated as Asset Acquisition

If a corporation purchases 80% of a second corporation's (the target corporation) voting stock and 80% of nonvoting stock (other than nonvoting, preferred stock) within a 12-month period, it is permitted to make an irrevocable election to treat the stock purchase as an asset acquisition. The election must be made within 8½ months of the end of the month during which the corporation first satisfies the 80% requirement(s) (the acquisition date). This special election applies to stock purchases made after August 31, 1982.

The election causes the target corporation to be treated as having sold all of its assets in a single transaction at the close of business on the acquisition date. This transaction is treated as having satisfied all of the requirements of the 12-month liquidation rules even though the target corporation is not formally liquidated, except for tax purposes.

The target corporation is treated as a new corporation that purchased all of its assets at the beginning of the first day following the acquisition date. The "new" and "old" corporation designations exist only within the tax laws. No formal liquidation or reincorporation occurs under state law, nor does a physical transfer of the assets occur. The "new" corporation elects all new accounting periods and methods, but cannot carryover any of the tax attributes of the "old" corporation. The sale/purchase price for the assets equals the fair market value of the target corporation's assets.

The transaction is not entirely tax-free to the target corporation. The various exceptions to the nonrecognition of gain or loss rules for a 12-month liquidation (e.g., the LIFO inventory and depreciation recapture items) and the investment tax credit recapture requirement may cause the target corporation to incur a tax liability on the sale.

The acquiring corporation's basis for the assets equals the purchasing corporation's basis in the target corporation stock plus any liabilities of the target corporation assumed or acquired. Included in the liability total are any tax liabilities arising from the deemed sale. If the purchasing corporation acquires less than 100% of the target corporation's stock, then an adjustment to the basis must be made in order to increase the acquiring corporation's basis for the assets to the amount that would have been paid to acquire 100 percent of the target corporation's stock.

**Example 12-5.**  Assume the facts remain the same as in Example 12-1 except that the stock purchase took place on July 1, 1983. TAV Corporation has 8½ months from July 31 to make an election to treat the stock purchase as an asset acquisition. If the election is made, RLG must recognize a $344,000 gain on the deemed sale of the inventory, building, and equipment. The corporation's tax liability on the gain at a 46% tax rate is $158,240. The deemed sale/purchase price is the fair market value of RLG's assets, or $1,400,000. This amount also becomes the total basis [$1,091,760 (basis) + $150,000 (mortgage) + $158,240 (tax liability)] for the "new" corporation's assets, which means that each asset's basis should equal its fair market value.

### Collapsible Corporations

A collapsible corporation is a corporation formed, or availed of, principally for the manufacture, construction, or production, or for the purchase, of certain "collapsible" assets (i.e., inventory, property held primarily for sale while conducting a trade or business, unrealized receivables or fees, and Section 1231 trade or business property) with a view toward either sale or exchange of the corporation's stock, or a distribution of property to its shareholders, before the corporation has realized a substantial portion (two-thirds) of the taxable (ordinary) income from the property. The collapsible corporation rules convert the long-term capital gain realized on a sale or exchange of a collapsible corporation's stock, or on a distribution of its property to a shareholder, into ordinary income. These rules do not alter the tax consequences of the transaction to the corporation itself, but prevent the shareholder from converting ordinary income into capital gain by engaging in certain sale or exchange transactions prior to the recognition of most of its profit for tax purposes.

EXAMPLE 12-6.    Tax A. Voider forms a corporation to subdivide some land that it has purchased into 40 lots. She has invested $250,000 to acquire all of the corporation's stock. The corporation is liquidated after operating for 15 months and Tax A. Voider receives $800,000 of property, including 24 lots held in inventory that have a fair market value of $480,000. Tax A. Voider realizes a $550,000 ($800,000 − $250,000) gain on the liquidation. Normally this gain is a capital gain. However, the profit realized from the sale of the 16 lots prior to liquidation does not represent the realization of two-thirds of the corporation's potential income from the project. Since the corporation is deemed collapsible, the $550,000 gain must be recognized as ordinary income.

## PARTNERSHIP LIQUIDATING DISTRIBUTIONS

As noted in Chapter 11, the rules which govern the taxation of a liquidating distribution from a partnership are slightly different from the rules which apply to a current distribution. The liquidating distribution rules apply whether the entire partnership is liquidating or a single partner is liquidating his interest in the partnership. In this chapter the tax results to the partners and the partnership of a liquidation of the entire partnership will be presented.

### Effects on Partnership

Under the laws of many states, a partnership terminates whenever there is a general partner who dies, withdraws, files for bankruptcy, or becomes incompetent. This termination arises from the agency relationship among general partners and is a logical extension of that theory. However, for tax purposes, there is little reason to predicate the termination of the partnership upon the actions of a single general partner. Instead, the Code provides that a partnership terminates for tax purposes only under two conditions. First, the partnership terminates if no part of any business or venture of the partnership continues to be carried on by any of the partners in a partnership. The courts have liberally interpreted what constitutes the business of a partnership and have allowed a partnership to continue even when the partnership sells off all its assets and reinvests the proceeds in a totally different business activity. The second condition which results in a termination of the partnership is the sale or exchange of 50% or more of the total interest in partnership capital and profits within a 12-month period.

Termination of a partnership originating from a cessation of all business activity really has very little tax effect. The limited effect is the direct result of the minimal level of activity required to avoid termination. The termination is likely to occur when the partnership has virtually no assets. The termination is likely to be the result of a final distribution in liquidation of the partnership. Accordingly, the only significant result of this kind of termination is the closing of the partnership taxable year. This closing could cause a bunching of income in a partner's return if the partner and the partnership have different taxable years.

This bunching of income is not generally a problem since the taxable-year requirements for a partnership normally result in the partners and the partnership having the same year-end. However, if bunching of income is a potential problem, it can normally be avoided by maintaining minimal business activity by the partnership until the partner's next taxable year begins. At least two Circuit Court of Appeals cases suggest that the partnership continues even if it holds only notes received on the sale of its assets, collects interest on the notes, and makes minor investments of the interest. However, common sense strongly suggests that maintenance of such *de minimis* (insignificant) assets is rather risky.

### Effects on Partners

Each partner must include in income his distributive share of all income, gain, and loss realized by the partnership in its final taxable year. Income, gain, or loss must be included, whether it is from normal partnership business activity or whether it arises from the disposition of partnership assets. There are no special provisions which allow nonrecognition of gain on the termination of a partnership. This is logical since the corporate provisions were enacted to avoid double taxation on the termination, and no possibility of double taxation exists in the partnership setting.

In addition to including his share of income for the final tax year, each partner must determine the tax result of any liquidating distribution he receives. Remember that any reduction in a partner's share of partnership liabilities is considered a cash distribution to the partner, so most partners receive some kind of liquidating distribution. As explained in Chapter 11, a liquidating distribution results in gain to a partner only if cash (or the liability reduction) exceeds the partner's basis in his partnership interest. Loss can be recognized only if the partner receives only cash, unrealized receivables, and inventory. If the partner receives property, the rules for a liquidating distribution, which were explained in Chapter 11, are the rules for determining the basis of the property received.

The holding period of property received by a partner when a partnership liquidates includes the partnership's holding period for the property. The partnership's holding period is used, regardless of the partner's holding period for his partnership interest. This holding period rule applies even when the property's basis is determined from the partner's basis in his partnership interest, rather than as a strict carryover basis from the partnership books. This holding period rule provides an opportunity for tax planning.

**EXAMPLE 12-7.** Tax A. Voider has a $5,000 basis in her partnership interest before receiving a liquidating distribution. She purchased her partnership interest on April 1, 19X1. On July 1, 19X1 she received a liquidating distribution of a piece of land having a basis of $3,000. The partnership had purchased the land 4 years earlier. Tax A. Voider's $5,000 basis for the land references her basis for the partnership interest, but the holding period of the land is based on the partnership's holding period for the land. If Tax A. Voider sells the land on the day she receives it, any gain or loss she recognizes is long-term. In effect Tax A. Voider has turned a short-term investment (April 1, 19X1 to July 1, 19X1) into a long-term gain or loss.

# 13

# TAX SHELTERS

Tax shelters are what you say they are. Probably no tax-related concept incites as much interest among taxpayers and the IRS as does the idea of tax shelters. Depending on who you listen to, tax shelters may be characterized as anything from "the only salvation from an almost unbearable tax burden" to "the loophole through which the rich avoid paying their fair share of the nation's tax bill." Emotions and interest run rampant in this area of the tax law.

So what is all the hoopla about? What exactly is a tax shelter? It is, first of all, an investment which will provide a reduction in your tax bill. However, this definition is woefully incomplete since bad investments which result in economic losses may also reduce your tax bill. No one would be likely to consciously choose a bad investment as a way to shelter income. Instead, we shall define a tax shelter as an investment which is economically sound and which also provides a reduction in your tax bill from what it would have been without this investment.

At this point, we should remember that investments which produce tax-exempt income (such as municipal bonds or qualified pension plans) do result in a lower tax bill than investments in stocks and bonds which produce taxable income. Nevertheless, these investments have traditionally not been considered tax shelters since they do not reduce the taxes due from the taxpayer's other economic endeavors (i.e., salary, dividends, royalties, etc.). They do not "shelter" other income. Our discussion for the remainder of the chapter will ignore such investment forms, but a wise taxpayer in a high marginal tax bracket will not.

## ENTITY FORMS FOR TAX SHELTER INVESTMENTS

One of the basic premises upon which most tax shelters are founded is the idea that tax losses generated by the shelter activity can be used to lower the investor's personal taxable income and thereby lower his tax bill. Given this fact, it is essential to the viability of most tax shelters that the tax laws not consider the entity to be a regular corporation. Losses incurred by regular corporations create net operating losses that can only be carried back or forward and can not be passed through to the shareholders. This leaves several possible business forms in which tax shelter activities can be organized.

Sole proprietorships can be tax shelters and, in fact, this is a common business form for investing in small real estate activities. The major advantages of this business form are its simplicity and the ability of the owner to maintain control of his investment. However, there are two risks which must be considered with a sole proprietorship. First, the investor assumes all of the economic risks of ownership and is likely to be fully liable for all debts that are incurred. While insurance may reduce his liability from some unforeseen events, there still remains substantial economic risk. In addition, a single investor must be quite wealthy before he can afford to properly diversify his investments. For example, a single real estate investment is subject to risks from accidents, condemnation, unfavorable changes in the neighborhood, and changes in the available supply of similar property—which may adversely affect the value of his holdings. Diversification into different types of property (i.e., residential and commercial real estate) and into different geographical areas minimizes the risks to the investor but clearly requires a substantial dollar investment.

A partnership between two or more investors is the most common business form for tax shelter investments. The partnership form of doing business offers a number of advantages. First, the pooling of resources of two or more investors provides a larger amount of capital and can allow for greater diversification of holdings. More importantly for most investors, a limited partnership interest provides a shield between the liabilities and risks of the tax shelter activities and the other business and personal holdings of the investor. The limited partner may lose his investment if the shelter activity is unsuccessful, but he does not risk any of his wealth beyond the amount of his investment. It is no wonder that most tax shelters are organized as limited partnerships, with a corporate entity functioning as a general partner and assuming the risks. Many of the widely marketed limited partnerships have substantial minimum net worth requirements for potential investors and have minimum investment amounts between $5,000 and $20,000.

One danger with the limited partnership form of investment, as it is frequently marketed, is that the partnership may assume so many of the characteristics of a corporation that the IRS considers the business to be an association (taxed as a regular corporation). Prospectuses for syndicated partnership interests include an attorney's report which normally addresses this question. Nevertheless, each investor should satisfy himself or herself that the tests are met.

For tax years after 1982, the taxation of S corporations is similar in many respects to that of a partnership and has potential use for tax shelter investments. Because S corporations are limited to 35 shareholders, it is most useful for closely held tax shelter operations. One clear advantage this business form has is the limitation of liability to the corporate assets. However, as was pointed out in Chapter 5, there are numerous procedural rules which must be followed. Failure to follow the procedures will result in the loss of S corporation status, and thereby the loss of the shelter benefits. An S corporation also has a second type of disadvantage. The pass-through of losses to a shareholder is limited to the shareholder's capital contribution and any amounts owed by the corporation to the shareholder. A partnership's limitation is usually higher because it includes the partner's pro rata share of all partnership liabilities. Thus, if large losses are expected, the S corporation may be at a disadvantage.

## TAX SHELTER BENEFITS

Shelter benefits normally arise from some combination of the following four significant features.

1. The effect of leverage.
2. The deferral of income.
3. The permanent reduction of the taxes due to tax credits.
4. The conversion of ordinary income into capital gains.

At this point in time it should be emphasized that, in large part, tax shelters depend upon provisions which were written into the Code to provide incentives for certain taxpayer behavior. While there is always the possibility that Congress (or a court) will change its mind and rescind the provisions, use of these provisions to minimize tax liability is relatively free of the risk of an IRS attack. On the other hand, some shelters have benefits which depend upon "creative" valuations of property or "creative" interpretations of existing tax laws. These shelters have a substantial risk of close IRS scrutiny and, potentially, a total disallowance of tax benefits from the investment. A prudent investor will remember that if it seems too good to be true, it probably is.

### Leverage

Typically, tax shelters involve an investment by more than one taxpayer to obtain a pooling of funds, in order to increase the size and diversify the type of property that can be acquired. Frequently, a substantial portion of the purchase price is financed with borrowed money. This use of borrowed funds, or leverage, is economically profitable as long as the borrowed money earns more than its interest cost. From a tax standpoint there are several potential advantages which accrue to the leveraged property owner. First, of course, the interest paid (or accrued) is a deductible expense, subject to the investment interest limitation discussed in Chapter 3. Secondly, if the asset is a depreciable asset, the full purchase price of the asset is its basis for depreciation purposes so that the depreciation deductions claimed in the early years may exceed the taxpayer's investment. (If the borrowing is paid off in future years, then of course the taxpayer's investment equals the total depreciation deductions.) Still another tax benefit exists for leveraged investments in property which qualify for an investment tax credit, a business energy credit, or a credit for rehabilitation of a 30 to 40 year old building or a certified historic structure. These credits are normally calculated on the total investment in such property including the borrowed funds.

**EXAMPLE 13-1.** Mark and Mary formed an equal partnership (MM) to begin raising horses. Each invested $40,000 in cash and the partnership borrowed an additional $100,000 on a full recourse basis. Mark can deduct his share of partnership losses up to $90,000 ($40,000 cash investment + $50,000 share of liabilities for which he is at risk).

Before you drop this book and call your broker in excitement over the tax benefits of leveraged investments, you must obtain some additional information about the at-risk rules. Essentially, these rules prevent taxpayers from taking more deductions from an investment than the amount the taxpayer has "at risk." While the at-risk rules are quite complex, the general idea is that the amount the taxpayer has at risk is the amount he would lose if the investment suddenly became totally worthless. Clearly, the taxpayer would lose any amounts he has invested outright in the property and he would also have to pay off any outstanding debt for which he is liable. He would not stand to lose the amount of any nonrecourse liability since, by definition, this kind of liability is one in which the lender has no recourse in the event of nonpayment except the taking of the property itself. Regardless of the taxable entity doing the investing, these at-risk rules apply to all investments with the single, very important exception of real estate. There are no at-risk rules for real estate investments, and this fact accounts for much of the favor with which these investments are viewed as tax shelters. There is also a minor exception to the at-risk rules for certain closely held corporations actively engaged in equipment leasing.

As discussed in Chapter 8, the at-risk rules also limit the amount of investment tax credits (ITC) which can be claimed by individual investors, partnerships, S corporations, and certain closely held corporations. The taxpayer can claim an ITC only on the amount of the investment for which he is at risk. However, there is a significant difference between the definitions of the amounts at risk for calculating the ITC and for loss limitation purposes.

### Deferral of Income

Much of the tax benefit from shelter investments results from the deferral of income that comes about from taking heavy deductions early in the life of the investment. These heavy deductions normally produce tax losses in the early years and therein lies the "shelter" of other income. These large deductions most frequently arise from use of accelerated depreciation methods for buildings, machinery, and equipment. Other major sources of early deductions include the immediate expensing of intangible drilling costs for oil and gas investments and the immediate expensing of certain research and development costs. High initial interest costs and the normal start-up losses of a new business both increase the amount of losses that can be claimed early in the life of some investments.

EXAMPLE **13-2.**    On January 1, 1983 Tax A. Voider buys a rental house for $100,000 ($20,000 down; $80,000 borrowed from her bank at 9% annual interest for 30 years) with principal and interest payments of $8,057 per year. The rental property qualifies as 15-year recovery property because of its acquisition date. Rental income minus all expenses (except for interest and depreciation) is projected to be $9,000 each year. Cash flow and taxable income (loss) for year 1 from the investment can be computed as follows:

|  | Net Cash Inflow (Outflow) | Taxable Income (Loss) |
|---|---|---|
| Income minus operating expenses | $9,000 | $ 9,000 |
| Less: Depreciation |  | (12,000) |
| Interest | (7,164) | ( 7,164) |
| Principal | ( 893) |  |
| Net amount | $ 943 | ($10,164) |

Under our assumptions, the cash flow will remain $943 per year until the mortgage is paid off. The amount of the deductible loss will decrease as follows for years 1 through 16.

| Year | Depreciation | Interest | Taxable Income (Loss)[a] |
|---|---|---|---|
| 1 | $12,000 | $7,164 | $(10,164) |
| 2 | 10,000 | 7,080 | (8,080) |
| 3 | 9,000 | 6,988 | (6,988) |
| 4 | 8,000 | 6,888 | (5,888) |
| 5 | 7,000 | 6,779 | (4,779) |
| 6 | 6,000 | 6,659 | (3,659) |
| 7 | 6,000 | 6,527 | (3,527) |
| 8 | 6,000 | 6,384 | (3,384) |
| 9 | 6,000 | 6,227 | (3,227) |
| 10 | 5,000 | 6,055 | (2,055) |
| 11 | 5,000 | 5,868 | (1,868) |
| 12 | 5,000 | 5,662 | (1,662) |
| 13 | 5,000 | 5,438 | (1,438) |
| 14 | 5,000 | 5,192 | (1,192) |
| 15 | 5,000 | 4,923 | (923) |
| 16 | 0 | 4,768 | 4,232 |

[a] $9,000 − (Depreciation + Interest)

If Tax A. Voider's marginal tax rate is 50%, then her tax savings from this investment range from $5,082 in Year 1 down to $461.50 in Year 15. In Year 16 she begins to have taxable income and will continue to have positive income until her investment is disposed of. Note, however, that for 15 years she has enjoyed both positive cash flow from her investment and a reduction in her tax bill. If this investment is like most real estate, she can also expect to realize a substantial gain on her ultimate sale of the property even though she has enjoyed a significant deferral of income from this shelter.

Not all tax shelters throw off long-run income deferrals. Some tax shelters are based upon the use of the cash method of accounting and the ability to deduct certain expenses when they are paid, even though the item purchased remains on hand as an asset and does not represent an accounting expense.

A cash method of accounting taxpayer's ability to use the payment of the expense as the authority for deducting the outlay has been restricted by the 1984 Tax Act. As was discussed in Chapter 1, expenses are generally to be treated by the cash method of accounting taxpayer as being incurred at the point in time when economic performance has occurred (e.g., payments for services would be deductible when provided). For many types of outlays incurred by a tax shelter, this will deny a deduction for expenses which have been prepaid but not yet incurred by the end of the taxable year.

### Permanent Reduction of Taxes

A permanent reduction of taxes occurs whenever the taxpayer becomes eligible for a credit against his taxes. The major credits that are found in tax shelter investments are the investment tax credit, the credit for the rehabilitation of buildings 30 years of age or older and the credit for the rehabilitation of certified historic structures. The precise workings of these credits were explained in Chapter 8.

Rehabilitation of older buildings does provide a substantial shelter when the credit is taken but the size of this shelter cannot be increased by accelerated depreciation. In order to claim the rehabilitation credit, the taxpayer must agree to use the straight-line capital recovery method with respect to the rehabilitation costs. Nevertheless, the credit itself is large enough that combined with 15-year or 18-year depreciation and interest deductions, it provides significant potential for shelter.

Some of the impact of credits for investment and rehabilitation has been blunted by the requirement that the depreciable basis of the property be reduced by part or all of the credit taken. Even though this reduces the benefit of the credit, it certainly does not negate it. The credit is a dollar-for-dollar reduction in taxes due. The worst that the basis reduction can mean is a loss of ability to deduct that amount.

### The Conversion of Ordinary Income into Capital Gains

In years past, the conversion of ordinary income into capital gains was one of the most common features of tax shelters. Investors took large current deductions for expenses and depreciation which of course offset ordinary income. The depreciation reduced the basis of the property but, if gain on the later sale of that property could be reported as capital gain, the taxpayer had earned a substantial advantage—an immediate reduction in ordinary income in exchange for deferred income that is taxed as a capital gain. Congress, however, greatly reduced the opportunity to make such a conversion by enacting recapture provisions like Sections 1245 and 1250. Virtually no conversion is possible if accelerated depreciation was used for tangible personalty or nonresidential real estate purchased after 1980, since they are Section 1245 properties. If the taxpayer chooses straight-line depreciation for his nonresidential real estate all of his gain will be Section 1231 gain and, if he is careful, will be taxed as a long-term capital gain. Some sheltering is possible also with residential rental properties where only the excess depreciation amount must be recaptured.

There are numerous investments other than real estate which can result in a similar conversion of ordinary income into capital gains. While many of the details are beyond the scope of this book, this conversion is one of the basic premises of tax shelters in cattle breeding, citrus groves, timber, and oil and gas properties.

## CAVEATS—THE TAX
## DANGERS OF SHELTERS

### Alternative Minimum Tax (AMT)

A number of years ago there was a large public outcry when it became increasingly clear that some U.S. citizens paid far less than their proportionate share of taxes. Congress enacted a minimum tax which was designed to insure that a larger number of U.S. citizens paid at least some minimum amount of taxes. While the provisions of the minimum tax have been frequently changed, the underlying concept has remained. Taxpayers who greatly reduce their tax bills with use of preferentially taxed provisions (like capital gains and accelerated depreciation) will be taxed under the minimum tax provisions. There is a separate minimum tax for corporations but that is discussed in Chapter 4; here we shall discuss only the minimum tax assessed for individual taxpayers or trusts or estates.

The AMT limits the taxpayer's ability to reduce his federal income tax liability by taking advantage of tax preference deductions. The AMT is paid by an individual, trust, or estate whenever it exceeds the regular federal income tax liability.

The starting point for the AMT computation is the taxpayer's adjusted gross income. This amount is reduced by certain itemized deductions, including medical expenses in excess of 10% of A.G.I., casualty losses in excess of 10% of A.G.I., charitable contributions, interest expense incurred with respect to the taxpayer's personal residence, other interest expenses (but not in excess of net investment income), and so on. The taxpayer's tax preference items are added to this total to produce the "alternative minimum taxable income" amount. Tax preferences are just what the name implies; items which receive preferential treatment under our tax law. Some of the more common tax preference items include: the 60% deduction available for long-term capital gains, accelerated depreciation claimed (in excess of straight-line depreciation) on all real estate and any personal property that is subject to a net lease, percentage depletion claimed in excess of a property's adjusted basis, intangible drilling costs, and the bargain element of incentive stock options.

The alternative minimum taxable income is reduced by a $40,000 statutory exemption ($30,000 for single taxpayers and $20,000 for married taxpayers filing separate returns). A 20% tax is then imposed on this base. If the AMT (reduced by the foreign tax credit, the earned income credit, and the nonhighway gasoline usage credit) exceeds the regular income tax, the taxpayer must pay the higher AMT.

**EXAMPLE 13-3.**  Tax A. Voider earns $100,000 in salary and reports a net long-term capital gain of $200,000 in 19X4. His deductions and exemptions are $80,000 for federal income tax purposes, and $60,000 for AMT purposes. The $20,000 difference in the deduction totals is due to certain itemized deductions such as personal interest and state income taxes that cannot be deducted when determining the AMT. Tax A. Voider reports A.G.I. and taxable income of $180,000 and $100,000, respectively. His federal income tax liability (at 1984 rates) is $32,400. The alternative minimum taxable income is $240,000 ($180,000 − $60,000 deductions + $120,000 LTCG tax preference). The AMT liability is $40,000 [($240,000 − $40,000) × 0.20]. Tax A. Voider would owe $32,400 in regular federal income taxes plus $7,600 in AMT.

A taxpayer who finds himself in the situation of being subject to the AMT will find that normal tax planning techniques of accelerating deductions may not reduce his tax liability. For example, Tax A. Voider can invest in a tax shelter in 19X4 that produces $20,000 in deductions. These $20,000 of additional deductions will reduce his taxable income to $80,000 and his income tax liability to $23,568 (an $8,832 savings). If these tax shelter deductions represent a tax preference item, his alternative minimum taxable income and AMT will not change. Tax A. Voider will still owe $40,000 in total taxes, but they will now represent $23,568 in income taxes and $16,432 in AMT. The deductions can be more valuable to Tax A. Voider if they are deferred to a taxable year when he is not subject to the AMT. The tax shelter deductions will reduce Tax A. Voider's 19X4 tax bill only to the extent that they do not represent a tax preference item which must be added back for AMT purposes.

## Abusive Tax Shelters

For years the IRS was at a definite disadvantage in trying to stem the growth of abusive tax shelters based on overvaluation of assets, creative accounting and other similar tactics. The IRS defines abusive and nonabusive tax shelters in the following manner:

> Abusive tax shelters involve transactions with little or no economic reality, inflated appraisals, unrealistic allocations, etc., where the claimed tax benefits are disproportionate to the economic benefits. Such shelters typically seek to evade taxes.

> Nonabusive tax shelters involve transactions with legitimate economic reality, where the economic benefits outweigh the tax benefits. Such shelters seek to defer or minimize taxes.

Beginning in October 1983, abusive tax shelters are subject to special scrutiny on a national scale. District coordinators search magazines, newspapers, other IRS investigations, federal, state, and local information agencies, and any other available source to identify shelters which may be abusive. The coordinator turns his information over to a committee made up of IRS employees with legal, criminal, and auditing experience to determine whether the investigation should be continued. In making their decision the committee will consider factors such as: the past activity of the promoter; the type of shelter involved; the size of the promotion; and the total amount of deductions or credits which could be claimed. If the committee determines that further investigation is warranted, a revenue agent is assigned to the case to gather further information and to determine the course of IRS action.

The IRS has three possible penalty actions which can be taken. First, the IRS can assert a penalty of the greater of $1,000 or 20% of the promoter's income from the shelter against the promoter and/or anyone who assists him in the tax shelter project. Second, the IRS can seek an injunction against the promoter of an abusive tax shelter to terminate shelter sales. Finally, if the IRS concludes that investors who claim promised tax benefits from this abusive shelter are not in compliance with the law, the IRS can notify each investor before his tax return is filed. This IRS letter warns the investors that the IRS does not consider the tax shelter deductions or credits to be in conformity with law and that, if the investor claims these tax shelter benefits on his return, the return will be audited. If these prefiling letters are sent, the IRS notifies the filing district for each investor to watch the notified investors' returns to be certain that such tax benefits are not claimed unchallenged.

The IRS is increasingly aggressive in challenging abusive tax shelters. While the overall percentage of returns that have been audited has dropped in recent years, the investigation of tax shelters has increased. A shelter which uses overvaluation of assets or false or fraudulent statements as a basis for making available tax deductions should be considered an extremely poor investment.

The 1984 Tax Act added a number of penalty provisions aimed specifically at tax shelter activities. First, the interest rate imposed on underpayments of taxes that are attributed to tax-motivated transactions (e.g., overstated valuations, disallowance of deductions or credits because of the application of the at-risk rules, etc.) is increased to 120% of the normal interest rate imposed on underpayments. This higher interest rate applies to all interest accruing in 1985 and later years. Second, any person who organizes a potentially abusive tax shelter (or sells an interest in such a shelter) must maintain a list identifying each person who purchased an interest in the shelter. The list must meet certain requirements and be made available for IRS inspection for a 7-year period. Third, tax shelter promoters are required to register certain shelters with the IRS. Registration is required when (1) the tax benefits received in the first five years are expected to exceed the investor's cash and property investment, or (2) the investment is (a) registered under federal or state securities laws, (b) sold under an exemption from registration requiring the filing of a notice with a federal or state agency regulating the offering or sale of securities, or (c) offered for sale for an amount in excess of $250,000 (in total) and there are expected to be 5 or more investors. The minimum requirements associated with the registration include providing information identifying and describing the tax shelter and the tax benefits represented to investors. All of these provisions are designed to make enforcement easier for the IRS and to make these investments less attractive for an investor.

## ANALYSIS OF A SHELTER

First and foremost, tax shelters are investments which must be evaluated based on expected economic benefits outside of their tax benefits. If you would not invest in a project except for its expected tax benefits, you should very carefully weigh your decision to invest. Throwing money away on bad investments may reduce your taxes but it reduces your bankroll even more. You should evaluate your tax shelter investment based upon your normal investment criterion such as expected return, risk of loss, promoter reputation, minimum (and maximum) required investment, and timing of returns. Remember in analyzing your expected return to separate your economic return earned on the investment from your cash flow derived from the tax savings. The shelter must be a viable investment without depending on tax savings, since tax laws can and do regularly change. Furthermore, the IRS has successfully challenged some shelters on the premise that the transactions were not "entered into for a profit" but solely for the available tax benefits. If a venture is not entered into for a profit, total deductions are limited to the venture's income under the hobby loss rules.

Once you have identified an investment (or investments) which has potential as a tax shelter you need to know how to evaluate the tax benefits from the shelter or how to interpret your tax advisor's evaluation. Evaluation of the economic benefit of a shelter requires some analysis of the expected returns from the investment. Of course there is nothing certain about expected returns, but the astute investor will establish both the amounts and timing of what he/she anticipates receiving from the investment. The investors can then use traditional finance tools for evaluating the investment such as the payback method, the Internal Rate of Return method (IRR), or the present value method. The use of these methods for tax shelter analysis is illustrated in the next section.

### Payback Method

The payback method is the simplest but, unfortunately, the least useful method of evaluation. The investor simply compares his investment with the expected cash flow from the investment (which, of course, includes any tax benefits) to see when he will have received back as much as he invested. Any additional cash flow beyond the payback point will represent gain or income.

**EXAMPLE 13-4.** In 19X1 Tax A. Voider is considering making a $10,000 investment in a shelter that will produce the following cash flows:

| Year | Annual Cash Inflows (Outflows) |
|---|---|
| 19X1 | ($10,000) |
| 19X2 | 5,000 |
| 19X3 | 3,000 |
| 19X4 | 2,000 |
| 19X5 and thereafter | 1,500 |

Tax A. Voider's payback period is 3 years ($5,000 + $3,000 + $2,000 = $10,000 the initial investment amount). All cash flows received after 19X4 represents a return that is in excess of his original investment.

The payback method does not consider the timing of returns within the payback period. The problem can cause true differences in investment potential to be masked.

**EXAMPLE 13-5.** At the same time Tax A. Voider is considering the investment in the preceding example, he is also considering another investment which would be expected to yield the following cash flows:

| Year | Annual Cash Inflows (Outflows) |
|---|---|
| 19X1 | ($10,000) |
| 19X2 | 0 |
| 19X3 | 0 |
| 19X4 | 10,000 |
| 19X5 and thereafter | 1,500 |

The payback period for this investment is also 3 years

In each of these two examples Tax A. Voider has a payback period of 3 years, but few investors would consider the two investments to have equal potential. The cash flow in Example 13-4 provides the investor with $5,000 in 19X2 and $3,000 in 19X3 which can be invested to earn additional income. No such returns are available in Example 13-5. The two examples have similar solutions only because the time value of money is ignored under the payback method.

### Internal Rate of Return Method

The Internal Rate of Return (IRR) method finds the investment yield which is earned by the funds retained in the investment. Realistically, the IRR is the percentage yield which makes cash inflows and outflows exactly equal, given the timing differences.

**EXAMPLE 13-6.**   Tax A. Voider is considering a $10,000 investment on December 31, 19X1 which will yield the following cash flows. All cash payments will occur on the last day of the year.

| Tax Year | Annual Cash Inflows (Outflows) |
|----------|-------------------------------|
| 19X1 | ($10,000) |
| 19X2 | 3,000 |
| 19X3 | 4,000 |
| 19X4 | 5,000 |
| 19X5 | 5,000 |
| 19X6 | 2,000 |

The IRR for this investment is 26.08%.

The correct IRR can be determined by trial and error, but many personal computers include a function which will readily calculate an IRR for you. However, the IRR tells you only what the level of earnings will be for capital retained in the investment. All cash which is withdrawn from the investment ceases to earn at the rate of return provided by the investment.

### Present Value Method

The present value method requires that an investor decide what minimum yield he must have on an investment and then he can proceed to evaluate his cash flows. The cash flows to be received in future years are discounted at the predetermined yield to establish what those flows are worth today. If the discounted cash flows exceed the investment required in the current period, the investment provides more than the required yield.

EXAMPLE **13-7.** Tax A. Voider is considering the following investment and knows that she must have a yield of at least 10% in order to go ahead with her investment plans.

| Year | Annual Cash Inflows (Outflows) | Present Value Factor | Present Value |
|------|-------------------------------|----------------------|---------------|
| 19X1 | $(10,000) | 1.000 | ($10,000) |
| 19X2 | 4,000 | 0.90909 | 3,636.36 |
| 19X3 | 3,000 | 0.82645 | 2,479.35 |
| 19X4 | 4,000 | 0.75131 | 3,005.24 |
| 19X5 | 2,000 | 0.68301 | 1,366.02 |
| 19X6 | 3,000 | 0.62092 | 1,862.76 |
| Total | $ 6,000 | | $ 2,349.73 |

Since the present value of the cash inflows is positive, Tax A. Voider knows that this investment will yield more than her required 10%.

The IRR and present value methods both permit an investor to analyze the yield of a single investment. One way to make an investment choice is to invest in any shelter which yields more than the required rate. However, any investor who has less than an unlimited amount of funds to invest must choose between several alternative investments. In such a situation, the general rule is to choose the investment with the higher IRR or with the larger present value when all other factors are equal.

Next, it is necessary to look at the cash flow numbers we have been using and consider the impact of tax savings on those numbers.

At this stage the full complexity of analyzing a tax shelter can be appreciated. For purposes of illustration (and for being able to complete this analysis within the pages of a reasonably sized volume) we shall use a short, simple analysis. Let us return to Example 13-2 and analyze Tax A. Voider's investment in a $100,000 rental house for 10 years.

**EXAMPLE 13-8.** Let's assume that Tax A. Voider's income from all sources other than this property is stable at $110,000 per year and that Tax A. Voider is single with no dependents and uses the zero bracket amount. Accordingly, the tax shelter will save him taxes at his marginal rate of 50%. Let us further assume that he has no items of tax preference other than the accelerated depreciation that is claimed with respect to this house. Therefore, Tax A. Voider is not subject to the alternative minimum tax. Assume a 10% discount rate, and that all inflows and outflows will be occurring at the end of the year, except for the sale which occurs on January 1, 19Y1.

| Year | Operating Cash Inflows (Outflows) | Taxable Income (Loss)[a] | Tax Savings | Annual Cash Inflows (Outflows) | Discount Factor | Present Value |
|---|---|---|---|---|---|---|
| | (1) | (2) | (3) = (2) × .50 | (4) = (1) + (3) | (5) | (6) = (4) × (5) |
| 19X1 | ($20,000) | | 0 | ($20,000) | 1.00 | ($20,000) |
| 19X2 | 943 | $(10,164) | 5,082 | 6,125 | .909 | 5,568 |
| 19X3 | 943 | (8,080) | 4,040 | 4,983 | .826 | 4,116 |
| 19X4 | 943 | (6,988) | 3,494 | 4,437 | .751 | 3,332 |
| 19X5 | 943 | (5,888) | 2,944 | 3,887 | .683 | 2,655 |
| 19X6 | 943 | (4,779) | 2,390 | 3,333 | .621 | 2,070 |
| 19X7 | 943 | (3,659) | 1,830 | 2,773 | .564 | 1,564 |
| 19X8 | 943 | (3,527) | 1,764 | 2,707 | .513 | 1,389 |
| 19X9 | 943 | (3,384) | 1,692 | 2,635 | .467 | 1,231 |
| 19Y0 | 943 | (3,227) | 1,614 | 2,557 | .424 | 1,084 |
| 19Y1 Sale | 21,818[b] | 60,000[c] | (15,000)[d] | 6,818 | .386 | 2,632 |
| Total | 11,305 | 10,304 | 9,850 | 20,255 | XX | $ 5,641 |

[a] Calculations for the tax results of the sale on January 1, 19Y1 and the cashflows are as follows:

[b]                                                         Cash Flow

| | | |
|---|---|---|
| 1. | Original mortgage balance | $80,000 |
| Less: | Principal reductions | (11,818) * |
| Equals: | Unpaid mortgage balance | $68,182 |

| | | |
|---|---|---|
| 2. | Sales price | $90,000 |
| Less: | Unpaid mortgage balance | (68,182) |
| Equals: | Pretax cash flow from sale | $21,818 |

(*continued*)

| * | Total payments | $72,513 |
|---|---|---|
| Less: | Interest payments | (60,695) |
| Equals: | Principal reductions | $11,818 |

c | | Tax Consequences | |
|---|---|---|
| | Acquisition cost | $100,000 |
| Less: | Depreciation taken years X2–Y0 | (70,000) |
| Equals: | Adjusted basis | $ 30,000 |
| | Sales price | $ 90,000 |
| Less: | Adjusted basis | 30,000 |
| Equals: | Realized gain | $ 60,000 |

Section 1250 recapture calculation:

| Accelerated depreciation | $ 70,000 |
|---|---|
| Less: Straight-line depreciation [($100,000 ÷ 15) × 9] | (60,000) |
| Equals: Ordinary income | $ 10,000 |

| Realized gain | $ 60,000 |
|---|---|
| Less: Ordinary income | (10,000) |
| Equals: Section 1231 gain (capital gain) | $ 50,000 |

d

| Type of Income | Additional Income | Marginal Tax Rate | Additional Tax |
|---|---|---|---|
| Ordinary | $10,000 | 50% | $ 5,000 |
| Capital Gain | 50,000 | 20% (50% × 40%) | 10,000 |
| Total | $60,000 | | $15,000 |

While the calculations required for Example 13-8 are numerous, the problem is a great deal more complex if all the income sheltered is not in the 50% marginal bracket. This can easily happen if the taxpayer's annual income fluctuates, if the tax rates change, or even if the shelter is so good that it fully offsets income at the 50% marginal rate and also shelters some income at lower marginal rates. In fact, many taxpayers are not sure that all shelter losses will save taxes at a 50% rate so it is necessary to expand our model to incorporate this change. The total tax savings should always represent the taxpayers best estimate of the *change* in his tax bill, because of the investment.

**EXAMPLE 13-9.** Tax A. Voider invests in the same property described in Example 13-8 except that his taxable income from all sources other than this property is $82,000. For year 19X2 the tax savings would be calculated as follows.

|        | Tax due on $82,000 at 1984 rates          | $28,935   |
|--------|-------------------------------------------|-----------|
| Less:  | Tax due on $71,836 ($82,000 − $10,164)    | (24,052)  |
| Equals: | Tax savings from investment              | $ 4,884   |

The calculation of tax savings which occurs with the investment must, of course, include the impact of any alternative minimum tax which is imposed on the individual investor because of the investment. In addition, the taxpayer should remember that additional differences in the taxes that are due with and without the shelter may also arise from changes in charitable contribution limits, nondeductible medical and casualty loss deduction amounts, and any similar amounts where the calculation is based on A.G.I. Rarely could a taxpayer forecast precisely the impact of changes in the itemized deduction amounts and limits, so for practical reasons they are not normally part of the model. However, the investor should remember that a tax shelter investment will lower his A.G.I., and therefore increase the deductible amounts of medical expenses and casualty losses and decrease the amounts of charitable contributions which can be deducted. Other amounts, such as the exclusions for Social Security benefits and unemployment benefits, may also be changed by the tax shelter investment which lowers his A.G.I.

In short, it is not accurate to measure the tax savings generated by a tax shelter by multiplying the tax losses by the marginal tax rate. Rather the investor should, in theory, calculate his entire projected tax bill with and without the investment to see the full impact of the shelter. Unfortunately, the theory is impractical for most investors to apply. (Use of a personal computer with the appropriate tax software would make the calculation quite simple.) Practically, investors should at least consider just how much of an impact the change in the other items will be. If the impact seems small, the increased accuracy may not be worth the effort expended, especially when one considers the large number of estimates that are used to make this analysis. However, if an investor suspects that the impact of changing his A.G.I. may be significant, it would be wise to fully calculate the impact for at least the first year or two of the investment to get a feel for the accuracy of the tax savings numbers.

## MATCHING SHELTERS AND INVESTORS

There are many kinds of tax shelters. The tax savings provided by the various kinds of tax shelters typically have different timing patterns. Briefly, let's look at several common kinds of shelters and consider the usual time frames over which an investor can expect to reap their benefits. Then the problems of matching an investor with an appropriate kind of tax shelter can be discussed.

### Real Estate

Investments in real estate include investments in residential real property (rental houses, duplexes, and apartments), nonresidential real property (office buildings and commercial property), and raw land. Real estate is probably the most popular tax shelter for several reasons—one of which is the tradition that real estate is a good economic investment.

From a tax viewpoint real estate has several advantages. First, most real estate investments are leveraged and have the resulting benefit that was previously explained. Some of the borrowings may be on a nonrecourse basis so that the investor limits his potential loss. Because the at-risk rules do not apply to real estate, the investor can still claim the full amount of these tax losses as would not be the case with certain other types of investments.

The second tax benefit from real estate is the income deferral that results from the use of accelerated depreciation and from the deduction of interest expense. Ordinarily this tax benefit accrues for a number of years without any need for changing the investment. Further, a real estate investment has a high probability of having all or a large amount of the gain on the sale of the property taxed as capital gain. Residential real estate depreciated using the ACRS tables is likely to generate a small amount of ordinary income, but nonresidential real estate depreciated using the straight-line method will result only in Section 1231 gain.

Some real estate investments result in the availability of tax credits in the early years of the investment. For example, rehabilitation expenditures for 30-year-old structures, 40-year-old structures, and certified historic structures immediately result in substantial tax credits. Certain costs incurred in an investment in nonresidential real estate will qualify for an investment tax credit. Examples of qualifying costs are the costs of drapes, carpets, movable partitions, special lighting, elevators and escalators and so on, but only if they are in nonresidential real estate. Coin washing machines and dryers are among the few qualifying costs for investment tax credit purposes which can be incurred for residential real property.

As you can see, real estate investments provide all four of the benefits which are found in tax shelters. In addition, there is a wide range of investments which can vary from an individual's purchase of a rental house to a syndicated limited partnership investing in vast real estate holdings.

### Oil and Gas

For many of us, investments in oil and gas tax shelters epitomize the glamour of tax shelter investments. While we may be dazzled by dreams of striking it rich, the reality is that oil and gas shelters have a high degree of risk. It is commonly said that only one of every 10 wildcat wells is successful so there may be a substantial risk of losing the entire investment in an oil and gas exploration shelter. Accordingly, any investment in an oil and gas shelter should be made after careful consideration.

There are several different kinds of oil and gas shelters and they are not equally risky. An *exploratory drilling* shelter is one in which the investors' funds will be used to explore one or more potential oil and gas areas. These shelters essentially are wildcatting operations where the odds favor dry holes instead of producing wells. The risk is, of course, less if the operation is undertaken by very experienced, successful operators in an area which is very close to proven reserves. *Developmental* drilling shelters are those which drill wells on leases where oil and gas reserves have already been proven. While these are less risky, there is no guarantee that a producing well will be the result. Some oil and gas shelters are investments in operations which will involve both *exploration* and *development*.

The tax benefits from an oil and gas tax shelter arise from four sources, which are as follows:

1.  Intangible drilling costs deductions.
2.  Percentage depletion deductions.
3.  Investment tax credits.
4.  Capital gain potential.


Many of the costs of drilling an oil well must be incurred before any production is possible. For accounting purposes, these production costs would normally be capitalized and amortized for a producing well and would be written off for nonproducing wells when it is determined that the hole is dry. The tax laws allow a taxpayer to expense these intangible drilling costs (IDC) in the year in which they are incurred which, of course, provides very large writeoffs in the first year or two of an investment in a drilling shelter. Alternatively, the investor can choose to capitalize these intangible drillings costs and include them in the depletable basis of the property. The IDC costs—along with the purchase price of the oil and gas property—could then be depleted using cost depletion. However, capitalizing the IDC is frequently not advantageous, because it only increases the available cost depletion. Each year the investor calculates both cost depletion and percentage depletion and chooses the method which yields the greater depletion. Since percentage depletion is usually greater, the investor will choose percentage depletion and receive little (if any) benefit from capitalizing the IDC amounts.

**Example 13-10.**    Tax A. Voider invested in an oil and gas property. The drilling activities incurred $100,000 in intangible drilling costs in 19X1. Her other depletable costs for the property were $300,000 and engineers estimated there were 1,000,000 barrels of oil which could be produced from this well. In 19X1 30,000 barrels of oil were sold from this well. Percentage depletion for 19X1 is $60,000. If Tax A. Voider deducts her IDC she claims deductions for 19X1 as follows:

| | | |
|---|---|---|
| Intangible drilling costs | | $100,000 |
| Depletion: | | |
| Larger of: Percentage depletion | $60,000 | |
| or | | |
| Cost depletion | 30,000[a] | 60,000 |
| Total deductions | | $160,000 |

[a] $\dfrac{\$300,000}{100,000 \text{ bls.}} \times 10,000 \text{ bls.} = \$30,000$

If Tax A. Voider chooses to capitalize her IDC, the 19X1 deductions are as follows:

| | | |
|---|---|---|
| Intangible drilling costs | | $    0 |
| Depletion: | | |
| Larger of: Percentage depletion | $60,000 | |
| or | | |
| Cost depletion | 40,000[b] | 60,000 |
| Total deductions | | $ 60,000 |

[b] $\dfrac{\$300,000 + \$100,000}{100,000 \text{ bls.}} \times 10,000 \text{ bls.} = \$40,000$

In fact, Tax A. Voider has given up her immediate deduction of IDC and has not increased her depletion allowance unless her cost depletion deduction exceeds her percentage depletion deduction (which is unlikely except in the well's initial years).

After a producing well is established, the percentage depletion rules provide incentives for many investors, as noted before. While many uses of percentage depletion were repealed in 1975, the exception for independent producers allows small producers and royalty owners (those whose average daily production of oil and gas is 1,000 barrels or less) to continue to use percentage depletion. For most tax shelter investors, percentage depletion represents a deduction which has little, if any, relationship to the amount of capital investment and can readily result in depletion deductions in excess of investment. Percentage depletion on oil and gas in 1984 and later years is 15% of the value of minerals produced and sold. The percentage depletion deduction is limited to 50% of the taxable income from the *property* (before depletion deductions). In addition, the deduction for a given investor is limited to 65% of his taxable income before the percentage depletion deduction (and certain other adjustments). Depletion in excess of the 65% limit can be carried forward and deducted in later years but remains subject to the 65% of taxable income limit for the year of the deduction.

**EXAMPLE 13-11.** Tax A. Voider invests $40,000 in an oil and gas drilling shelter. In 19X3 Tax A. Voider's share of oil produced has a value of $200,000 and his share of taxable income from the property before depletion deductions is $50,000. His percentage depletion deduction is calculated as follows:

| | |
|---|---|
| Tentative deduction: | 15% × $200,000 = $30,000 |
| Property taxable income limit: | 50% of taxable income from the property ($50,000) = $25,000 |

If Tax A. Voider's taxable income from salary and so on (without the percentage depletion deduction) is at least $40,000, he can deduct the full $25,000 in 19X3 since it is less than the 65% limit. If Tax A. Voider's taxable income before considering the percentage depletion deduction is instead $35,000, he can deduct only $22,750 ($35,000 × 65%) in 19X3 and the remaining $2,250 ($25,000 − $22,750) can be carried forward and deducted in the future.

Investment tax credits may also be a significant tax saving feature of some oil and gas wells. A producing oil and gas well requires the purchase and use of significant amounts of equipment. Depending on the type of drilling program in which the taxpayer invests, he may be eligible to claim the 10% credit on a pass-through of part of the equipment purchases.

When a producing oil and gas well is sold, there is potential for recognizing long-term capital gains. However, if intangible drilling costs have been expensed for this property, part or all of the gain on the sale of the property may be changed from capital gain to ordinary income by the recapture provisions. The amount of gain which will be taxed as ordinary income because of the intangible drilling cost recapture provisions equals the difference between the intangible drilling costs which were actually expensed and the intangible drilling costs which would have been deducted had such costs been capitalized and deducted using cost depletion. Accordingly, the longer the well has been operating, the greater the amount of IDC which would have been deducted using the cost depletion approach and, therefore, the smaller the IDC recapture of gain as ordinary income.

**EXAMPLE 13-12.** Tax A. Voider invested in an oil and gas well in 19X1 and expensed $20,000 of IDC in that year. If she had chosen to capitalize the $20,000 of IDC, cost depletion would have been increased by $3,000 in 19X1, $5,000 in 19X2, and $5,000 in 19X3. Early in 19X4 Tax A. Voider sells her interest in the well for a $30,000 gain. She must recapture $7,000 of the $30,000 gain as ordinary income [$20,000 IDC expensed − ($3,000 + $5,000 + $5,000) which would have been deducted if she had capitalized and used cost depletion on the IDC amount]. The remaining $23,000 of her gain ($30,000 − $7,000) will be taxed as capital gain (assuming she has no depreciation or other forms of recapture).

### Equipment Leasing

There are two basic types of leases: financing leases and operating leases. A financing lease is typically one where the lessor owns the equipment and enters into a noncancellable lease agreement with a term (including, perhaps, renewable options) long enough for the lease payments to provide a full recovery of the lessor's investment and a reasonable return. The lease is almost always on a net basis so that the lessee pays for maintenance, property taxes, insurance and other normal operating expenses in addition to his rental payment. An operating lease does not normally provide lease payments which allow full recovery of the lessor's cost over the life of the original lease. With an operating lease, the lessor generally expects to lease the equipment a second or even a third time since the original lease term usually is significantly shorter than the equipment's useful life. Because of the need to negotiate an additional lease, an operating lease generally is riskier than a financing lease.

Three tax benefits provide the shelter opportunities for equipment leasing shelters. They are depreciation deductions, interest deductions, and investment tax credits. Under the ACRS rules, leased equipment is ordinarily 3-year or 5-year property. The recovery period depends only on the kind of equipment that is leased and not on the length of the lease agreement.

Interest deductions are available if money is borrowed by the lessor to finance his purchase of the leased equipment. However, the interest deductions are subject to the investment interest limits discussed in Chapter 3 if the lease is considered a net lease. For purposes of applying the investment interest limitation, a lease is a net lease if, for the taxable year, the sum of the ordinary and necessary business expenses (other than interest, depreciation, taxes, and certain other expenses) is less than 15% of the rental income. Additionally, property is considered subject to a net lease if the lessor is either guaranteed a specific return or is guaranteed against loss of income. Since most tax shelter leases fall into the first category, this limitation may reduce the tax shelter potential of equipment leasing for some taxpayers.

While the potential for receiving investment tax credits is a part of the allure of equipment leasing, an individual lessor will probably not be able to claim the credit. Noncorporate and S corporation lessors can claim the investment tax credit *only* if one of the following two conditions is met:

1. The leased equipment has been manufactured or produced by the lessor.
2. (a) The ordinary and necessary business expenses (other than depreciation, interest, and taxes) related to the first 12 months of the lease is greater than 15% of the rental income from that same 12-month period, and
   (b) The equipment is leased for less than half its expected useful life.

Realistically, the first condition is highly unlikely to be met by individual taxpayers since they generally are not the manufacturer or producer of the product to be leased. The second condition is not much easier to meet since most of the ordinary expenses of lease transactions are excluded from the test. Remaining lease expenses such as maintenance, repairs, and possibly fees to a manager for the leasing endeavor are unlikely to exceed 15% of the rental income. While operating leases may have terms short enough to satisfy the second part of this condition, the restriction ensures that a lessor will be assuming substantial amounts of risk before an investment tax credit is allowed.

Even if the lessor can not qualify for the investment tax credit under these conditions, it is possible to pass the investment tax credit benefits on to the lessee if the leased equipment is new. This pass-through to the lessee provides a feasible solution for preserving some of the investment tax credit benefits because the lessor can command a higher rental price if the lessee claims the credit. It is clearly possible to make a lease agreement which can benefit both the lessor and the lessee under these conditions.

### Other Shelters

Numerous other kinds of tax shelters exist. Some, such as investments in motion pictures were once high-flying shelter activities which have been greatly altered after the enactment of the at-risk rules. Now, films still provide significant numbers of shelters but the investors generally must assume substantial economic risk in order to get the tax benefits. Investment tax credits are available only on amounts which qualify as U.S. production costs. Motion picture films qualify as 5-year recovery class properties, but frequently the income forecast method of depreciation is used instead. This depreciation method yields depreciation for each year equal to the capitalized cost of the film multiplied by a fraction made up of the net recepits for the current tax year divided by the expected net receipts from all tax years. Since net receipts are greatest in the first year after release, this income forecasting method yields very rapid cost recovery. However, if the income forecasting method of depreciation is used, a reduced 6⅔% investment tax credit must be claimed. The full 10% investment tax credit can be claimed, but if the 10% credit is selected, the unearned credit must be recaptured when the film is disposed of or when 90% of the film's cost have been recovered through depreciation, whichever is earlier. As long as the investor is prepared to assume the economic risks, shelters are available which produce movies, which advertise and distribute completed films, and which both produce and distribute a film or group of films.

Another kind of shelter which has not yet gained wide popularity is the research and development shelter. Typically, the general partner in such a shelter is a subsidiary of a major corporation which wishes to undertake a specific project or group of projects but wants to minimize its investment. Clearly, there is substantial economic risk that no marketable product will result from the research effort, but if the research is successful the partners may realize substantial royalty income or gain when the product or process is sold. The tax shelter of such a partnership arises largely because all research and development expenses can be written off as they are incurred. Further, if the product or process which is produced can be patented, the investors may have their gain on the sale of the product taxed at capital gains rates. Like all other shelters except real estate, the at-risk rules apply and require the investor to assume economic risk in order to deduct losses from the partnership.

### Shelters and Investors

After this overview of several different kinds of shelters, it is obvious that two factors differ widely. First, the economic risks inherent in different shelters vary. Oil and gas exploration shelters in new geographical areas are probably the most risky, but there are also very risky and relatively safe investments to be found within each of the other types of shelters that were mentioned. The investor should carefully match his own risk preferences and the risks encountered in the available shelter investments. (It should go without saying that an investment in a shelter should only be made out of funds the taxpayer can afford to lose.)

Secondly, the pattern of tax losses generated varies among the types of shelter. For example, oil and gas shelters produce large losses in the first one or two years if the IDC is expensed and much smaller losses in later years. If an investor has stable, high income, an investment in a single oil and gas shelter probably is not the type of investment that is needed. However, one or more investments in oil and gas shelters made in a single year might be perfect to shelter a professional athlete's one-time signing bonus. The timing of expected tax losses from a shelter must be carefully matched with the expected pattern of the taxpayer's income from other sources.

Third, investors should be wary of tax shelter promoters bearing year-end gifts. Many taxpayers reach December needing to find the "right" tax shelter investment to quickly reduce their taxes. Some promoters will promise large deductions based on a partnership that is already in operation. A taxpayer can not obtain a full year's losses (retroactive to the beginning of the taxable year) by making a year-end investment except in very rare circumstances.

## BURNED-OUT SHELTERS

It is not possible to leave the subject of tax shelters without at least mentioning a commonly overlooked feature of virtually all shelters. Most shelters derive some or all of their attractiveness from a mismatching of expenses and revenues. While this seems wonderful to the investor as he lowers his tax bill with the losses in the early years, he finds it considerably less wonderful when his tax bill is increased by the later years' revenues. In fact, an investor's excellent tax shelter can (and will) turn on him—sometimes even to the extent that the cash flow from the shelter is less than the additional tax due on the investor's allocable share of the shelter's income. This is a burned-out shelter.

If an investor holds an investment long enough, it will burn out. If he sells the shelter, he will have a low basis and probably a significant gain. As discussed throughout the book, the various recapture provisions are likely to come into play and result in at least some of the gain being taxed as ordinary income. (Real estate investments provide some exceptions to this rule. Residential real estate held for 10 or more years will have relatively small recapture amounts and other real estate which has been depreciated on a straight-line basis will have no recapture.) If the taxpayer exchanges his burned-out shelter in a tax-free exchange he will simply keep his low basis and transfer it to a different property. Even giving a burned-out shelter away may not have the desired result since, to the extent the investor is relieved of liability, he is treated as having sold the property. Further, since the donee would receive the property with its low basis and attendant problems, few willing recipients will be found.

There is one way out—die. Admittedly, the solution is a drastic one and it is unlikely to be an investor's choice of tax planning. However, it is a realistic fact to be considered by elderly investors since the heirs will receive a fair market value basis for the property.

A somewhat more palatable, but quite risky solution for most investors, is to pyramid investments. The idea is that when one shelter burns out, the taxpayer purchases a new shelter which produces losses large enough to shelter both the taxpayer's original income plus the taxable income of the burned-out shelter. When this new shelter burns out a still larger one must be purchased. This pyramiding can continue as long as the financial resources and credit rating of the investor hold out. Since most such investments involve borrowed funds, this technique is inherently dangerous if there is a downturn in economic conditions. Any investor contemplating such a scheme should carefully consider the risk of building this house of cards.

## TAX ADVISORS AND SHELTERS

Advice from your own tax advisor is highly recommended on numerous issues in tax shelter investments, and excellent tax advice should be a prerequisite to all tax shelter investment. What you pay for tax advice is almost certainly very small in proportion to what you could lose in a bad shelter. Nevertheless, any investor must be realistic in his expectations from his tax advisor. No advisor can look into the future and predict the outcome of an investment. The best advisors will clearly outline for you the risks inherent in the investment, but the ultimate decision of whether to accept these risks must lie with the investor.

# 1984 TAX RATE SCHEDULES[a]

## Married Individuals Filing Joint Returns and Surviving Spouses

| If taxable income is | The tax is: |
|---|---|
| Not over $3,400 . . . . . . . . . . . . . | No tax. |
| Over $3,400 but not over $5,500 . . . . | 11% of the excess over $3,400. |
| Over $5,500 but not over $7,600 . . . . | $231, plus 12% of the excess over $5,500. |
| Over $7,600 but not over $11,900 . . . | $483, plus 14% of the excess over $7,600. |
| Over $11,900 but not over $16,000 | $1,085, plus 16% of the excess over $11,900. |
| Over $16,000 but not over $20,200 . . | $1,741, plus 18% of the excess over $16,000. |
| Over $20,200 but not over $24,600 . . | $2,497, plus 22% of the excess over $20,200. |
| Over $24,600 but not over $29,900 . . | $3,465, plus 25% of the excess over $24,600. |
| Over $29,900 but not over $35,200 . . | $4,790, plus 28% of the excess over $29,900. |
| Over $35,200 but not over $45,800 . . | $6,274, plus 33% of the excess over $35,200. |
| Over $45,800 but not over $60,000 . . | $9,772, plus 38% of the excess over $45,800. |
| Over $60,000 but not over $85,600 . . | $15,168, plus 42% of the excess over $60,000. |
| Over $85,600 but not over $109,400 . | $25,920, plus 45% of the excess over $85,600. |
| Over $109,400 but not over $162,400 . | $36,630, plus 49% of the excess over $109,400. |
| Over $162,400 . . . . . . . . . . . . . | $62,600, plus 50% of the excess over $162,400. |

[a] The tax brackets and zero bracket amount are to be adjusted annually for changes in the Consumer Price Index starting in 1985. The 1985 change increases the 1984 zero bracket amounts by 4.1%. Similar changes to the tax brackets shown for 1984 will occur.

## Married Individuals Filing Separately

| If taxable income is | The tax is: |
|---|---|
| Not over $1,700 | No tax. |
| Over $1,700 but not over $2,750 | 11% of the excess over $1,700. |
| Over $2,750 but not over $3,800 | $115.50, plus 12% of the excess over $2,750. |
| Over $3,800 but not over $5,950 | $241.50, plus 14% of the excess over $3,800. |
| Over $5,950 but not over $8,000 | $542.50, plus 16% of the excess over $5,950. |
| Over $8,000 but not over $10,100 | $870.50, plus 18% of the excess over $8,000. |
| Over $10,100 but not over $12,300 | $1,248.50, plus 22% of the excess over $10,100. |
| Over $12,300 but not over $14,950 | $1,732.50, plus 25% of the excess over $12,300. |
| Over $14,950 but not over $17,600 | $2,395, plus 28% of the excess over $14,950. |
| Over $17,600 but not over $22,900 | $3,137, plus 33% of the excess over $17,600. |
| Over $22,900 but not over $30,000 | $4,886, plus 38% of the excess over $22,900. |
| Over $30,000 but not over $42,800 | $7,584, plus 42% of the excess over $30,000. |
| Over $42,800 but not over $54,700 | $12,960, plus 45% of the excess over $42,800. |
| Over $54,700 but not over $81,200 | $18,315, plus 49% of the excess over $54,700. |
| Over $81,200 | $31,300, plus 50% of the excess over $81,200. |

## Heads of Household

| If taxable income is | The tax is: |
|---|---|
| Not over $2,300 | No tax. |
| Over $2,300 but not over $4,400 | 11% of the excess over $2,300. |
| Over $4,400 but not over $6,500 | $231, plus 12% of the excess over $4,400. |
| Over $6,500 but not over $8,700 | $483, plus 14% of the excess over $6,500. |
| Over $8,700 but not over $11,800 | $791, plus 17% of the excess over $8,700. |
| Over $11,800 but not over $15,000 | $1,318, plus 18% of the excess over $11,800. |
| Over $15,000 but not over $18,200 | $1,894, plus 20% of the excess over $15,000. |
| Over $18,200 but not over $23,500 | $2,534, plus 24% of the excess over $18,200. |
| Over $23,500 but not over $28,800 | $3,806, plus 28% of the excess over $23,500. |
| Over $28,800 but not over $34,100 | $5,290, plus 32% of the excess over $28,800. |
| Over $34,100 but not over $44,700 | $6,986, plus 35% of the excess over $34,100. |
| Over $44,700 but not over $60,600 | $10,696, plus 42% of the excess over $44,700. |
| Over $60,600 but not over $81,800 | $17,374, plus 45% of the excess over $60,600. |
| Over $81,800 but not over $108,300 | $26,914, plus 48% of the excess over $81,800. |
| Over $108,300 | $39,634, plus 50% of the excess over $108,300. |

## Single Taxpayers

| If taxable income is | The tax is: |
|---|---|
| Not over $2,300 | No tax. |
| Over $2,300 but not over $3,400 | 11% of the excess over $2,300. |
| Over $3,400 but not over $4,400 | $121, plus 12% of the excess over $3,400. |
| Over $4,400 but not over $6,500 | $241, plus 14% of the excess over $4,400. |
| Over $6,500 but not over $8,500 | $535, plus 15% of the excess over $6,500. |
| Over $8,500 but not over $10,800 | $835, plus 16% of the excess over $8,500. |
| Over $10,800 but not over $12,900 | $1,203, plus 18% of the excess over $10,800. |
| Over $12,900 but not over $15,000 | $1,581, plus 20% of the excess over $12,900. |
| Over $15,000 but not over $18,200 | $2,001, plus 23% of the excess over $15,000. |
| Over $18,200 but not over $23,500 | $2,737, plus 26% of the excess over $18,200. |
| Over $23,500 but not over $28,800 | $4,115, plus 30% of the excess over $23,500. |
| Over $28,800 but not over $34,100 | $5,705, plus 34% of the excess over $28,800. |
| Over $34,100 but not over $41,500 | $7,507, plus 38% of the excess over $34,100. |
| Over $41,500 but not over $55,300 | $10,319, plus 42% of the excess over $41,500. |
| Over $55,300 but not over $81,800 | $16,115, plus 48% of the excess over $55,300. |
| Over $81,800 | $28,835, plus 50% of the excess over $81,800. |

# INDEX